D0001718

TURBO C®

Reference Guide

**This manual was produced in its entirety with
Sprint: The Professional Word Processor,®
available from Borland.**

Borland International, Inc.
4585 Scotts Valley Drive
Scotts Valley, California 95066

Copyright ©1987
All Rights Reserved. First Printing, 1987
Printed in U.S.A.

10 9 8 7 6

Table of Contents

This is the second volume of documentation in the Turbo C package. This volume, the *Turbo C Reference Guide*, contains definitions of all the Turbo C library routines, common variables, and common defined types, along with example program code to illustrate how to use many of these routines, variables, and types.

If you are new to C programming, you should first read the other book in your Turbo C package—the *Turbo C User's Guide*. In that book you'll find instructions on how to install Turbo C on your system, an overview of Turbo C's window and menu system, and tutorial-style chapters designed to get you started programming in Turbo C. The user's guide also summarizes Turbo C's implementation of the C language and discusses some advanced programming techniques. For those of you who are Turbo Pascal and Turbo Prolog programmers, the user's guide provides information to help you integrate your understanding of those languages with your new knowledge of C.

You should refer to the Introduction in the user's guide for information on the Turbo C implementation, a summary of the contents of Volume I, and a short bibliography.

Volume II: The Reference Guide

The *Turbo C Reference Guide* is written for experienced C programmers; it provides implementation-specific details about the language and the run-time environment. In addition, it provides definitions for each of the Turbo C functions, listed in alphabetical order.

These are the chapters and appendixes in the programmer's reference guide:

Chapter 1: Using Turbo C Library Routines summarizes Turbo C's input/output (I/O) support, and lists and describes the #include (.h) files.

Chapter 2: The Turbo C Library is an alphabetical reference of all Turbo C library functions. Each definition gives syntax, include files, related functions, an operative description, return values, and portability information for the function.

Appendix A: The Turbo C Interactive Editor gives a more thorough explanation of the editor commands—for those who need more information than that given in Chapter 2 of the *Turbo C User's Guide*.

Appendix B: Compiler Error Messages lists and explains each of the error messages and summarizes the possible or probable causes of the problem that generated the message.

Appendix C: Options describes each of the Turbo C user-selectable compiler options.

Appendix D: Turbo C Utilities discusses the MAKE utility, CPP, and the Turbo Link Utility. The section on CPP summarizes how the Turbo C preprocessor functions. The section on the stand-alone MAKE utility documents when, where, and how to use MAKE for rebuilding program files. The section on TLINK, the stand-alone Turbo Link Utility, summarizes how to use the command-line version of Turbo C's built-in linker.

Appendix E: Language Syntax Summary uses modified Backus-Naur Forms to detail the syntax of all Turbo C constructs.

Appendix F: Customizing Turbo C guides you through the installation program (TCINST), which lets you customize your keyboard, modify default values, change your screen colors, resize your Turbo C windows, and more.

Appendix G: MicroCalc introduces the spreadsheet program included with your Turbo C package and gives directions for compiling and running the program.

Typographic Conventions

All typefaces used in this manual were produced by Borland's Sprint: The Professional Word Processor, on an Apple LaserWriter Plus. Their special uses are as follows:

`Monospaced type`	This typeface represents text as it appears on the screen or in your program and anything you must type (such as command-line options).
[ ]	Square brackets in text or DOS command lines enclose optional input or data that depends on your system, which should not be typed verbatim.
< >	Angle brackets in the function reference section enclose the names of include files.
Boldface	Turbo C function names (such as **printf**) are shown in boldface when mentioned within text (but not in program examples).
Italics	Italics indicate variable names (identifiers) within sections of text and to emphasize certain words (especially new terms).
`Bold monospaced`	This typeface represents Turbo C keywords (such as `char`, `switch`, `near`, and `cdecl`.
Keycaps	This special typeface indicates a key on your keyboard. It is often used when describing a particular key you should type, e.g., "press *Esc* to cancel a menu."

Borland's No-Nonsense License Statement

This software is protected by both United States Copyright Law and International Treaty provisions. Therefore, you must treat this software *just like a book* with the following single exception: Borland International authorizes you to make archival copies of Turbo C for the sole purpose of backing up your software and protecting your investment from loss.

By saying, "just like a book," Borland means, for example, that this software may be used by any number of people and may be freely moved from one computer location to another so long as there is **no possibility** of its being used at one location while it's being used at another. Just like a book that can't be read by two different people in two different places at the same time, neither can the software be used by two different people in two different places at the same time. (Unless, of course, Borland's copyright has been violated.)

Acknowledgments

In this manual, we refer to several products:

- Turbo Pascal, Turbo Prolog and Sprint: The Professional Word Processor are registered trademarks of Borland International Inc.
- WordStar is a trademark of MicroPro Inc.
- IBM PC, XT, and AT are trademarks of International Business Machines Inc.
- MS-DOS is a registered trademark of Microsoft Corporation.
- UNIX is a registered trademark of American Telephone and Telegraph

How to Contact Borland

If, after reading these manuals and using Turbo C, you would like to contact Borland with comments, questions, or suggestions, we suggest the following procedures:

The best way to contact Borland is to log on to Borland's Forum on CompuServe: Type GO BOR from the main CompuServe menu and select "Enter Language Products Forum" from the Borland main menu. Leave your questions or comments there for the support staff to process.

If you prefer, write a letter detailing your comments and send it to

Technical Support Department
Borland International
4585 Scotts Valley Drive
Scotts Valley, CA
95066, USA

As a last resort, if, for some reason, you cannot write to us, you can telephone our Technical Support department. If you're calling with a problem, please have the following information handy before you call:

- product name and version number

- computer make and model number
- operating system and version number

1

Using Turbo C Library Routines

Turbo C comes equipped with over 300 library routines—functions and macros that you call from within your C programs to perform a wide variety of tasks, including low- and high-level I/O, string and file manipulation, memory allocation, process control, data conversion, mathematical calculations, and much more.

Turbo C's routines are contained in the library files (Cx.LIB and MATHx.LIB). Because Turbo C supports six distinct memory models, each model has its own library file and math file, containing versions of the routines written for that particular model.

Turbo C supports the draft ANSI C standard which, among other things, allows function prototypes to be given for the routines in your C programs. All of Turbo C's library routines are declared with prototypes in one or more header file (these are the .H or "include" files that you copied from the distribution disks into your INCLUDE directory).

In This Chapter...

This first part of the *Turbo C Reference Guide* provides an overview of the Turbo C library routines and include files.

In this chapter, we:

- list and describe the include files
- summarize the different categories of tasks performed by the library routines
- describe (in look-up fashion) common global variables implemented in many of the library routines

The Library Routine Lookup Section

The second part of this reference guide is an alphabetical lookup; it contains descriptions for each of the Turbo C routines. Many of the routines are grouped by "family" (such as memory-allocation routines, formatted-output routines, etc.) because they perform similar or related tasks.

However, since you might not intuitively know which family of related routines a particular one belongs to, we have included an individual entry in the lookup for each and every routine. For instance, if you want to look up information about the **free** routine, you would first look under **free**; there you would find a listing for **free** that:

- summarizes what **free** does
- gives the Usage (syntax) for calling **free**
- tells you which header file contains the prototype for **free**
- refers you to **malloc** (the "family" listing) for a detailed description of how **free** is implemented and how it relates to the other memory-allocation routines

The last part of this reference guide contains several appendices designed to give you detailed reference and usage information about some of Turbo C's special features; the editor, error messages, and the stand-alone utilities.

Why You Should License the Turbo C Run-Time Library Source Code

The Turbo C Run-Time Library contains over 300 functions, covering a broad range of areas: low-level control of your IBM PC, interfacing with DOS, input/output, process management, string and memory manipulations, math, sorting and searching, and so on.

Using Turbo C, you may find that the particular function you want to write is similar to, but not the same as, a function in the library. With access to the Run-Time Library source code, you can tailor that function to your own needs.

Sometimes, when you have trouble debugging code, you may wish that you knew more about the internals of a library function. This is a time when having the source code to the Run-Time Library would be of great help.

When you can't figure out what a library function is really supposed to do, it is very useful to be able to take a quick look at that function's source code.

You may dislike the underscore convention on C symbols, and wish you had a version of the libraries without leading underscores. Again, access to the source code to the Run-Time Library will let you eliminate leading underscores.

You can also learn a lot from studying tight, professionally written library source code.

For all these reasons, and more, you will want to have access to the Turbo C Run-Time Library source code. Because Borland deeply believes in the concepts of "open architecture," the Turbo C Run-Time Library source code is available for licensing. All you have to do is fill out the order form distributed with this documentation, include your payment, and we'll ship you the Turbo C Run-Time Library source code.

The Turbo C Include Files

ALLOC.H   Declares memory management functions (allocation, deallocation, etc.).

ASSERT.H   Defines the **assert** debugging macro.

BIOS.H   Declares various functions used in calling IBM-PC ROM BIOS routines.

CONIO.H   Declares various functions used in calling the DOS console I/O routines.

CTYPE.H   Contains information used by the character classification and character conversion macros (such as **isalpha** and **toascii**).

DIR.H   Contains structures, macros and functions for working with directories and path names.

DOS.H   Defines various constants and gives declarations needed for MS-DOS and 8086-specific calls.

ERRNO.H   Defines constant mnemonics for the error codes.

FCNTL.H   Defines symbolic constants used in connection with the library routine **open**.

FLOAT.H   Contains parameters for floating-point routines.

IO.H   Contains structures and declarations for low-level Input/Output routines.

LIMITS.H   Contains environmental parameters, information about compile-time limitations, and ranges of integral quantities.

MATH.H   Declares prototypes for the math functions; also defines the macro HUGE_VAL, and declares the exception structure used by the **matherr** and **_matherr** routines.

MEM.H   Declares the memory-manipulation functions. (Many of these are also defined in STRING.H.)

PROCESS.H   Contains structures and declarations for **spawn...** and **exec...** functions.

SETJMP.H	Defines a type *jmp_buf* used by the **longjmp** and **setjmp** functions and declares the routines **longjmp** and **setjmp**.
SHARE.H	Defines parameters used in functions which make use of file-sharing.
SIGNAL.H	Defines the constants SIG_IGN and SIG_DFL, and declares the **ssignal** and **gsignal** functions.
STDARG.H	Defines macros used for reading the argument list in functions declared to accept a variable number of arguments (such as **vprintf**, **vscanf**, etc.).
STDDEF.H	Defines several common data types and macros.
STDIO.H	Defines types and macros needed for the Standard I/O Package defined in Kernighan and Ritchie and extended under UNIX System V. Defines the standard I/O predefined streams *stdin*, *stdout*, and *stderr*, and declares stream-level I/O routines.
STDLIB.H	Declares several commonly used routines; conversion routines, search/sort routines, and other miscellany.
STRING.H	Declares several string-manipulation and memory-manipulation routines.
SYS\STAT.H	Defines symbolic constants used for opening and creating files.
TIME.H	Defines a structure filled in by the time-conversion routines **asctime**, **localtime** and **gmtime**, and a type used by the routines **ctime**, **difftime**, **gmtime**, **localtime**, and **stime**; also provides prototypes for these routines.
VALUES.H	Defines important constants, including machine dependencies; provided for UNIX System V compatibility.

Library Routines by Category

The Turbo C library routines perform a variety of tasks. In this section, we list the routines, and the include files in which they are declared, under several general categories of task performed.

Classification Routines

These routines classify ASCII characters as letters, control characters, punctuation, uppercase, etc.

isalnum	(ctype.h)	isdigit	(ctype.h)	ispunct	(ctype.h)
isalpha	(ctype.h)	isgraph	(ctype.h)	isspace	(ctype.h)
isascii	(ctype.h)	islower	(ctype.h)	isupper	(ctype.h)
iscntrl	(ctype.h)	isprint	(ctype.h)	isxdigit	(ctype.h)

Conversion Routines

These routines convert characters and strings: from alpha to different numeric representations (floating-point, integers, longs), and vice versa; and from uppercase to lowercase (and vice versa).

atof	(stdlib.h)	strtod	(stdlib.h)
atoi	(stdlib.h)	strtol	(stdlib.h)
atol	(stdlib.h)	toascii	(ctype.h)
ecvt	(stdlib.h)	_tolower	(ctype.h)
fcvt	(stdlib.h)	tolower	(ctype.h)
gcvt	(stdlib.h)	_toupper	(ctype.h)
itoa	(stdlib.h)	toupper	(ctype.h)
ltoa	(stdlib.h)	ultoa	(stdlib.h)

Directory Control Routines

These routines manipulate directories and path names.

chdir	(dir.h)	getdisk	(dir.h)
findfirst	(dir.h)	mkdir	(dir.h)
findnext	(dir.h)	mktemp	(dir.h)
fnmerge	(dir.h)	rmdir	(dir.h)
fnsplit	(dir.h)	searchpath	(dir.h)
getcurdir	(dir.h)	setdisk	(dir.h)
getcwd	(dir.h)		

Diagnostic Routines

These routines provide built-in troubleshooting capability.

assert	(assert.h)
matherr	(math.h)
perror	(errno.h)

Input/Output Routines

These routines provide stream-level and DOS-level I/O capability.

access	(io.h)	**fputc**	(stdio.h)	**puts**	(stdio.h)
cgets	(conio.h)	**fputchar**	(stdio.h)	**putw**	(stdio.h)
_chmod	(io.h)	**fputs**	(stdio.h)	**read**	(io.h)
chmod	(io.h)	**fread**	(stdio.h)	**read**	(io.h)
clearerr	(stdio.h)	**freopen**	(stdio.h)	**remove**	(stdio.h)
close	(io.h)	**fscanf**	(stdio.h)	**rename**	(stdio.h)
_close	(io.h)	**fseek**	(stdio.h)	**rewind**	(stdio.h)
cprintf	(conio.h)	**fstat**	(sys\stat.h)	**scanf**	(stdio.h)
cputs	(conio.h)	**ftell**	(stdio.h)	**setbuf**	(stdio.h)
creat	(io.h)	**fwrite**	(stdio.h)	**setftime**	(io.h)
_creat	(io.h)	**getc**	(stdio.h)	**setmode**	(io.h)
creatnew	(io.h)	**getch**	(conio.h)	**setvbuf**	(stdio.h)
creattemp	(io.h)	**getchar**	(stdio.h)	**sopen**	(io.h)
cscanf	(conio.h)	**getche**	(conio.h)	**sprintf**	(stdio.h)
dup	(io.h)	**getftime**	(io.h)	**sscanf**	(stdio.h)
dup2	(io.h)	**getpass**	(conio.h)	**ssignal**	(signal.h)
eof	(io.h)	**gets**	(stdio.h)	**stat**	(sys\stat.h)
fclose	(stdio.h)	**getw**	(stdio.h)	**strerror**	(stdio.h)
fcloseall	(stdio.h)	**gsignal**	(signal.h)	**tell**	(io.h)
fdopen	(stdio.h)	**ioctl**	(io.h)	**ungetc**	(stdio.h)
feof	(stdio.h)	**isatty**	(io.h)	**ungetc**	(stdio.h)
ferror	(stdio.h)	**kbhit**	(conio.h)	**ungetch**	(conio.h)
fflush	(stdio.h)	**lock**	(io.h)	**unlock**	(io.h)
fgetc	(stdio.h)	**lseek**	(io.h)	**vfprintf**	(stdio.h)
fgetchar	(stdio.h)	**_open**	(io.h)	**vfscanf**	(stdio.h)
fgets	(stdio.h)	**open**	(io.h)	**vprintf**	(stdio.h)
filelength	(io.h)	**perror**	(stdio.h)	**vscanf**	(stdio.h)
fileno	(stdio.h)	**printf**	(stdio.h)	**vsprintf**	(stdio.h)
flushall	(stdio.h)	**putc**	(stdio.h)	**vsscanf**	(io.h)
fopen	(stdio.h)	**putch**	(conio.h)	**_write**	(io.h)
fprintf	(stdio.h)	**putchar**	(stdio.h)	**write**	(io.h)

Interface Routines (DOS, 8086, BIOS)

These routines provide DOS, BIOS and machine-specific capabilities.

absread	(dos.h)	geninterrupt	(dos.h)	keep	(dos.h)
abswrite	(dos.h)	getcbrk	(dos.h)	MK_FP	(dos.h)
bdos	(dos.h)	getdfree	(dos.h)	outport	(dos.h)
bdosptr	(dos.h)	getdta	(dos.h)	outportb	(dos.h)
bioscom	(bios.h)	getfat	(dos.h)	parsfnm	(dos.h)
biosdisk	(bios.h)	getfatd	(dos.h)	peek	(dos.h)
biosequip	(bios.h)	getpsp	(dos.h)	peekb	(dos.h)
bioskey	(bios.h)	getvect	(dos.h)	poke	(dos.h)
biosmemory	(bios.h)	getverify	(dos.h)	pokeb	(dos.h)
biosprint	(bios.h)	harderr	(dos.h)	randbrd	(dos.h)
biostime	(bios.h)	hardresume	(dos.h)	randbwr	(dos.h)
country	(dos.h)	hardretn	(dos.h)	segread	(dos.h)
ctrlbrk	(dos.h)	inport	(dos.h)	setcbrk	(dos.h)
disable	(dos.h)	inportb	(dos.h)	setdta	(dos.h)
dosexterr	(dos.h)	int86	(dos.h)	setvect	(dos.h)
enable	(dos.h)	int86x	(dos.h)	setverify	(dos.h)
FP_OFF	(dos.h)	intdos	(dos.h)	sleep	(dos.h)
FP_SEG	(dos.h)	intdosx	(dos.h)	unlink	(dos.h)
freemem	(dos.h)	intr	(dos.h)		

Manipulation Routines (String, Memory)

These routines handle strings and blocks of memory; copying, comparing, converting, and searching.

memccpy	(mem.h) and (string.h)	strcat	(string.h)	strncpy	(string.h)
memchr	(mem.h) and (string.h)	strchr	(string.h)	strnicmp	(string.h)
memcmp	(mem.h) and (string.h)	strcmp	(string.h)	strnset	(string.h)
memcpy	(mem.h) and (string.h)	strcpy	(string.h)	strpbrk	(string.h)
memicmp	(mem.h) and (string.h)	strcspn	(string.h)	strrchr	(string.h)
memmove	(mem.h) and (string.h)	strdup	(string.h)	strrev	(string.h)
memset	(mem.h) and (string.h)	strerror	(string.h)	strset	(string.h)
movebytes	(mem.h)		stricmp	(string.h)	strspn	(string.h)
movedata	(mem.h) and (string.h)	strlen	(string.h)	strstr	(string.h)
movmem	(mem.h) and (string.h)	strlwr	(string.h)	strtok	(string.h)
setmem	(mem.h)		strncat	(string.h)	strupr	(string.h)
stpcpy	(string.h)		strncmp	(string.h)		

Math Routines

These routines perform mathematical calculations and conversions.

abs	(stdlib.h)	exp	(math.h)	matherr	(math.h)
acos	(math.h)	fabs	(math.h)	modf	(math.h)
asin	(math.h)	fcvt	(stdlib.h)	poly	(math.h)
atan	(math.h)	floor	(math.h)	pow	(math.h)
atan2	(math.h)	fmod	(math.h)	pow10	(math.h)
atof	(stdlib.h)	_fpreset87	(float.h)	rand	(stdlib.h)
atof	(math.h)	frexp	(math.h)	sin	(math.h)
atoi	(stdlib.h)	gcvt	(stdlib.h)	sinh	(math.h)
atol	(stdlib.h)	hypot	(math.h)	sqrt	(math.h)
cabs	(math.h)	itoa	(stdlib.h)	srand	(stdlib.h)
ceil	(math.h)	labs	(stdlib.h)	_status87	(float.h)
_clear87	(float.h)	ldexp	(math.h)	strtod	(stdlib.h)
_control87	(float.h)	log	(math.h)	strtol	(stdlib.h)
cos	(math.h)	log10	(math.h)	tan	(math.h)
cosh	(math.h)	ltoa	(stdlib.h)	tanh	(math.h)
ecvt	(stdlib.h)	_matherr	(math.h)	ultoa	(stdlib.h)

Memory Allocation Routines

These routines provide dynamic memory allocation in the small-data and large-data models.

allocmem	(dos.h)	farmalloc	(alloc.h)
brk	(alloc.h)	farrealloc	(alloc.h)
calloc	(alloc.h)	free	(alloc.h) and (stdlib.h)
coreleft	(alloc.h) and (stdlib.h)	malloc	(alloc.h) and (stdlib.h)
farcalloc	(alloc.h)	realloc	(alloc.h) and (stdlib.h)
farcoreleft	(alloc.h)	sbrk	(alloc.h)
farfree	(alloc.h)	setblock	(dos.h)

Miscellaneous Routines

These routines provide non-local goto capabilities.

setjmp	(setjmp.h)
longjmp	(setjmp.h)

Process Control Routines

These routines invoke and terminate new processes from within another.

abort	(process.h)	exit	(process.h)
execl	(process.h)	spawnl	(process.h)
execle	(process.h)	spawnle	(process.h)
execlp	(process.h)	spawnlp	(process.h)
execlpe	(process.h)	spawnlpe	(process.h)
execv	(process.h)	spawnv	(process.h)
execve	(process.h)	spawnve	(process.h)
execvp	(process.h)	spawnvp	(process.h)
execvpe	(process.h)	spawnvpe	(process.h)
_exit	(process.h)	system	(process.h)

Standard Routines

These are standard routines.

abort	(stdlib.h)	fcvt	(stdlib.h)	putenv	(stdlib.h)
abs	(stdlib.h)	free	(stdlib.h)	qsort	(stdlib.h)
atexit	(stdlib.h)	gcvt	(stdlib.h)	rand	(stdlib.h)
atof	(stdlib.h)	getenv	(stdlib.h)	realloc	(stdlib.h)
atoi	(stdlib.h)	itoa	(stdlib.h)	srand	(stdlib.h)
atol	(stdlib.h)	labs	(stdlib.h)	strtod	(stdlib.h)
bsearch	(stdlib.h)	lfind	(stdlib.h)	strtol	(stdlib.h)
calloc	(stdlib.h)	lsearch	(stdlib.h)	swab	(stdlib.h)
ecvt	(stdlib.h)	ltoa	(stdlib.h)	system	(stdlib.h)
_exit	(stdlib.h)	malloc	(stdlib.h)	ultoa	(stdlib.h)
exit	(stdlib.h)				

Time and Date Routines

These are time-conversion and time-manipulation routines.

asctime	(time.h)	localtime	(time.h)
ctime	(time.h)	setdate	(dos.h)
difftime	(time.h)	settime	(dos.h)
dostounix	(dos.h)	stime	(time.h)
getdate	(dos.h)	time	(time.h)
gettime	(dos.h)	tzset	(time.h)
gmtime	(time.h)	unixtodos	(dos.h)

Variable Argument List Routines

These routines are for use when accessing variable argument lists (such as with **vprintf**, etc).

va_arg	(stdarg.h)
va_end	(stdarg.h)
va_start	(stdarg.h)

The main Function

Every C program must have a **main** function; where you place it is a matter of preference. Some programmers place **main** at the beginning of the file, others at the very end. But regardless of its location, the following points about **main** always apply.

The Arguments to main

Three parameters (arguments) are passed to main by the Turbo C start-up routine: *argc, argv* and *env*.

- *argc*, an integer, is the number of command-line arguments passed to **main**.

- *argv* is an array of strings

    under 3.x versions of DOS, *argv*[0] is defined as the full path name of the program being run

    under versions of DOS before 3.0, *argv*[0] points to the null string (*""*).

    argv[1] contains the first string typed on the DOS command line after the program name

    argv[2] contains the second string typed after the program name

    ...

    argv[*argc*] contains NULL

- *env* is also an array of strings. Each element of *env*[] holds a string of the form ENVVAR=value

    ENVVAR is the name of an environment variable, such as PATH, or 87.

    value is the value to which an ENVVAR is set, such as C:\DOS;C\TURBOC (for PATH), or YES (for 87)

The Turbo C start-up routine always passes these three arguments to **main**: You have the option of whether or not to declare them in your program. If you declare some (or all) of these arguments to **main**, they are made available as local variables to your **main** routine.

Note, however, that if you do declare any of these parameters, you *must* declare them exactly in the order given: *argc, argv, env*.

For example, the following are all valid declarations of **main** 's arguments:

```
main()
main(int argc)                                    /* legal but very unlikely */
main(int argc, char * argv[])
main(int argc, char * argv[], char * env[])
```

Note: The declaration `main(int argc)` is legal, but it's very unlikely that you would use *argc* in your program without also using the elements of *argv*.

Another Note: The argument *env* is also available via the global variable *environ*. Refer to the *environ* lookup entry (in this chapter) and the **putenv** and **getenv** lookup entries (in Chapter 2) for more information.

An Example Program Using argc, argv and env

Here is an example program, named ARGS.EXE, that demonstrates a simple way of implementing these arguments passed to **main**.

```
/* Program name ARGS.EXE */

#include <stdio.h>
#include <stdlib.h>

main(int argc, char *argv[], char *env[])
{
   int i;

   printf("The value of argc is %d \n\n",argc);
   printf("These are the %d command-line arguments passed to main:\n\n",argc);

   for (i = 0; i <= argc; i++)
      printf("   argv[%d]: %s\n", i, argv[i]);

   printf("\nThe environment string(s) on this system are:\n\n");

   for (i = 0; env[i] != NULL; i++)
      printf("   env[%d]: %s\n", i, env[i]);
}
```

Suppose you run ARGS.EXE at the DOS prompt with the following command line:

```
> args first_argument "argument with blanks" 3  4 "last but one" stop!
```

Note that you can pass arguments with embedded blanks by surrounding the with double quotes, as shown by `"argument with blanks"` and `"last but one"` in this example command line.

The output of ARGS.EXE (assuming that the environment variables are set as shown here) would then be like this:

```
The value of argc is 7

These are the 7 command-line arguments passed to main:

    argv[0]: C:\TURBOC\TESTARGS.EXE
    argv[1]: first_argument
    argv[2]: argument with blanks
    argv[3]: 3
    argv[4]: 4
    argv[5]: last but one
    argv[6]: stop!
    argv[7]: (null)

The environment string(s) on this system are:

    env[0]: COMSPEC=C:\COMMAND.COM
    env[1]: PROMPT=$p $g
    env[2]: PATH=C:\SPRINT;C:\DOS;C:\TURBOC
```

Note: The maximum combined length of the command-line arguments passed to **main** (including the space between adjacent arguments) is 128 characters: this is a DOS limit.

When You Compile Using –p (Pascal Calling Conventions)

If you compile your program using Pascal calling conventions (which are described in detail in Chapter 9), you *must* remember to explicitly declare **main** as being a C type.

You do this with the **cdecl** keyword, like this:

```
cdecl  main(int argc, char * argv[], char * envp[])
```

The Value main Returns

In all but two instances, the value returned by **main** is the status code of the program: an `int`. If, however, your program uses the routine **exit** (or **_exit**) to terminate, the value returned by **main** is the argument passed to the call to **exit** (or to **_exit**).

For example, if your program contains the call

```
exit(1)
```

the status is 1.

If you are using the Integrated Environment version of Turbo C (TC.EXE) to run your program, you can display the return value from **main** by pressing *Alt-V* when the `"Press any key"` message appears (after you run the program).

Global Variables

daylight, timezone

Names	*daylight, timezone*
Usage	extern int *daylight*; extern long *timezone*;
Declared in	time.h
Description	These variables are used by the time-and-date functions.

daylight: This variable = 1 for Daylight Savings Time, 0 for Standard Time.

timezone: This variable is a calculated value; it is assigned a long value that is the difference, in seconds, between the current local time and Greenwich Mean Time.

errno, _doserrno, sys_errlist, sys_nerr

Names	*errno, _doserrno, sys_errlist, sys_nerr*	
Usage	extern int *errno*; extern int *_doserrno*; extern char * *sys_errlist*[ ]; extern int *sys_nerr*;	
Declared in	errno.h	(*errno, _doserrno, sys_errlist, sys_nerr*)
	dos.h	(*_doserrno*)

Description   Three of these variables (*errno*, *sys_errlist*, and *sys_nerr*) are used by the **perror** function to print error messages when certain library routines fail to accomplish their appointed tasks. *_doserrno* is a variable that maps many MS-DOS error codes to *errno*; however, **perror** does not use *_doserrno* directly.

_doserrno: When an MS-DOS system call results in an error, *_doserrno* is set to the actual MS-DOS error code. *errno* is a parallel error variable inherited from UNIX.

errno: Whenever an error in a system call occurs, *errno* is set to indicate the type of error. Sometimes *errno* and *_doserrno* are equivalent. Other times, *errno* does not contain the actual DOS error code (which is contained in *_doserrno*). Still other errors might occur which set only *errno*, not *_doserrno*.

sys_errlist: To provide more control over message formatting, the array of message strings is provided in *sys_errlist*. *errno* can be used as an index into the array to find the string corresponding to the error number. The string does not include any newline character.

sys_nerr: This variable is defined as the number of error message strings in *sys_errlist*.

The following table gives mnemonics for the values stored in *sys_errlist* and their meanings.

mnemonic	Meaning
E2BIG	Arg list too long
EACCES	Permission denied
EBADF	Bad file number
ECONTR	Memory blocks destroyed
ECURDIR	Attempt to remove CurDir
EDOM	Domain error
EINVACC	Invalid access code
EINVAL	Invalid argument
EINVDAT	Invalid data
EINVDRV	Invalid drive specified
EINVENV	Invalid environment
EINVFMT	Invalid format
EINVFNC	Invalid function number

EINVMEM	Invalid memory block address
EMFILE	Too many open files
ENMFILE	No more files
ENODEV	No such device
ENOENT	No such file or directory
ENOEXEC	Exec format error
ENOFILE	No such file or directory
ENOMEM	Not enough core
ENOPATH	Path not found
ENOTSAM	Not same device
ERANGE	Result out of range
EXDEV	Cross-device link
EZERO	Error 0

The following list gives mnemonics for the actual DOS error codes to which _doserrno_ can be set. (This value of _doserrno_ may or may not be mapped—through _errno_—to an equivalent error message string in _sys_errlist_.

mnemonic	MS-DOS error code
EINVAL	Bad function
E2BIG	Bad environ
EACCES	Access denied
EACCES	Bad access
EACCES	Is current dir
EBADF	Bad handle
EFAULT	Reserved
EINVAL	Bad data
EMFILE	Too many open
ENOENT	File not found
ENOENT	Path not found
ENOENT	No more files
ENOEXEC	Bad format
ENOMEM	Mcb destroyed
ENOMEM	Out of memory
ENOMEM	Bad block
EXDEV	Bad drive
EXDEV	Not same device

Refer to the Microsoft *MS-DOS Programmer's Reference Manual* for more information about MS-DOS error returns.

_fmode

Name	*_fmode* – default file-translation mode
Usage	extern int *_fmode*;
Declared in	fcntl.h
Description	This variable determines in which mode (text or binary) files will be opened and translated. The value of *_fmode* is O_TEXT by default, which specifies that files will be read in text mode. If *_fmode* is set to O_BINARY, the files are opened and read in binary mode. (O_TEXT and O_BINARY are defined in fcntl.h.)

In text mode, on input, carriage-return/line-feed (CR/LF) combinations are translated to a single line-feed character (LF). On output, the reverse is true: LF characters are translated to CR/LF combinations.

In binary mode, no such translation occurs.

You can override the default mode as set by *_fmode* by specifying a *t* (for text mode) or *b* (for binary mode) in the argument *type* in the library routines **fopen**, **fdopen**, and **freopen**. Also, in the routine **open**, the argument *access* can include either O_BINARY or O_TEXT, which will explicitly define the file being opened (given by the **open** *pathname* argument) to be in either binary or text mode.

_psp, environ

Names	_psp, environ
Usage	extern unsigned int _psp; extern char * environ[ ];
Declared in	dos.h (_psp) dos.h (environ)
Description	_psp: This variable contains the segment address of the program segment prefix (PSP) for the current program. The PSP is an MS-DOS process descriptor; it contains initial DOS information about the program.

Refer to the Microsoft *MS-DOS Programmer's Reference Manual* for more information on the PSP.

environ: This is an array of strings; it is used to access and alter a process environment. Each string is of the form

 envvar = varvalue

where *envvar* is the name of an environment variable (such as PATH), and *varvalue* is the string value to which *envvar* is set (such as C:\BIN;C:\DOS). The string *varvalue* may be empty.

When a program begins execution, the MS-DOS environment settings are passed directly to the program. Note that *envp*, the third argument to **main**, is equal to the initial setting of *environ*.

The *environ* array can be accessed by **getenv**; however, the **putenv** function is the only routine that should be used to add, change or delete the *environ* array entries. (This is because modification can resize and relocate the process environment array, but *environ* is automatically adjusted so that it always points to the array.)

_stklen

Name	_stklen – stack length variable
Usage	int _stklen;
Description	In large data models (compact, large, and huge), _stklen is the exact stack size in bytes.

In small data models (tiny, small, and medium), the startup code uses _stklen to compute the minimum size of the DATA segment. The DATA segment includes initialized global data, uninitialized data, and the stack.

```
min DATA segment size =

  size of _DATA segment
+ size of _BSS segment
+ _stklen
+ MINSTACK(128 words)
```

If the memory available is less than this, the startup aborts the program. The maximum DATA segment size is, of course, 64K.

_version, _osmajor, _osminor

Names	_version, _osmajor, _osminor
Usage	extern unsigned int _version;
	extern unsigned char _osmajor;
	extern unsigned char _osminor;
Declared in	dos.h

Description   _version contains the MS-DOS version number, with the major version number in the low byte and the minor version number in the high byte. (For MS-DOS version x.y, the x is the major version number, and y is the minor.)

The major and minor version numbers are also available individually through _osmajor and _osminor, where _osmajor is the major version number and _osminor is the minor version number.

These variables can be useful when you want to write modules that will run on MS-DOS versions 2.x and 3.x. Some library routines behave differently depending on the MS-DOS version number, while others only work under MS-DOS 3.x. (For example, refer to **_open**, **creatnew**, and **ioctl** in the lookup section of this reference guide.)

_8087

Name   _8087 – coprocessor chip flag

Usage   extern int _8087;

Description   The _8087 variable is set to 1 if the start-up code auto-detection logic detects a floating-point coprocessor (an 8087, 80287, or 80387), or if the 87 environment variable is set to Y (SET 87 = Y). The _8087 variable is set to 0 otherwise.
(Refer to Chapter 9 in the Turbo C User's Guide for more information about the 87 environment variable.)

You must have floating-point code in your program for the _8087 variable to be set to 1.

2

The Turbo C Library

This sample library look-up entry explains how to use this section of the *Turbo C Reference Guide*.

using library routine entries

Name	**routine** – summary of what the library routine does
Usage	#include <header.h> Only listed if it *must* be included routine(modifier *parameter*[, ...]); Declaration syntax
Related functions usage	routine2(modifier *parameter*[, ...]);
Prototype in	header.h File containing prototype for **routine**
Description	This describes what **routine** does, the parameters it takes, and any details you need to use **routine** and the related routines listed.
Return value	The value that **routine** returns (if any), is given here. If the global variable *errno* is set, that's also listed here.
Portability	Specifies systems **routine** is available on.
See also	Lists other routines you may wish to read about.

abort

Name	**abort** – abnormally terminates a process
Usage	void abort(void);
Prototype in	stdlib.h process.h
Description	This function writes a termination message on *stderr* and aborts the program via a call to **_exit**, with an exit code
Return value	This function does not return a value.
Portability	Available on UNIX systems.
See also	**assert, _exit, exec..., exit, spawn...**

abs

Name	**abs** – absolute value
Usage	int abs(int *i*);

Related functions usage	double cabs(struct complex *znum*);
	double fabs(double *x*);
	long labs(long *n*);

Prototype in	stdlib.h **(abs, labs)** math.h **(cabs, fabs)**
Description	**abs** returns the absolute value of the integer argument *i*. If **abs** is called when stdlib.h has been included, **abs** will be treated as a macro that expands to in-line code. If you don't include stdlib.h (or if you do include it and #undef **abs**) you will get the **abs** function rather than a macro.

cabs is a macro that calculates the absolute value of *znum*, a complex number. *znum* is a structure with type **complex**; the structure is defined in math.h as:

```
struct complex {
   double x, y;
};
```

Calling **cabs** is equivalent to calling **sqrt** with the real and imaginary components of *znum*, as shown here:

```
sqrt(znum.x*znum.x + znum.y*znum.y)
```

If you don't include math.h (or if you do include it and `#undef` **cabs**) you will get the **cabs** function rather than a macro.

fabs calculates the absolute value of *x*, a **double**.

labs calculates the absolute value of *n*, a **long** integer.

Return value

abs returns an integer in the range of 0 to 32767, with the exception that an argument of –32768 is returned as –32768.

cabs returns the absolute value of *znum*, a **double**. On overflow, **cabs** returns HUGE_VAL and sets *errno* to

    ERANGE   Result out of range

Error handling for **cabs** can be modified through the function **matherr**.

fabs returns the absolute value of *x*. **labs** returns the absolute value of *n*. There are no error returns.

Portability

Available on UNIX systems.

See also

matherr

absread

Name	**absread** – reads data
Usage	int absread(int *drive*, int *nsects*, int *sectno*, void **buffer*);
Related functions usage	int abswrite(int *drive*, int *nsects*, int *sectno*, void **buffer*);
Prototype in	dos.h
Description	These functions read and write specific disk sectors. They ignore the logical structure of a disk and pay no attention to files, FATs, or directories.

absread reads specific disk sectors via DOS interrupt 0x25; **abswrite** writes specific disk sectors via DOS interrupt 0x26.

> *drive* = drive number to read (0 = A, 1 = B, etc.)
> *nsects* = number of sectors to read
> *sectno* = beginning logical sector number
> *buffer* = memory address where the data is to be read or written

The number of sectors to read is limited to the amount of memory in the segment above *buffer*. Thus, 64K bytes is the largest amount of memory that can be read in a single call to **absread** or **abswrite**.

Return value	If successful, both routines return 0.

On error, the routines return –1 and set *errno* to the value of the AX register returned by the system call. See the MS-DOS documentation for the interpretation of *errno*.

Portability	Unique to MS-DOS.

abswrite

Name	**abswrite** – writes data
Usage	int abswrite(int *drive*, int *nsects*, int *sectno*, void **buffer*);
Prototype in	dos.h
Description	see **absread**

access

Name	**access** – determines accessibility of a file
Usage	int access(char **filename*, int *amode*);
Prototype in	io.h
Description	**access** checks a named file to determine if it exists and whether it can be read, written to, or executed. *filename* points to a string naming the file.

The bit pattern contained in *amode* is constructed as follows:

06	Check for read and write permission
04	Check for read permission
02	Check for write permission
01	Execute (ignored)
00	Check for existence of file

Note: Under MS-DOS, all existing files have read access (*amode* = 04), so 00 and 04 give the same result. In the same vein, *amode* values of 06 and 02 are equivalent because under MS-DOS, write access implies read access.

If *filename* refers to a directory, **access** simply determines whether the directory exists or not.

Return value	If the requested access is allowed, 0 is returned; otherwise, a value of –1 is returned and *errno* is set to one of the following:

        ENOENT   Path or file name not found
        EACCES   Permission denied

Portability	Available on UNIX systems.
See also	**chmod**

Example

```
#include <stdio.h>
#include <io.h>

/* returns 1 if filename exists, else 0 */

int file_exists(char *filename)
{
   return (access(filename, 0) == 0);
}

main()
{
   printf("Does NOTEXIST.FIL exist: %s\n",
          file_exists("NOTEXIST.FIL") ? "YES" : "NO");
}
```

Program output

```
Does NOTEXIST.FIL exist: NO
```

acos

Name	**acos** – trigonometric function
Usage	double acos(double *x*);
Prototype in	math.h
Description	see **trig**

allocmem

Name	**allocmem** – allocates DOS memory segment
Usage	int allocmem(unsigned *size*, unsigned **seg*);
Related functions usage	int freemem(unsigned *seg*); int setblock(int *seg*, int *newsize*);
Prototype in	dos.h
Description	**allocmem** uses the MS-DOS system call 0x48 to allocate a block of free memory and returns the segment address of the allocated block.

size is the desired size in paragraphs. *seg* is a pointer to a word which will be assigned the segment address of the newly allocated block. No assignment is made to the word pointed to by *seg* if not enough room is available.

All allocated blocks are paragraph aligned.

freemem frees a memory block allocated by a previous call to **allocmem**. *seg* is the segment address of that block.

setblock modifies the size of a memory segment. *seg* is the segment address returned by a previous call to **allocmem**. *newsize* is the new, requested size in paragraphs.

Return value   **allocmem** returns –1 on success. In the event of error, a number (the size of the largest available block) is returned.

freemem returns 0 on success. In the event of error, –1 is returned and *errno* is set to

    ENOMEM   Insufficient memory

setblock returns –1 on success. In the event of error, the size of the largest possible block is returned.

An error return from any **allocmem** or **setblock** will set _doserrno_ and will set the global variable _errno_ to

ENOMEM   Not enough core

Portability   Unique to MS-DOS.

See also   **malloc**

asctime

Name   **asctime** – converts date and time to ASCII

Usage   #include <time.h>
char *asctime(struct tm *tm);

Prototype in   time.h

Description   see **ctime**

asin

Name   **asin** – trigonometric function

Usage   double asin(double x);

Prototype in   math.h

Description   see **trig**

assert

Name   **assert** – tests a condition and possibly aborts

Usage   #include <asssert.h>
                void assert(int *test*);

Prototype in assert.h

Description   **assert** is a macro that expands to an **if** statement which, if the *test* fails, will print a message and abort the program. The message is:

```
Assertion failed: file filename, line linenum
```

The *filename* and *linenum* listed are the source file name and line number where the **assert** macro appears. A call to **abort** is used to abort the program.

If you place the #define NDEBUG directive in the source code before the #include assert.h directive, the effect is to "comment out" the **assert** statement.

Return value None

Portability   This macro is available on some UNIX systems including Systems III and V.

See also   **abort**

Example

```
/* add an item to a list.  verify the item is not NULL. */

#include <assert.h>
#include <stdio.h>

struct ITEM {
   int   key;
   int   value;
};
```

```
void additem(struct ITEM *itemptr)
{
   assert(itemptr != NULL);
   /* ... add the item ... */
}

main()
{
   additem(NULL);
}
```

Program output

```
Assertion failed: file C:\TURBOC\ASSERT.C, line 13
```

atan

Name	**atan** – trigonometric arctangent function
Usage	double atan(double x);
Prototype in	math.h
Description	see **trig**

atan2

Name	**atan** – trigonometric function
Usage	double atan2(double y, double x);
Prototype in	math.h
Description	see **trig**

atexit

Name   **atexit** – registers termination function

Usage   #include <stdlib.h>
                     int atexit(atexit_t *func*)

Prototype in   stdlib.h

Description   **atexit** registers the function pointed to by *func* as an "exit function". Upon normal termination of the program, **exit** calls **func* (without arguments) just before returning to the operating system. The called function is of type *atexit_t*, which is defined in a **typedef** in stdlib.h.

Each call to **atexit** registers another exit function; up to 32 functions can be registered, and they are executed on a last in, first out basis.

Return value   **atexit** returns 0 on success and non-zero on failure (no space left to register the function).

See also   **exec...**, **exit, spawn...**

Example

```
#include <stdlib.h>
#include <stdio.h>
void exit_fn1()
{
   printf("Exit Function 1 called\n");
}

void exit_fn2()
{
   printf("Exit Function 2 called\n");
}

main()
{
   atexit(exit_fn1);      /* post exit_fn1 */
   atexit(exit_fn2);      /* post exit_fn2 */
   printf("Main quitting ...\n");
}
```

Program output

```
Main quitting ...
Exit Function 2 called
Exit Function 1 called
```

atof

Name	**atof** – converts a string to a floating point number
Usage	double atof(char *nptr);
Related functions usage	int atoi(char *nptr); long atol(char *nptr);
Prototype in	math.h (**atof**) stdlib.h (**atof, atoi, atol**)
Description	**atof** converts a string pointed to by *nptr* to **double**; this function recognizes

- an optional string of tabs and spaces
- an optional sign
- then a string of digits and an optional decimal point
- then an optional *e* or *E* followed by an optional signed integer

atoi converts a string pointed to by *nptr* to **int**; **atol** converts the string to **long**. **atoi** and **atol** recognize

- an optional string of tabs and spaces
- an optional sign
- then a string of digits

In all three of these functions, the first unrecognized character ends the conversion.

There are no provisions for overflow in any of these functions.

Return value	These functions return the converted value of the input string. If the string cannot be converted to a number of the corresponding type (**double** for **atof**, **int** for **atoi**, **long** for **atol**), the return value is 0.
Portability	Available on UNIX systems.
See also	**scanf**

atoi

Name	**atoi** – converts a string to an integer
Usage	int atoi(char *nptr);
Prototype in	stdlib.h
Description	see **atof**

atol

Name	**atol** – converts a string to a long
Usage	long atol(char *nptr);
Prototype in	stdlib.h
Description	see **atof**

bdos

Name	**bdos** – MS-DOS system call
Usage	int bdos(int *dosfun*, unsigned *dosdx*, unsigned *dosal*);
Related functions usage	int bdosptr(int *dosfun*, void **argument*, unsigned *dosal*);
Prototype in	dos.h
Description	These calls provides direct access to many of the MS-DOS system calls. Refer to the *MS-DOS Programmer's Reference Manual* for details of each system call.

Those system calls which require an integer argument use **bdos**, while those which require a pointer argument use **bdosptr**.

For the small data models (tiny, small and medium), **bdos** and **bdosptr** are similar. In the large data models (compact, large and huge), it is important to use **bdosptr** for system calls that require a pointer as the call argument.

dosfun is defined in the *MS-DOS Programmer's Reference Manual*.

In the small data models, the *argument* parameter to **bdosptr** specifies DX; in the large data models, it gives the DS:DX values to be used by the system call.

dosdx is the value of register DX for the **bdos** call.

dosal is the value of register AL.

For an example that demonstrates the use of **bdosptr**, refer to **harderr**.

Return value

The return value of **bdos** is the value of AX set by the system call.

The return value of **bdosptr** is the value of AX on success, or −1 on failure. On failure *errno* and *_doserrno* are set.

Portability

Unique to MS-DOS.

Example

```
#include <stdio.h>
#include <dos.h>

/* get current drive as 'A', 'B', ... */

char current_drive(void)
{
   char curdrive;

   curdrive = bdos(0x19,0,0);   /* get current disk as 0, 1, ... */
   return( 'A' + curdrive );
}

main()
{
      printf("The current drive is %c:\n", current_drive());
}
```

Program output

```
The current drive is C:
```

bdosptr

Name   **bdosptr** – MS-DOS system call

Usage   int bdosptr(int *dosfun*, void **argument*, unsigned *dosal*);

Prototype in dos.h

Description   see **bdos**

bioscom

Name	**bioscom** – communications I/O
Usage	int bioscom(int *cmd*, char *byte*, int *port*);
Prototype in	bios.h
Description	**bioscom** performs various RS232 communications over the I/O port given in *port*.

A *port* value of 0 corresponds to COM1, 1 corresponds to COM2, and so forth.

The value of *cmd* can be one of the following:

0 Sets the communications parameters to the value in *byte*

1 Sends the character in byte out over the communications line

2 Receives a character from the communications line

3 Returns the current status of the communications port

byte is a combination of the following bits:

0x02	7 data bits
0x03	8 data bits
0x00	1 stop bit
0x04	2 stop bits
0x00	No parity
0x08	Odd parity
0x18	Even parity

0x00	110 baud
0x20	150 baud
0x40	300 baud
0x60	600 baud
0x80	1200 baud
0xA0	2400 baud
0xC0	4800 baud
0xE0	9600 baud

For example, giving a value for *byte* of 0xEB (0xE0 | 0x08 | 0x00 | 0x03) sets the communications port to 9600 baud, odd parity, 1 stop bit, and 8 data bits.

Return value   For all values of *cmd*, the return value is a 16-bit integer where the upper 8 bits are status bits, and the lower 8 bits vary depending on the value of *cmd*. The upper bits of the return value are defined as follows:

bit 15	Time out
bit 14	Transmit shift register empty
bit 13	Transmit holding register empty
bit 12	Break detect
bit 11	Framing error
bit 10	Parity error
bit 9	Overrun error
bit 8	Data ready

With a *cmd* value of 1, and *if* bit 15 is set, the *byte* value could not be transmitted. Otherwise, the remaining upper and lower bits are appropriately set.

With a *cmd* value of 2, the byte read is in the lower bits of the return value if there was no error.

If an error occurred, at least one of the upper bits are set. If no upper bits are set, the byte was received without error.

With a *cmd* value of 0 or 3, the return value has the upper bits set as defined, and the lower bits are defined as follows:

bit 7   Received line signal detect
bit 6   Ring indicator
bit 5   Data set ready
bit 4   Clear to send
bit 3   Delta receive line signal detector
bit 2   Trailing edge ring detector
bit 1   Delta data set ready
bit 0   Delta clear to send

Portability   This function works only with IBM PCs or compatibles.

biosdisk

Name   **biosdisk** – hard disk/floppy I/O

Usage   int biosdisk(int *cmd*, int *drive*, int *head*, int *track*,
                int *sector*, int *nsects*, void **buffer*);

Prototype in   bios.h

Description   This function uses interrupt 0x13 to issue disk operations directly to the BIOS.

drive is a number that specifies which disk drive is to be used: 0 for the first floppy disk drive, 1 for the second floppy disk drive, 2 for the third, etc. For hard disk drives, a *drive* value of 0x80 specifies the first drive, 0x81 specifies the second, 0x82 the third, etc.

For hard disks, the physical drive is specified, not the disk partition. The application program must interpret the partition table information itself if it needs to do so.

cmd indicates the operation to perform. Depending on the value of *cmd*, the other parameters may or may not be needed. The following are the possible values for *cmd* for any IBM PC, XT, or AT.

0	Resets diskette system. This forces the drive controller to do a hard reset. All other parameters are ignored.
1	Returns the status of the last disk operation. All other parameters are ignored.
2	Reads one or more disk sectors into memory. The starting sector to read is given by *head*, *track*, and *sector*. The number of sectors is given by *nsects*. The data is read, 512 bytes per sector, into *buffer*.
3	Writes one or more disk sectors from memory. The starting sector to write is given by *head*, *track*, and *sector*. The number of sectors is given by *nsects*. The data is written, 512 bytes per sector, from *buffer*.
4	Verifies one or more sectors. The starting sector is given by *head*, *track*, and *sector*. The number of sectors is given by *nsects*.
5	Formats a track. The track is specified by *head* and *track*. *buffer* points to a table of sector headers to be written on the named *track*. See the *Technical Reference Manual* for the IBM PC for a description of this table and the format operation.

The following *cmd* values are allowed only for an XT or AT:

6	Formats a track and sets bad sector flags
7	Formats the drive beginning at a specific track
8	Returns the current drive parameters

> The drive information is returned in *buffer* in the first four bytes.

9	Initializes drive-pair characteristics
10	Does a long read, which reads 512 plus 4 extra bytes per sector
11	Does a long write, which writes 512 plus 4 extra bytes per sector
12	Does a disk seek
13	Alternates disk reset
14	Reads sector buffer
15	Writes sector buffer
16	Tests whether the named drive is ready
17	Recalibrates the drive
18	Controller RAM diagnostic
19	Drive diagnostic
20	Controller internal diagnostic

Return value   These operations return a status byte composed of the following bits:

0x00	Operation successful
0x01	Bad command
0x02	Address mark not found
0x04	Record not found
0x05	Reset failed
0x07	Drive parameter activity failed
0x09	Attempt to DMA across 64K boundary
0x0B	Bad track flag detected
0x10	Bad ECC on disk read
0x11	Ecc corrected data error
0x20	Controller has failed
0x40	Seek operation failed
0x80	Attachment failed to respond
0xBB	Undefined error occurred
0xFF	Sense operation failed

Note that 0x11 is not an error because the data is correct. The value is returned anyway to give the application an opportunity to decide for itself.

Portability   This function works with IBM PCs and compatibles, only.

biosequip

Name	**biosequip** – checks equipment
Usage	int biosequip(void);
Prototype in	bios.h
Description	This function returns an integer describing the equipment connected to the system. BIOS interrupt 0x11 is used for this.
Return value	The return value is interpreted as a collection of bit-sized fields. The values for the IBM PC are:

bit 15   Numbers of printers
bit 14   Numbers of printers
bit 13   Serial printer attached
bit 12   Game I/O attached

bit 11   Number of RS232 ports
bit 10   Number of RS232 ports
bit 9   Number of RS232 ports

bit 8   NOT DMA

       bit 8 = 0 machine has DMA
       bit 8 = 1 machine does not have DMA; for example, PC Jr.

bit 7   Number of diskettes
bit 6   Number of diskettes

       00 = 1 drive
       01 = 2 drives
       10 = 3 drives
       11 = 4 drives, only if bit 0 is 1

bit 5   Initial
bit 4   Video mode

       00 = Unused
       01 = 40x25 BW with color card
       10 = 80x25 BW with color card

                        11 = 80x25 BW with mono card

            bit 3   Motherboard
            bit 2   Ram size

                     00 = 16K
                     01 = 32K
                     10 = 48K
                     11 = 64K

            bit 1   Floating-point coprocessor
            bit 0   Boot from diskette

Portability   This function works with IBM PCs and compatibles, only.

bioskey

Name   **bioskey** – keyboard interface

Usage   int bioskey(int *cmd*);

Prototype in bios.h

Description   This function performs various keyboard operations using BIOS interrupt 0x14. The parameter *cmd* determines the exact operation.

0   Returns the next key struck at the keyboard. If the lower 8 bits are non-zero, that is the ASCII character struck. If the lower 8 bits are zero, the upper 8 bits are the extended keyboard codes defined in the *Technical Reference Manual* for the IBM PC.

1   This tests whether a keystroke is available to be read. A return value of zero means no key is available. Otherwise, the value of the next keystroke is returned. The keystroke itself is kept to be returned by the next call to **bioskey** that has a *cmd* value of zero.

2 Requests the current shift key status. The value is composed from ORing the following values together:

0x80	*Insert* toggled
0x40	*Caps* toggled
0x20	*Num Lock* toggled
0x10	*Scroll Lock* toggled
0x08	*Alt* down
0x04	*Ctrl* down
0x02	*Left Shift* down
0x01	*Right Shift* down

Portability   This function works with IBM PCs and compatibles, only.

Example

```
#include <stdio.h>
#include <bios.h>
#include <ctype.h>

#define RIGHT 0x0001
#define LEFT  0x0002
#define CTRL  0x0004
#define ALT   0x0008

main ()
{
   int key; int modifiers;
   /* function 1 returns 0 until a key is struck. Wait
      for an input by repeatedly checking for a key.
   */
   while(bioskey(1) == 0) ;

   /* now use function 0 to get return value of the key. */
   key = bioskey(0);
   printf("Key Pressed was: ");

   /* use function 2 to determine if shift keys were used */
   modifiers = bioskey(2);
   if (modifiers) {
      printf("[");
      if (modifiers & RIGHT) printf("RIGHT ");
      if (modifiers & LEFT ) printf("LEFT ");
      if (modifiers & CTRL ) printf("CTRL ");
      if (modifiers & ALT  ) printf("ALT ");
      printf("] ");
   }
   if (isalnum(key & 0xFF))
      printf("'%c'\n",key);
   else
      printf("%#02x\n",key);
}
```

Program output

```
Key Pressed was: [LEFT ] 'T'
```

biosmemory

Name	**biosmemory** – returns memory size
Usage	int biosmemory(void);
Prototype in	bios.h
Description	This function returns the memory size using BIOS interrupt 0x12.
Return value	The return value is the size of memory in 1K blocks.
Portability	This function works with IBM PCs and compatibles, only.

biosprint

Name	**biosprint** – printer I/O
Usage	int biosprint(int *cmd*, int *byte*, int *port*);
Prototype in	bios.h
Description	This function performs various printer functions on the printer identified by the parameter *port*.

A *port* value of 0 corresponds to LPT1, *port* value of 1 corresponds to LPT2, etc.

The value of *cmd* can be one of the following:

0   Print the character in *byte*
1   Initialize the printer port
2   Read the printer status

The value of *byte* can be 0 to 255.

Return value	The value returned from any of these operations is the current printer status composed by ORing these bit values together:

0x01	Device time out
0x08	I/O error
0x10	Selected
0x20	Out of paper
0x40	Acknowledge
0x80	Not busy

With *cmd* equal to 0, a return value with *device time out* set indicates an output error.

Portability This function works with IBM PCs and compatibles, only.

---

biostime

Name	**biostime** – returns time of day
Usage	long biostime(int *cmd*, long *newtime*);
Prototype in	bios.h
Description	This function either reads or sets the BIOS timer. This is a timer counting ticks since midnight at a rate of roughly 18.2 ticks per second.
	If *cmd* = 0, **biostime** returns the current value of the timer.
	If *cmd* = 1, the timer is set to the **long** value in *newtime*.
Return value	When **biostime** reads the BIOS timer, (*cmd* = 0), it returns the timer's current value.
Portability	This function works with IBM PCs and compatibles, only.

brk

Name	**brk** – changes data-segment space allocation
Usage	int brk(void *endds*);
Related functions usage	char *sbrk(int *incr*);
Prototype in	alloc.h
Description	**brk** is used to dynamically change the amount of space allocated to the calling program's data segment. The change is made by resetting the program's *break value*, which is the address of the first location beyond the end of the data segment. The amount of allocated space increases as the break value increases.
	brk sets the break value to *endds* and changes the allocated space accordingly.
	sbrk adds *incr* bytes to the break value and changes the allocated space accordingly. *incr* can be negative, in which case the amount of allocated space is decreased.
	Both functions will fail without making any change in the allocated space if such a change would result in more space being allocated than is allowable.
Return value	Upon successful completion, **brk** returns a value of 0, and **sbrk** returns the old break value.
	On failure, both functions return a value of –1, and *errno* is set to
	ENOMEM Not enough core
Portability	**brk** is available on UNIX systems.
See also	**coreleft**

bsearch

Name	**bsearch** – binary search
Usage	void *bsearch(void *key, void *base, int *nelem, int width, int (*fcmp)( ));

Related
functions usage
	void *lfind(void *key, void *base, int *nelem,
	    int width, int (*fcmp)( ));
	void *lsearch(void *key, void *base,
	    int *nelem, int width, int (*fcmp)( ));

Prototype in	stdlib.h
Description	**bsearch** is a binary search algorithm designed to search an arbitrary table of information. The entries in the table must be sorted into ascending order before **bsearch** is called.

lfind and **lsearch** also search a table for information. However, because these are *linear* searches, the table entries do not need to be sorted before a call to **lfind** or **lsearch**. If the item that *key* points to is not in the table, **lsearch** appends that item to the table, but **lfind** does not.

- *base* points to the base (0th element) of the search table.
- *nelem* points to an integer containing the number of entries in the table.
- *width* contains the number of bytes in each entry.
- *key* points to the item to be searched for (the "search key").

The argument *fcmp* points to a user-written comparison routine. That routine compares two items and returns a value based on the comparison.

To search the table, these three search functions make repeated calls to the routine whose address is passed in *fcmp*.

On each call to the comparison routine, the search functions pass two arguments: *key*, a pointer to the item being searched for; and *elem*, a pointer to the element of *base* being compared.

fcmp is free to interpret the search key and the table entries any way it likes.

Return value   Each function returns the address of the first entry in the table that matches the search key. If no match is found, **bsearch** and **lfind** return 0.

In **bsearch**

If the search key is	*fcmp* returns
Greater than *elem*	An integer < 0
Identical to *elem*	0
Less than *elem*	An integer > 0

In **lsearch** and **lfind**

If the search key is	*fcmp* returns
Not identical to *elem*	An integer != 0
Identical to *elem*	0

Portability   Available on UNIX systems.

See also   **qsort**

Example

```
#include <stdio.h>
#include <stdlib.h>

#define NELEMS(arr)    (sizeof(arr) / sizeof(arr[0]))

int numarray[] = { 123, 145, 512, 627, 800, 993 };
int numeric(int *p1, int *p2)
{
   return(*p1 - *p2);
}
```

```
/* return 1 if key is in the table, 0 if not */
int lookup(int key)
{
    int *itemptr;

    /* bsearch() returns a pointer to the item that is found */
    itemptr = (int *) bsearch(&key, numarray, NELEMS(numarray),
                    sizeof(int), numeric);
    return (itemptr != NULL);
}

main()
{
    printf("Is 512 in table? ");
    printf("%s\n", lookup(512) ? "YES" : "NO");
}
```

Program output

```
Is 512 in table? YES
```

Another Example

```
#include <stdlib.h>
#include <stdio.h>
#include <string.h>  /* for strcmp declaration */

char *colors[10] = { "red", "blue", "green" };
int ncolors = 3;
/* return 1 if already in the table, 0 if not and was added */
/* assumes there is room for new additions */

int addelem(char *color)
{
    int oldn = ncolors;

    lsearch(color, colors, &ncolors, sizeof(colors[0]), strcmp);
    return (ncolors == oldn);
}

main()
{
    if (addelem("purple"))
        printf("purple already in colors table\n");
    else
        printf("purple added to colors table, now %d colors\n",
                ncolors);
}
```

Program output

```
purple added to colors table, now 4 colors
```

cabs

Name	**cabs** – absolute value of complex number
Usage	#include <math.h> double cabs(struct complex *znum*);
Prototype in	math.h
Description	see **abs**

calloc

Name	**calloc** – allocates main memory
Usage	void *calloc(unsigned *nelem*, unsigned *elsize*);
Prototype in	stdlib.h and alloc.h
Description	see **malloc**

ceil

Name	**ceil** – rounds up
Usage	double ceil(double *x*);
Prototype in	math.h
Description	see **floor**

cgets

Name	**cgets** – reads string from console
Usage	char *cgets(char *string);
Prototype in	conio.h
Description	see **gets**

chdir

Name	**chdir** – changes working directory
Usage	int chdir(char *path);
Prototype in	dir.h
Description	**chdir** causes the directory specified by *path* to become the current working directory. *path* must specify an existing directory.
	A drive can also be specified in the *path* argument, such as:

```
chdir("a:\\turboc")  or  chdir("a:/turboc")
```

Return value	Upon successful completion, **chdir** returns a value of 0. Otherwise, a value of –1 is returned and *errno* is set to
	ENOENT Path or file name not found
Portability	**chdir** is available on UNIX systems.
See also	**mkdir**

_chmod

Name	**_chmod** – changes access mode of file
Usage	#include <dos.h>
	int _chmod(char *filename, int func [, int attrib]);
Prototype in	io.h
Description	see **chmod**

chmod

Name	**chmod** – changes access mode of file
Usage	#include <sys\stat.h>
	int chmod(char *filename, int permiss);
Related functions usage	int _chmod(char *filename, int func [, int attrib]);
Prototype in	io.h
Description	**chmod** sets the file-access permissions of the file filename according to the mask given by *permiss*. *filename* points to a string naming the file.

permiss can contain one or both of the symbolic constants S_IWRITE and S_IREAD (defined in sys\stat.h).

Value of *permiss*	Access Permission
S_IWRITE	Permission to write
S_IREAD	Permission to read
S_IREAD|S_IWRITE	Permission to read and write

The **_chmod** function may either fetch or set the MS-DOS file attributes. If *func* is 0, the function returns the current MS-DOS attributes for the file. If *func* is 1, the attribute is set to *attrib*.

attrib can be one of the following symbolic constants (defined in dos.h).

FA_RDONLY   Read only attribute
FA_HIDDEN   Hidden file
FA_SYSTEM   System file

Return value

Upon successfully changing the file-access mode, **chmod** returns 0. Otherwise, **chmod** returns a value of –1.

Upon successful completion, **_chmod** returns the file attribute word; otherwise, it returns a value of –1.

In the event of an error, *errno* is set to one of the following:

ENOENT   Path or file name not found
EACCES   Permission denied

Portability

chmod is available on UNIX systems.
_chmod is unique to MS-DOS.

See also

access, open, unlink

Example

```
#include <stdio.h>
#include <sys\stat.h>
#include <io.h>

void make_read_only(char *filename)
{
   int stat;

   stat = chmod(filename, S_IREAD);
   if (stat)
      printf("couldn't make %s read-only\n", filename);
   else
      printf("made %s read-only\n", filename);
}

main()
{
   make_read_only("NOTEXIST.FIL");
   make_read_only("MYFILE.FIL");
}
```

Program output

```
couldn't make NOTEXIST.FIL read-only
made MYFILE.FIL read-only
```

_clear87

Name	**_clear87** – clears floating-point status word
Usage	unsigned int _clear87 (void);
Prototype in	float.h
Description	**_clear87** clears the floating-point status word, which is a combination of the 8087/80287 status word and other conditions detected by the 8087/80287 exception handler.
Return value	The bits in the value returned indicate the old floating-point status. See float.h for a complete definition of the bits returned by **_clear87**.
See also	**_fpreset, _status87**

clearerr

Name	**clearerr** – resets error indication
Usage	#include <stdio.h> void clearerr(FILE *stream);
Prototype in	stdio.h
Description	see **ferror**

_close

Name	**_close** – closes a file handle
Usage	int _close(int *handle*);
Prototype in	io.h
Description	see **close**

close

Name	**close** – closes a file handle
Usage	int close(int *handle*);
Related functions usage	int _close(int *handle*);
Prototype in	io.h
Description	**close** and **_close** both close the file handle indicated by *handle*. *handle* is a file handle obtained from a **_creat**, **creat**, **creatnew**, **creattemp**, **dup**, **dup2**, **_open**, or **open** call.
	Note: These functions do not write a *Ctrl-Z* character at the end of the file. If you want to terminate the file with a *Ctrl-Z*, you must explicitly output one.
Return value	Upon successful completion, **close** and **_close** return 0. Otherwise, a value of –1 is returned.
	Both fail if *handle* is not a valid, open file handle, and set *errno* to
	EBADF Bad file number

Portability   **close** is available on UNIX systems.
                   _close is unique to MS-DOS.

See also   **creat, dup, fclose, fcntl, open**

_control87

Name   **_control87** – manipulates floating-point control word

Usage   unsigned int _control87(unsigned int *newvals*,
                       unsigned int *mask*);

Prototype in   float.h

Description   This function is used to retrieve or change the floating-point control word.

The floating-point control word is an **unsigned int** that, bit by bit, specifies certain modes in the floating-point package; namely, the precision, infinity and rounding modes. Changing these modes allows you to mask or unmask floating-point exceptions.

_control87 matches the bits in *mask* to the bits in *newvals*. If a *mask* bit = 1, the corresponding bit in *newvals* contains the new value for the same bit in the floating-point control word, and **_control87** sets that bit in the control word to the new value.

Here's a simple illustration of how this works:

```
Original control word: 0100 0011 0110 0011

       mask      1000  0001  0100  1111
       newvals   1110  1001  0000  0101

Changing bits  1---  ---1  -0--  0101
```

If *mask* = 0, **_control87** returns the floating-point control word without altering it.

Return value   The bits in the value returned reflect the new floating-point control word. For a complete definition of the bits returned by **_control87**, see float.h.

See also   _clear87, _fpreset, _status87

coreleft

Name	**coreleft** – returns a measure of unused memory
Usage	*In the tiny, small, and medium models:* unsigned coreleft(void);
	In the compact, large, and huge models: unsigned long coreleft(void);
Prototype in	alloc.h
Description	see **malloc**

cos

Name	**cos** – trigonometric function
Usage	double cos(double *x*);
Prototype in	math.h
Description	see **trig**

cosh

Name	**cosh** – hyperbolic functions
Usage	double cosh(double *x*);
Prototype in	math.h
Description	see **hyperb**

country

Name	**country** – returns country-dependent information
Usage	#include <dos.h> struct country *country(int *countrycode*, struct country **countryp*);
Prototype in	dos.h
Description	**country** specifies how certain country-dependent data, such as dates, times, and currency, will be formatted. The values set by this function depend on the version of DOS being used.

If *countryp* has a value of –1, the current country is set to the value of *countrycode*, which must be non-zero. Otherwise, the **country** structure pointed to by *countryp* is filled with the country-dependent information of

- the current country (if *countrycode* is set to 0), or
- the country given by *countrycode*.

The structure **country** is defined as follows:

```
struct  country {
     int co_date;                          /* Date format */
     char co_curr[5];                      /* Currency symbol */
     char co_thsep[2];                   /* Thousand separator */
     char co_desep[2];                   /* Decimal separator */
     char co_dtsep[2];                    /* Date separator */
     char co_tmsep[2];                    /* Time separator */
     char co_currstyle;                   /* Currency style */
     char co_digits;              /* Number of significant */
                                          /* digits in currency */
     int(far *co_case)();                /* Case map function */
     char co_dasep;                       /* Data separator */
     char co_fill[10];                           /* Filler */
};
```

The date format in *co_date* is

0 for the USA style of month, day, year
1 for the European style of day, month, year
2 for the Japanese style of year, month, day

Currency display style is given by *co_currstyle* as follows:

0 Currency symbol precedes value with no spaces between the symbol and the number.
1 Currency symbol follows value with no spaces between the number and the symbol.
2 Currency symbol precedes value with a space after the symbol.
3 Currency symbol follows the number with a space before the symbol.

Return value   **country** returns the pointer argument *countryp*.

Portability   Unique to MS-DOS.

cprintf

Name   **cprintf** – sends formatted output to the console

Usage   int cprintf(char *format*[, *argument*, ...]);

Prototype in conio.h

Description   see **printf**

cputs

Name	**cputs** – writes a string to the console
Usage	void cputs(char *string);
Prototype in	conio.h
Description	see **puts**

_creat

Name	**_creat** – creates a new file or rewrites an existing one
Usage	#include <dos.h> int _creat(char *filename, int attrib);
Prototype in	io.h
Description	see **creat**

creat

Name	**creat** – creates a new file or rewrites an existing one
Usage	#include <sys\stat.h> int creat(char *filename, int permiss);

Related
functions usage
	int _creat(char *filename, int attrib);
	int creatnew(char *filename, int attrib);
	int creattemp(char *filename, int attrib);

Prototype in	io.h

Description   **creat** creates a new file or prepares to rewrite an existing file named by the string pointed to by *filename*. *permiss* only applies to newly created files.

If the file exists and the write attribute is set, **creat** truncates the file to a length of zero bytes, leaving the file attributes unchanged. If the existing file has the read-only attribute set, the **creat** call fails, and the file remains unchanged.

The **creat** call examines only one bit of the access-mode word *permiss*; this is the UNIX owner-write permission bit.

If the owner-write permission bit is 1, the file is writable. If the bit is 0, the file is marked as read-only. All other MS-DOS attributes are set to 0.

permiss can be one of the following (defined in sys\stat.h):

Value of *permiss*	Access Permission
S_IWRITE	Permission to write
S_IREAD	Permission to read
S_IREAD|S_IWRITE	Permission to read and write

Note: In DOS, write permission implies read permission.

A file created with **_creat** is always created in the translation mode specified by the global variable *_fmode* (O_TEXT or O_BINARY).

To create a file in a particular mode, you can either assign to *_fmode*, or call **open** with the O_CREAT and O_TRUNC option ORed with the translation mode desired. For example, the call

```
open("xmp",O_CREAT|O_TRUNC|O_BINARY,S_IREAD)
```

will create a binary-mode, read-only file named XMP, truncating its length to 0 bytes if it already existed.

_creat accepts *attrib*, an MS-DOS attribute word. Any attribute bits may be set in this call. The file is always opened in binary mode. Upon successful file creation, the file pointer is set to the beginning of the file. The file is opened for both reading and writing.

creatnew is identical to **_create**, with the exception that, if the file exists, the **creatnew** call returns an error and leaves the file untouched.

creattemp is similar to **_creat** except that the *filename* is a path name ending with a backslash (\). A unique file name is selected in the directory given by *filename*. The newly created file name is stored in the *filename* string supplied. *filename* should be long enough to hold the resulting file name. The file is not automatically deleted when the program terminates.

The *attrib* argument to **_creat**, **creatnew**, and **creattemp** can be one of the following constants (defined in dos.h):

FA_RDONLY	Read only attribute
FA_HIDDEN	Hidden file
FA_SYSTEM	System file

Return value   Upon successful completion, the new file handle, a non-negative integer, is returned; otherwise, a –1 is returned.

In the event of error, *errno* is set to one of the following:

ENOENT	Path or file name not found
EMFILE	Too many open files
EACCES	Permission denied

Portability   **creat** is available on UNIX systems. **_creat** is unique to MS-DOS. **creatnew** and **creattemp** are unique to MS-DOS 3.0 and will not work on earlier DOS versions.

See also   **bsearch, close, dup,** *_fmode* (variable), **open, read, write**

creatnew

Name	**creatnew** – creates a new file
Usage	#include <dos.h> int creatnew(char *filename*, int *attrib*);
Prototype in	io.h
Description	see **creat**

creattemp

Name	**creattemp** – creates a new file or rewrites an existing one
Usage	#include <dos.h> int creattemp(char *filename, int attrib);
Prototype in	io.h
Description	see **creat**

cscanf

Name	**cscanf** – performs formatted input from console
Usage	int cscanf(char *format[, argument, ...]);
Prototype in	conio.h
Description	see **scanf**

ctime

Name	**ctime** – converts date and time to a string
Usage	char *ctime(long *clock);

Related functions usage	char *asctime(struct tm *tm);
	double difftime(time_t time2, time_t time1);
	
	struct tm *gmtime(long *clock);
	struct tm *localtime(long *clock);
	
	void tzset(void);

Prototype in	time.h
Description	**ctime** converts a time pointed to by *clock* (such as returned by the function **time**) into a 26-character string in the following form:

```
Mon Nov 21 11:31:54 1983\n\0
```

All the fields have constant width.

asctime converts a time stored as a structure to a 26-character string of the same form as the **ctime** string.

difftime calculates the elapsed time, in seconds, from *time1* to *time2*.

localtime and **gmtime** return pointers to structures containing the broken-down time. **localtime** corrects for the time zone And possible daylight savings time; **gmtime** converts directly to GMT.

The global long variable *timezone* contains the difference in seconds between GMT and local standard time (in EST, *timezone* is 5*60*60). The global variable *daylight* is non-zero *if and only if* the standard U.S.A. Daylight Savings Time conversion should be applied.

The program knows about the peculiarities of this conversion in 1974 and 1975; if necessary, a table for these years can be extended.

tzset is provided for UNIX compatibility and does nothing in this implementation.

The structure declaration from the time.h include file is:

```
struct  tm  {
    int tm_sec;
    int tm_min;
    int tm_hour;
    int tm_mday;
    int tm_mon;
    int tm_year;
    int tm_wday;
    int tm_yday;
    int tm_isdst;
};
```

These quantities give the time on a 24-hour clock, day of month (1-31), month (0-11), weekday (Sunday equals 0), year – 1900, day of year (0-365), and a flag that is non-zero if daylight savings time is in effect.

Return value   **ctime** and **asctime** return a pointer to the character string containing the date and time. This string is a static which is overwritten with each call.

difftime returns the result of its calculation as a double.

localtime and **gmtime** return the broken down time structure. This structure is a static which is overwritten with each call.

Portability   All functions are available on UNIX systems.

See also   **getdate, time**

Example

```
#include <stdio.h>
#include <time.h>

main()
{
    struct tm *tm_now;
    long secs_now;
    char *str_now;

    time(&secs_now);                /* in seconds */
    str_now = ctime(&secs_now);     /* make it a string */

    printf("The number of seconds since Jan 1, 1970 is %ld\n", secs_now);
    printf("In other words, the current time is %s\n", str_now);

    tm_now = localtime(&secs_now);  /* make it a structure */
    printf("From the structure: day %d  %02d-%02d-%02d %02d:%02d:%02d\n",
            tm_now->tm_yday, tm_now->tm_mon, tm_now->tm_mday, tm_now->tm_year,
            tm_now->tm_hour, tm_now->tm_min, tm_now->tm_sec);

    str_now = asctime(tm_now);      /* from structure to string */
    printf("Once more, the current time is %s\n", str_now);
}
```

Program output

```
The number of seconds since Jan 1, 1970 is 315594553
In other words, the current time is Tue Jan 01 12:09:13 1980

From the structure: day 0  00-01-80 12:09:13
Once more, the current time is Tue Jan 01 12:09:13 1980
```

ctrlbrk

Name	**ctrlbrk** – sets control-break handler
Usage	void ctrlbrk(int (*_fptr_)(void));
Prototype in	dos.h
Description	**ctrlbrk** sets a new control-break handler function pointed to by _fptr_. The interrupt vector 0x23 is modified to call the named function.
	The named function is not called directly. **ctrlbrk** establishes a DOS interrupt handler that calls the named function.
	The handler function may perform any number of operations and system calls. The handler does not have to return; it may use **longjmp** to return to an arbitrary point in the program.
Return value	**ctrlbrk** returns nothing. The handler function returns 0 to abort the current program; any other value will cause the program to resume execution.
Portability	Unique to MS-DOS.
See also	**longjmp, setjmp**

Example

```
#include <stdio.h>
#include <dos.h>

#define ABORT 0

int c_break(void)
{
   printf("Control-Break hit.  Program aborting ...\n");
   return(ABORT);
}
```

```
main()
{
   ctrlbrk(c_break);
   for (;;) {  /* infinite loop */
      printf("Looping ...\n");
   }
}
```

Program output

```
Looping ...
Looping ...
Looping ...
^C
Control-Break hit.  Program aborting ...
```

difftime

Name	**difftime** – computes difference between two times
Usage	#include <time.h> double difftime(time_t *time2*, time_t *time1*);
Prototype in	time.h
Description	see **ctime**

disable

Name	**disable** – disables interrupts
Usage	#include <dos.h> void disable(void);
Related functions usage	void enable(void); void geninterrupt(int *intr_num*);
Prototype in	dos.h

Description	These macros are designed to provide a programmer with flexible hardware interrupt control.
	The **disable** macro disables interrupts. Only the NMI interrupt will still be allowed from any external device.
	The **enable** macro enables interrupts. This allows any device interrupts to occur.
	The **geninterrupt** macro triggers a software trap for the interrupt given by *intr_num*.
Return value	**disable** and **enable** return nothing. For **geninterrupt** the return value depends on the interrupt that was called.
Portability	These macros are unique to the 8086 architecture.
See also	**getvect**

dosexterr

Name	**dosexterr** – gets extended error
Usage	#include <dos.h>
int dosexterr(struct DOSERR *eblkp);
Prototype in	dos.h
Description	This function fills in the **DOSERR** structure pointed to by *eblkp* with extended error information after an MS-DOS call has failed. The structure is defined as follows:

```
struct  DOSERR {
   int exterror;                        /* Extended error */
   char class;                          /* Error class */
   char action;                           /* Action */
   char locus;                          /* Error locus */
};
```

The values in this structure are obtained via DOS call 0x59. An *exterror* value of 0 indicates the prior MS-DOS call did not result in an error.

Return value	**dosexterr** returns the value *exterror*.
Portability	Unique to MS-DOS 3.x; cannot be used on earlier releases of MS-DOS.

dostounix

Name	**dostounix** – converts date and time to UNIX time format
Usage	#include <dos.h> long dostounix(struct date *dateptr*, struct time *timeptr*);
Related functions usage	void unixtodos(long *utime*, struct date *dateptr*, struct time *timeptr*);
Prototype in	dos.h
Description	**dostounix** converts a date and time as returned from **getdate** and **gettime** into UNIX-format time. *dateptr* points to a **date** structure, and *timeptr* points to a **time** structure containing valid DOS date and time information.
	unixtodos converts the UNIX-format time given in *utime* to DOS format and fills in the **date** and **time** structures pointed to by *dateptr* and *timeptr*.
Return value	**dostounix** UNIX version of current time: number of seconds since 00:00:00 on January 1, 1970 (GMT).
	unixtodos returns nothing.
Portability	Both functions are unique to MS-DOS.
See also	**ctime, getdate, gettime**

dup

Name	**dup** – duplicates a file handle
Usage	int dup(int *handle*);
Related functions usage	int dup2(int *oldhandle*, int *newhandle*);
Prototype in	io.h

Description **dup** and **dup2** each return a new file handle that has the following in common with the original file handle:

- same open file or device
- same file pointer (that is, changing the file pointer of one changes the other)
- same access mode (read, write, read/write)

dup2 returns the next file handle available; **dup2** returns a new handle with the value of *newhandle*. If the file associated with *newhandle* is open when **dup2** is called, it is closed.

handle and *oldhandle* are file handles obtained from a **creat**, **open**, **dup**, **dup2**, or **fcntl** call.

Return value Upon successful completion, **dup** returns the new file handle, a non-negative integer; otherwise, **dup** returns –1.

dup2 returns 0 on successful completion, –1 otherwise.

In the event of error, *errno* is set to one of the following:

EMFILE	Too many open files
EBADF	Bad file number

Portability **dup** is available on all UNIX systems.
dup2 is available on some UNIX systems, but not System III.

See also **close, creat, open, read, write**

dup2

Name	**dup2** – duplicates a file handle
Usage	int dup2(int *oldhandle*, int *newhandle*);
Prototype in	io.h
Description	see **dup**

ecvt

Name	**ecvt** – converts a floating-point number to a string
Usage	char *ecvt(double *value*, int *ndigit*, int *decpt*, int *sign*);
Related functions usage	char *fcvt(double *value*, int *ndigit*, int *decpt*, int *sign*); char *gcvt(double *value*, int *ndigit*, char *buf*);
Prototype in	stdlib.h
Description	**ecvt** converts *value* to a null-terminated string of *ndigit* digits and returns a pointer to the string. The position of the decimal point relative to the beginning of the string is stored indirectly through *decpt* (a negative value for *decpt* means to the left of the returned digits). If the sign of the result is negative, the word pointed to by *sign* is non-zero; otherwise, it is 0. The low-order digit is rounded.

fcvt is identical to **ecvt**, except that the correct digit has been rounded for Fortran F-format output of the number of digits specified by *ndigit*.

gcvt converts *value* to a null-terminated ASCII string in *buf* and returns a pointer to *buf*. It attempts to produce *ndigit* significant digits in Fortran F-format if possible;

otherwise, E-format (ready for printing) is returned. Trailing zeros may be suppressed.

Return value	The return values of **ecvt** and **fcvt** point to static data whose content is overwritten by each call to **ecvt** or **fcvt**.
	gcvt returns the string pointed to by *buf*.
Portability	Available on UNIX.
See also	**printf**

enable

Name	**enable** – enables interrupts
Usage	#include <dos.h> void enable(void);
Prototype in	dos.h
Description	see **disable**

eof

Name	**eof** – detects end-of-file
Usage	int eof(int *handle*);
Prototype in	io.h
Description	**eof** determines whether the file associated with *handle* has reached end-of-file.
Return value	If the current position is end-of-file, **eof** returns the value 1; otherwise, it returns 0. A return value of –1 indicates an error; and *errno* is set to
	EBADF Bad file number
See also	**ferror, perror**

exec...

Name exec... – functions that load and run other programs

Usage int execl(char *pathname, char *arg0, arg1, ..., argn, NULL);

int execle(char *pathname, char *arg0, arg1, ..., argn, NULL, char *envp[]);

int execlp(char *pathname, char *arg0, arg1, ..., argn, NULL);

int execlpe(char *pathname, char *arg0, arg1, ..., argn, NULL, char *envp[]);

int execv(char *pathname, char *argv[]);

int execve(char *pathname, char *argv[], char *envp[]);

int execvp(char *pathname, char *argv[]);

int execvpe(char *pathname, char *argv[], char *envp[]);

Prototype in process.h

Description The functions in the **exec...** family load and run (execute) other programs, known as *child processes*. When an **exec...** call is successful, the child process overlays the *parent process*. There must be sufficient memory available for loading and executing the child process.

pathname is the file name of the called child process. The **exec...** functions search for *pathname* using the standard MS-DOS search algorithm:

- no extension or no period—search for exact file name; if not successful, add .exe and search again
- extension given—search only for exact file name
- period given—search only for file name with no extension

The suffixes *l*, *v*, *p*, and *e* added to the **exec...** "family name" specify that the named function will operate with certain capabilities.

p specifies that the function will search for the child in those directories specified by the DOS PATH environment variable. Without the *p* suffix, the function only searches the root and current working directory.

l specifies that the argument pointers (*arg0*, *arg1, ..., argn*) are passed as separate arguments. Typically, the *l* suffix is used when you know in advance the number of arguments to be passed.

v specifies that the argument pointers (*argv[0] ..., arg[n]*) are passed as an array of pointers. Typically, the *v* suffix is used when a variable number of arguments is to be passed.

e specifies that the argument *envp* may be passed to the child process, allowing you to alter the environment for the child process. Without the *e* suffix, child processes inherit the environment of the parent process.

Each function in the **exec...** family *must* have one of the two argument-specifying suffixes (either *l* or *v*). The *path search* and *environment inheritance* suffixes (*p* and *e*) are optional.

For example,

- **execl** is an **exec...** function that takes separate arguments, searches only the root or current directory for the child, and passes on the parent's environment to the child.

- **execvpe** is an **exec...** function that takes an array of argument pointers, incorporates PATH in its search for the child process, and accepts the *envp* argument for altering the child's environment.

The **exec...** functions must pass at least one argument to the child process (*arg0* or *argv[0]*): This argument is, by convention, a copy of *pathname*. (Using a different value for this zeroth argument won't produce an error.)

Under MS-DOS 3.x, *pathname* is available for the child process; under earlier versions, the child process cannot use the passed value of the zeroth argument (*arg0* or *argv[0]*).

When the *l* suffix is used, *arg0* usually points to *pathname*, and *arg1*, ..., *argn* point to character strings that form the new list of arguments. A mandatory NULL following *argn* marks the end of the list.

When the *e* suffix is used, you pass a list of new environment settings through the argument *envp*. This environment argument is an array of **char***. Each element points to a null-terminated character string of the form

   envvar = value

where *envvar* is the name of an environment variable, and *value* is the string value to which *envvar* is set. The last element in *envp[ ]* is NULL. When *envp[0]* is NULL, the child inherits the parents' environment settings.

The combined length of *arg0* + *arg1* + ... + *argn* (or of *argv[0]* + *argv[1]* + ... + *argn[n]*), including space characters that separate the arguments, must be less than 128 bytes. Null terminators are not counted.

When an **exec...** function call is made, any open files remain open in the child process.

Return value   If successful, the **exec...** functions return no value. On error, the **exec...** functions return –1, and *errno* is set to one of the following:

E2BIG	Arg list too long
EACCES	Permission denied
EMFILE	Too many open files
ENOENT	Path or file name not found
ENOEXEC	Exec format error
ENOMEM	Not enough core

See also   **abort, atexit, exit, searchpath, spawn, system**

Example

```
#include <stdio.h>
#include <process.h>

main()
{
   int stat;

   printf("About to exec child with arg1 arg2 ...\n");
   stat = execl("CHILD.EXE", "CHILD.EXE", "arg1", "arg2", NULL);
```

```
   /* execl will return only if it cannot run CHILD */
   printf("execl error = %d\n", stat);
   exit(1);
}

/* CHILD.C */
#include <stdio.h>

main(int argc, char *argv[])
{
   int i;

   printf("Child running ...\n");
   /* print out its arguments */
   for (i=0; i<argc; i++)
      printf("argv[%d]: %s\n", i, argv[i]);
}
```

Program output

```
About to exec child with arg1 arg2 ...
Child running ...
argv[0]: CHILD.EXE
argv[1]: arg1
argv[2]: arg2
```

_exit

Name	**_exit** – terminates program
Usage	void _exit(int *status*);
Prototype in	process.h
Description	see **exit**

exit

Name	**exit** – terminates program
Usage	void exit(int *status*);
Related functions usage	void _exit(int *status*);
Prototype in	process.h
Description	**exit** terminates the calling process. Before exiting, all files are closed, buffered output (waiting to be output) is written, and any registered "exit functions" (posted with **atexit**) are called.
	_exit terminates without closing any files, flushing any output, or calling any exit functions.
	In either case, *status* is provided for the calling process as the exit status of the process. Typically a value of 0 is used to indicate a normal exit, and a non-zero value indicates some error.
Return value	These functions never return a value.
Portability	**exit** and **_exit** are available on UNIX systems.
See also	**abort, atexit, exec..., spawn...**

exp

Name	**exp** – exponential function; returns e^x
Usage	double exp(double *x*);
Related functions usage	double frexp(double *value*, int **eptr*); double ldexp(double *value*, int *exp*);

double log(double *x*);
double log10(double *x*);

double pow(double *x*, double *y*);
double pow10(int *p*);

double sqrt(double *x*);

Prototype in	math.h
Description	**exp** calculates the exponential function e^x

frexp calculates the mantissa *x* (a double <1) and *n* (an integer) such that *value* = $x \cdot 2^n$. **frexp** stores *n* in the integer that *eptr* points to.

ldexp calculates the double *value* $\cdot 2^{exp}$

log calculates the natural logarithm of *x*

log10 calculates the base 10 logarithm of *x*

pow calculates x^y

pow10 computes 10^p

sqrt calculates $+\sqrt{x}$

Return value
All these functions, on success, return the value they calculated.

exp returns e^x

frexp returns *x* (< 1) where *value* = $x \cdot 2^n$

ldexp returns *x* where $x = value \cdot 2^{exp}$

log returns $ln(x)$

log10 returns $log_{10}(x)$

pow returns *p* where $p = x^y$

pow10 returns *x* where $x = 10^p$

sqrt returns *q* where $q = +\sqrt{x}$

Sometimes the arguments passed to these functions produce results that overflow or are incalculable. When the correct value would overflow, **exp** and **pow** return the value HUGE_VAL. Results of excessively large magnitude can cause *errno* to be set to

ERANGE   Result out of range

The following errors cause *errno* to be set to

EDOM   Domain error

- The argument x passed to **log** or **log10** is less than or equal to 0.

- The argument x passed to **pow** is less than or equal to 0 and y is not a whole number.

- The arguments x and y passed to **pow** are both 0.

- The argument x passed to **sqrt** is less than 0.

When these errors occur

- **log, log10,** and **pow** return the value negative HUGE_VAL.

- **sqrt** returns 0.

Error handling for these routines can be modified through the function **matherr**.

Portability   Available on UNIX systems.

See also   **hyperb, trig, matherr**

fabs

Name   **fabs** – absolute value

Usage   double fabs(double x);

Prototype in   math.h

Description   see **abs**

farcalloc

Name	**farcalloc** – allocates memory from the far heap
Usage	void far * farcalloc(unsigned long *nunits*, unsigned long *unitsz*);
Prototype in	alloc.h
Description	see **farmalloc**

farcoreleft

Name	**farcoreleft** – returns measure of unused memory in far heap
Usage	long farcoreleft(void);
Prototype in	alloc.h
Description	see **farmalloc**

farfree

Name	**farfree** – frees a block from far heap
Usage	void farfree(void far * *block*);
Prototype in	alloc.h
Description	see **farmalloc**

farmalloc

Name	**farmalloc** – allocates from far heap
Usage	void far *farmalloc(unsigned long *size*);
Related functions usage	void far *farcalloc(unsigned long *nunits*, unsigned long *unitsz*);
	long farcoreleft(void); void farfree(void far *block*);
	void far *farrealloc(void far *block*, unsigned long *newsize*);
Prototype in	alloc.h
Description	**farmalloc** allocates a block of memory *size* bytes long from the far heap.

farcalloc allocates memory from the far heap for an array containing *nunits* elements, each *unitsz* bytes long.

farcoreleft returns a measure of the amount of unused memory in the far heap beyond the highest allocated block.

farfree releases a block of previously allocated far memory.

farrealloc adjusts the size of the allocated block to *newsize*, copying the contents to a new location if necessary.

For allocating from the far heap, note that:

- all of available RAM can be allocated
- blocks larger than 64K can be allocated
- far pointers are used to access the allocated blocks

In the compact, large, and huge memory models, these functions are similar, though not identical, to the normal memory allocation functions. These functions take unsigned long parameters, while the normal ones (**malloc**, etc.) take unsigned. (Refer to **malloc**.)

The tiny model cannot make use of these functions because it cannot have any segment fixups, which are often produced by far pointers.

In the small and medium memory models, blocks allocated by **farmalloc** may not be freed via normal **free**, and blocks allocated via **malloc** cannot be freed via **farfree**. In these models the two heaps are completely distinct.

Return value   **farmalloc** and **farcalloc** return a pointer to the newly allocated block, or NULL if not enough space exists for the new block.

farrealloc returns the address of the reallocated block. This may be different than the address of the original block. If the block cannot be reallocated, **farrealloc** returns NULL.

farcoreleft returns the total amount of space left between the highest allocated block and the end of memory.

Portability   Unique to MS-DOS.

See also   **malloc**

Example

```
/*
    Far Memory Management

    farcoreleft - gets the amount of core memory left
    farmalloc   - allocates space on the far heap
    farrealloc  - adjusts allocated block in far heap
    farfree     - frees far heap
*/
#include <stdio.h>
#include <alloc.h>

main()
{
    char far * block;
    long size = 65000;

    /* Find out what's out there *s/

    printf("%lu bytes free\n", farcoreleft());
```

```
    /* Get a piece of it */

    block = farmalloc(size);
    if (block == NULL) {
        printf("failed to allocate\n");
        exit(1);
    }
    printf("%lu bytes allocated, ",size);
    printf("%lu bytes free\n", farcoreleft());

    /* Shrink the block */
    size /= 2;
    block = farrealloc(block, size);
    printf("block now reallocated to %lu bytes, ",size);
    printf("%lu bytes free\n", farcoreleft());

    /* Let it go entirely */
    printf("Free the block\n");
    farfree(block);
    printf("block now freed, ");
    printf("%lu bytes free\n", farcoreleft());

}
/* End of main */
```

Program output

```
359616 bytes free
65000 bytes allocated, 294608 bytes free
block now reallocated to 32500 bytes, 262100 bytes free
Free the block
Block now freed, 359616 bytes free
```

farrealloc

Name	**farrealloc** – adjusts allocated block in far heap
Usage	void far * farrealloc(void far * *block*, unsigned long *newsize*);
Prototype in	alloc.h
Description	see **farmalloc**

fclose

Name	**fclose** – closes a stream
Usage	#include <stdio.h> int fclose(FILE *stream);

Related functions usage	int fcloseall(void);
	int fflush(FILE * stream);
	int flushall(void);

Prototype in	stdio.h
Description	**fclose** closes the named *stream*; generally, all buffers associated with *stream* are flushed before closing. System-allocated buffers are freed upon closing. Buffers assigned with **setbuf** or **setvbuf** are not automatically freed.
	fcloseall closes all open streams except *stdin* and *stdout*.
	fflush causes the contents of the buffer associated with an open output stream to be written to *stream*, and clears the buffer contents if *stream* is an open input stream. *stream* remains open.
	flushall clears all buffers associated with open input streams, and writes all buffers associated with open output streams to their respective files. Any read operation following **flushall** reads new data into the buffers from the input files.
Return value	**fclose** and **fflush** return 0 on success; **fcloseall** returns the total number of streams it closed. **fclose**, **fcloseall**, and **fflush** return EOF if any errors were detected.
	flushall returns an integer, which is the number of open input and output streams.
Portability	These functions are available on UNIX systems.
See also	**close, fopen, setbuf**

fcloseall

Name	**fcloseall** – closes open streams
Usage	int fcloseall(void);
Prototype in	stdio.h
Description	see **fclose**

fcvt

Name	**fcvt** – converts a floating-point number to a string
Usage	char *fcvt(double *value*, int *ndigit*, int *decpt*, int *sign*);
Prototype in	stdlib.h
Description	see **ecvt**

fdopen

Name	**fdopen** – associates a stream with a file handle
Usage	#include <stdio.h> FILE *fdopen(int *handle*, char *type*);
Prototype in	stdio.h
Description	see **fopen**

feof

Name	**feof** – detects end-of-file on stream
Usage	#include <stdio.h> int feof(FILE * *stream*);
Prototype in	stdio.h
Description	see **ferror**

ferror

Name	**ferror** – detects errors on stream
Usage	#include <stdio.h> int ferror(FILE * *stream*);
Related functions usage	void clearerr(FILE * *stream*); int feof(FILE * *stream*);
Prototype in	stdio.h
Description	**ferror** is a macro that tests the given *stream* for a read or write error. If the *stream*'s error indicator has been set, it remains set until **clearerr** or **rewind** is called, or until the stream is closed. **clearerr** sets the *stream*'s error and end-of-file indicators to 0. **feof** is a macro that tests the given *stream* for an end-of-file indicator. Once the indicator is set, read operations on the file return the indicator until **rewind** is called or the file is closed.
Return value	**ferror** returns non-zero if an error was detected on the named *stream*.

clearerr resets the error and end-of-file indicators on the named *stream*; it returns nothing.

feof returns non-zero if an end-of-file indicator was detected on the last input operation on the named *stream*.

The end-of-file indicator is reset with each input operation.

Portability	These functions are available on UNIX systems.
See also	**eof, fopen, getc, gets, open, putc, puts**

fflush

Name	**fflush** – flushes a stream
Usage	#include <stdio.h> int fflush(FILE *stream);
Prototype in	stdio.h
Description	see **fclose**

fgetc

Name	**fgetc** – gets character from stream
Usage	#include <stdio.h> int fgetc(FILE *stream);
Prototype in	stdio.h
Description	see **getc**

fgetchar

Name	**fgetchar** – gets character from stream
Usage	int fgetchar(void);
Prototype in	stdio.h
Description	see **getc**

fgets

Name	**fgets** – gets a string from a stream
Usage	#include <stdio.h> char *fgets(char *string, int n, FILE *stream);
Prototype in	stdio.h
Description	see **gets**

filelength

Name	**filelength** – gets file size in bytes
Usage	long filelength(int handle);
Prototype in	io.h
Description	**filelength** returns the length (in bytes) of the file associated with handle.

Return value	On success, **filelength** returns a long value, the file length in bytes. On error, the return value is –1L and *errno* is set to

	EBADF	Bad file number

fileno

Name	**fileno** – gets file handle
Usage	#include <stdio.h> int fileno(FILE * *stream*);
Prototype in	stdio.h
Description	**fileno** is a macro that returns the file handle for the given *stream*. If *stream* has more than one handle, **fileno** returns the handle assigned to the stream when it was first opened.
Return value	**fileno** returns the integer file handle associated with the *stream*.
Portability	Available on UNIX systems.

findfirst

Name	**findfirst** – searches disk directory
Usage	#include <dir.h> #include <dos.h> int findfirst(char *pathname*, struct ffblk **ffblk*, int *attrib*);
Related functions usage	int findnext(struct ffblk **ffblk*);
Prototype in	dir.h
Description	**findfirst** begins a search of a disk directory by using the MS-DOS system call 0x4E.

pathname is a string with an optional drive specifier, path and file name of the file to be found. The file name portion may contain wildcard match characters (such as ? or *). If a matching file is found, the *ffblk* structure is filled with the file-directory information.

attrib is an MS-DOS file-attribute byte used in selecting eligible files for the search. *attrib* can be one of the following constants defined in dos.h.

FA_RDONLY	Read only attribute
FA_HIDDEN	Hidden file
FA_SYSTEM	System file
FA_LABEL	Volume label
FA_DIREC	Directory
FA_ARCH	Archive

For more detailed information about these attributes, refer to the *MS-DOS Programmer's Reference Manual*.

findnext is used to fetch subsequent files which match the *pathname* given in **findfirst**. *ffblk* is the same block filled in by the **findfirst** call. This block contains necessary information for continuing the search. One file name for each call to **findnext** will be returned until no more files are found in the directory matching the *pathname*.

The format of the structure *ffblk* is as follows:

```
struct ffblk {
    char ff_reserved[21];          /* Reserved by DOS */
    char ff_attrib;                /* Attribute found */
    int ff_ftime;                      /* File time */
    int ff_fdate;                      /* File date */
    long ff_fsize;                     /* File size */
    char ff_name[13];              /* Found file name */
};
```

Note that **findfirst** and **findnext** set the MS-DOS disk-transfer address (DTA) to the address of the **ffblk**.

If you need this DTA value, you should save it and restore it (using **getdta** and **setdta**) after each call to **findfirst** or **findnext**.

Return value

findfirst and **findnext** return 0 on successfully finding a file matching the search *pathname*. When no more files can be found or if there is some error in the file name, –1 is returned, and the global variable *errno* is set to one of the following:

ENOENT   Path or file name not found
ENMFILE   No more files

Portability   Unique to MS-DOS.

Example

```
#include <stdio.h>
#include <dir.h>

main()
{
   struct ffblk ffblk;
   int done;

   printf("Directory listing of *.*\n");
   done = findfirst("*.*",&ffblk,0);
   while (!done) {
      printf("  %s\n", ffblk.ff_name);
      done = findnext(&ffblk);
   }
}
```

Program output

```
Directory listing of *.*
  FINDFRST.C
  FINDFRST.OBJ
  FINDFRST.MAP
  FINDFRST.EXE
```

findnext

Name	**findnext** – fetches files which match **findfirst**
Usage	#include <dir.h> int findnext(struct ffblk *ffblk*);
Prototype in	dir.h
Description	see **findfirst**

floor

Name	**floor** – rounds down
Usage	double floor(double x);
Related functions usage	double ceil(double x);
Prototype in	math.h
Description	**floor** finds the largest integer not greater than x. **ceil** finds the smallest integer not less than x.
Return value	**floor** and **ceil** each return the integer found (as a `double`).
Portability	These functions are available on UNIX systems.
See also	**abs**

flushall

Name	**flushall** – clears all buffers
Usage	int flushall(void);
Prototype in	stdio.h
Description	see **fclose**

fmod

Name	**fmod** – calculates x modulo y, the remainder of x/y
Usage	double fmod(double x, double y);
Related functions usage	double modf(double *value*, double * *iptr*);
Prototype in	math.h
Description	**fmod** calculates x modulo y (the remainder f where $x = iy + f$ for some integer i and $0 \le f < y$).
	modf breaks the double *value* into two parts: the integer and the fraction. It stores the integer in *iptr* and returns the fraction.
Return value	**fmod** returns the remainder f where $x = iy + f$ (as described).
	modf returns the fractional part of *value*.

fnmerge

Name	**fnmerge** – makes new file name
Usage	#include <dir.h> void fnmerge(char *path, char * *drive*, char * *dir*, 　　　　　　char * *name*, char * *ext*);
Related functions usage	int fnsplit(char *path, char *drive*, char *dir*, 　　　　　　char *name*, char *ext*);
Prototype in	dir.h
Description	**fnmerge** makes a file name from its components. The new file's full path name is

```
X:\DIR\SUBDIR\NAME.EXT
```

where

> x is given by *drive*
> \DIR\SUBDIR\ is given by *dir*
> NAME.EXT is given by *name* and *ext*

fnsplit takes a file's full path name (*path*) as a string in the form

    X:\DIR\SUBDIR\NAME.EXT

and splits *path* into its four components. It then stores those components in the strings pointed to by *drive*, *dir*, *name* and *ext*. (Each component is required but can be a NULL, which means the corresponding component will be parsed but not stored.)

The maximum sizes for these strings are given by the constants MAXDRIVE, MAXDIR, MAXPATH, MAXNAME and MAXEXT, (defined in dir.h) and each size includes space for the null-terminator.

Constant	(**Max**.)	String
MAXPATH	(80)	*path*
MAXDRIVE	(3)	*drive*; includes colon (:)
MAXDIR	(66)	*dir*; includes leading and trailing backslashes (\)
MAXFILE	(9)	*name*
MAXEXT	(5)	*ext*; includes leading dot (.)

fnsplit assumes that there is enough space to store each non-NULL component. **fnmerge** assumes that there is enough space for the constructed path name. The maximum constructed length is MAXPATH.

When **fnsplit** splits *path*, it treats the punctuation as follows:

- *drive* keeps the colon attached (C:, A:, etc.)
- *dir* keeps the leading and trailing backslashes (\turboc\include\, \source\, etc.)
- *ext* keeps the dot preceding the extension (.c, .exe, etc.)

These two functions are invertible; if you split a given *path* with **fnsplit**, then merge the resultant components with **fnmerge**, you end up with *path*.

Return value	**fnsplit** returns an integer (composed of five flags, defined in dir.h) indicating which of the full path name components were present in *path*; these flags and the components they represent are:

EXTENSION	an extension
FILENAME	a filename
DIRECTORY	a directory (and possibly sub-directories)
DRIVE	a drive specification (see dir.h)
WILDCARDS	wildcards (* or ? cards)

Portability   Available on MS-DOS systems only.

See also

Example

```
#include <stdio.h>
#include <dir.h>

char drive[MAXDRIVE];
char dir[MAXDIR];
char file[MAXFILE];
char ext[MAXEXT];

main()
{
    char s[MAXPATH], t[MAXPATH];
    int flag;

    for (;;) {
        printf("> ");         /* print input prompt */
        if (!gets(s)) break;  /* while there is more input */

        flag = fnsplit(s,drive,dir,file,ext);

            /* print the components */
        printf("  drive: %s, dir: %s, file: %s, ext: %s, ",
                drive, dir, file, ext);
        printf("flags: ");
        if (flag & DRIVE)
            printf(":");
        if (flag & DIRECTORY)
            printf("d");
        if (flag & FILENAME)
            printf("f");
        if (flag & EXTENSION)
            printf("e");
        printf("\n");
```

```
        /* glue the parts back together and compare to original */
    fnmerge(t,drive,dir,file,ext);
    if (strcmp(t,s) != 0)                    /* shouldn't happen! */
      printf(" --> strings are different!");
  }
}
```

Program output

```
> C:\TURBOC\FN.C
  drive: C:, dir: \TURBOC\, file: FN, ext: .C, flags: :dfe
> FILE.C
  drive: , dir: , file: FILE, ext: .C, flags: fe
> \TURBOC\SUBDIR\NOEXT.
  drive: , dir: \TURBOC\SUBDIR\, file: NOEXT, ext: ., flags: dfe
> C:MYFILE
  drive: C:, dir: , file: MYFILE, ext: , flags: :f
> ^Z
```

fnsplit

Name	**fnsplit** – splits a full path name into its components
Usage	#include <dir.h> int fnsplit(char *path*, char *drive*, char *dir*, char *name*, char *ext*);
Prototype in	dir.h
Description	see **fnmerge**

fopen

Name	**fopen** – opens a stream
Usage	#include <stdio.h> FILE *fopen(char *filename, char *type);
Related functions usage	FILE *fdopen(int handle, char *type); FILE *freopen(char *filename, char *type, FILE *stream);
Prototype in	stdio.h
Description	**fopen** opens the file named by filename and associates a stream with it. **fopen** returns a pointer to be used to identify the stream in subsequent operations.

fdopen associates a stream with a file handle obtained from **creat**, **dup**, **dup2**, or **open**. The type of stream must match the mode of the open handle.

freopen substitutes the named file in place of the open stream. The original stream is closed, regardless of whether the open succeeds. **freopen** is useful for changing the file attached to stdin, stdout, or stderr.

The type string used in each of these calls is one of the following values:

r   Open for reading only.

w   Create for writing.

a   Append; open for writing at end of file or create for writing if the file does not exist.

r+   Open an existing file for update (reading and writing).

w+   Create a new file for update.

a+   Open for append; open (or create if the file does not exist) for update at the end of the file.

To specify that a given file is being opened or created in text mode, you can append a *t* to the value of *type* (*rt*, *w+t*, etc.); similarly, to specify binary mode, you can append a *b* to the *type* value (*wb*, *a+b*, etc.)

If a *t* or *b* is not given in *type*, the mode is governed by the global variable *_fmode*. If *_fmode* is set to O_BINARY, files will be opened in binary mode. If *_fmode* is set to O_TEXT, they will be opened in text mode. These O_... constants are defined in fcntl.h.

When a file is opened for update, both input and output may be done on the resulting *stream*. However, output may not be directly followed by input without an intervening **fseek** or **rewind**, and input may not be directly followed by output without an intervening **fseek**, **rewind**, or an input which encounters end-of-file.

Return value   On successful completion, each function returns the newly open *stream*. **freopen** returns the argument *stream*. In the event of error, each function returns NULL.

Portability   These functions are available on UNIX systems. **fopen** is defined by Kernighan and Ritchie.

See also   **creat**, **dup**, **fclose**, **ferror**, *_fmode* (variable), **fread**, **fseek**, **getc**, **gets**, **open**, **putc**, **puts**, **rewind**, **setbuf**, **setmode**

Example

```
#include <stdio.h>
#include <fcntl.h>        /* needed to define the mode used in open */

main()
{
   int handle, status;
   FILE *stream;
   /* open a file */
   handle = open("MYFILE.TXT", O_CREAT);
   /* now turn it into a stream */
   stream = fdopen(handle, "w");
   if (stream == NULL)
      printf("fdopen failed\n");
   else {
      fprintf(stream, "Hello, world\n");
      fclose(stream);
   }
}
```

FP_OFF

Name	**FP_OFF** – gets a far address offset
Usage	#include <dos.h> unsigned FP_OFF(void far * *farptr*);
Related functions usage	unsigned FP_SEG(void far **farptr*); void far * MK_FP(unsigned *seg*, unsigned *off*);
Prototype in	dos.h
Description	The **FP_OFF** macro can be used to get the offset of the far pointer *farptr*.
	FP_SEG is a macro used to get the segment value of the far pointer *farptr*.
	MK_FP is a macro that makes a **far** pointer from its component segment (*seg*) and offset (*off*) parts.
Return value	**FP_OFF** returns an unsigned integer value representing an offset value.
	FP_SEG returns an unsigned integer representing a segment value.
	MK_FP returns a far pointer.
See also	**movedata, segread**

Example

```
#include <stdio.h>
#include <dos.h>

main ()
{
   char far *ptr;
   unsigned seg, off;

   ptr = MK_FP(0xB000,0);
   seg = FP_SEG(ptr);
   off = FP_OFF(ptr);
   printf("far ptr %Fp, segment %04x, offset %04x\n",
          ptr,seg,off);
```

```
}
```

Program output

```
far ptr B000:0000, segment b000, offset 0000
```

FP_SEG

Name	**FP_SEG** – gets far address segment
Usage	#include <dos.h> unsigned FP_SEG(void far *farptr*);
Prototype in	dos.h
Description	see **FP_OFF**

_fpreset

Name	**_fpreset** – reinitializes floating-point math package
Usage	void _fpreset();
Prototype in	float.h
Description	**_fpreset** reinitializes the floating-point math package. This function is usually used in conjunction with **signal**, **system**, or the **exec...** or **spawn...** functions.
	Note: Under MS-DOS versions prior to 2.x and 3.x, if an 8087/80287 coprocessor is used in a program, a child process (executed by **system** or by an **exec...** or **spawn...** function) might alter the parent process's floating-point state.
	If you use an 8087/80287, take the following precautions:

- Do not call **system** or an **exec...**, or **spawn...** function while a floating-point expression is being evaluated.
- Call **_fpreset** to reset the floating-point state after using **system, exec...**, or **spawn...** if there is *any* chance that the child process performed a floating-point operation with the 8087/80287.

Return value   There is no return value.

See also   **exec..., longjmp, signal, spawn..., system**

fprintf

Name   **fprintf** – sends formatted output to a stream

Usage   #include <stdio.h>
int fprintf(FILE *stream, char *format[, argument, ...]);

Prototype in   stdio.h

Description   see **printf**

fputc

Name   **fputc** – puts a character on a stream

Usage   #include <stdio.h>
int fputc(int ch, FILE *stream);

Prototype in   stdio.h

Description   see **putc**

fputchar

Name	**fputchar** – puts a character on *stdout*
Usage	int fputchar(char *ch*);
Prototype in	stdio.h
Description	see **putc**

fputs

Name	**fputs** – puts a string on a stream
Usage	#inlcude <stdio.h> int fputs(char *string*, FILE *stream*);
Prototype in	stdio.h
Description	see **puts**

fread

Name	**fread** – reads data from a stream
Usage	#include <stdio.h> int fread(void *ptr*, int *size*, int *nitems*, FILE *stream*);
Related functions usage	int fwrite(void *ptr*, int *size*, int *nitems*, FILE *stream*);
Prototype in	stdio.h
Description	**fread** reads *nitems* of data, each of length *size* bytes, from the named input *stream* into a block pointed to by *ptr*.

fwrite appends *nitems* of data, each of length *size* bytes, to the named output *stream*. The data appended begins at *ptr*.

For both functions, the total number of bytes read is (*nitems* * *size*).

ptr in the declarations is a pointer to any object. *size* is the size of the object *ptr* points to. The expression `sizeof *ptr` will produce the proper value.

Return value   On successful completion, each function returns the number of items (not bytes) actually read or written. **fread** returns a short count (possibly 0) on end-of-file or error. **fwrite** returns a short count on error.

Portability   These functions are available on all UNIX systems.

See also   **fopen, getc, gets, printf, putc, puts, read, scanf, write**

free

Name   **free** – frees allocated block

Usage   void free(void *ptr*);

Prototype in   stdlib.h and alloc.h

Description   see **malloc**

freemem

Name   **freemem** – frees a previously allocated DOS memory block

Usage   int freemem(unsigned *seg*);

Prototype in   dos.h

Description   see **allocmem**

freopen

Name	**freopen** – replaces a stream
Usage	#include <stdio.h> FILE *freopen(char *filename, char *type, FILE *stream);
Prototype in	stdio.h
Description	see **fopen**

frexp

Name	**frexp** – splits a double number into mantissa and exponent
Usage	double frexp(double value, int *eptr);
Prototype in	math.h
Description	see **exp**

fscanf

Name	**fscanf** – performs formatted input from a stream
Usage	#include <stdio.h> int fscanf(FILE *stream, char *format[, argument, ...]);
Prototype in	stdio.h
Description	see **scanf**

fseek

Name	**fseek** – repositions a file pointer on a stream
Usage	#include <stdio.h> int fseek(FILE * *stream*, long *offset*, int *fromwhere*);
Related functions usage	long ftell(FILE **stream*); int rewind(FILE **stream*);
Prototype in	stdio.h
Description	**fseek** sets the file pointer associated with *stream* to a new position that is *offset* bytes beyond the file location given by *fromwhere*.

fromwhere must be one of the values 0, 1 or 2, which represent three symbolic constants (defined in stdio.h) as follows:

fromwhere		File Location
SEEK_SET	(0)	file beginning
SEEK_CUR	(1)	current file pointer position
SEEK_END	(2)	end-of-file

fseek discards any character pushed back using **ungetc**.

ftell returns the current file pointer located in *stream*. The offset is measured in bytes from the beginning of the file.

rewind(*stream*) is equivalent to **fseek**(*stream*, 0L, SEEK_SET), except that **rewind** clears the end-of-file and error indicators, while **fseek** only clears the end-of-file indicator.

After **fseek** or **rewind**, the next operation on an update file may be either input or output.

Return value   **fseek** and **rewind** return 0 if the pointer successfully moved and a non-zero value on failure.

ftell returns the current file-pointer position on success or –1L on error.

Portability These functions are available on all UNIX systems.

See also **fopen, ftell, getc, lseek, setbuf, ungetc**

Example

```
#include <stdio.h>

/* returns the number of bytes in file stream */

long filesize(FILE *stream)
{
   long curpos,length;

   curpos = ftell(stream);
   fseek(stream, 0L, SEEK_END);
   length = ftell(stream);
   fseek(stream, curpos, SEEK_SET);
   return(length);
}

main ()
{
   FILE *stream;

   stream = fopen("MYFILE.TXT", "r");
   printf("filesize of MYFILE.TXT is %ld bytes\n", filesize(stream));
}
```

Program output

```
filesize of MYFILE.TXT is 15 bytes
```

fstat

Name **fstat** – gets open file information

Usage #include <sys\stat.h>
int fstat(char *handle, struct stat *buff)

Prototype in sys\stat.h

Description See **stat**

ftell

Name	**ftell** – returns the current file pointer
Usage	#include <stdio.h>
	long ftell(FILE *stream);
Prototype in	stdio.h
Description	see **fseek**

fwrite

Name	**fwrite** – writes to a stream
Usage	#include <stdio.h>
	int fwrite(void *ptr, int size, int nitems, FILE *stream);
Prototype in	stdio.h
Description	see **fread**

gcvt

Name	**gcvt** – converts floating-point number to string
Usage	#include <dos.h>
	char *gcvt(double value, int ndigit, char *buf);
Prototype in	stdlib.h
Description	see **ecvt**

geninterrupt

Name	**geninterrupt** – generates software interrupt
Usage	#include <dos.h>
	void geninterrupt(int *intr_num*);
Prototype in	dos.h
Description	see **disable**

getc

Name	**getc** – gets character from stream
Usage	#include <stdio.h>
	int getc(FILE *stream*);
Related functions usage	int fgetc(FILE *stream*);
	int fgetchar(void);
	int getch(void);
	int getchar(void);
	int getche(void);
	int getw(FILE *stream*);
	int ungetc(char *c*, FILE *stream*);
	int ungetch(int *c*);
Prototype in	stdio.h
	conio.h (**getch, getche, ungetch**)
Description	**getc** is a macro that returns the next character on the named input *stream*.
	getchar is a macro defined to be **getc**(*stdin*).
	ungetc pushes the character *c* back onto the named input *stream*. This character will be returned on the next

call to **getc** or **fread** for that *stream*. One character may be pushed back in all situations. A second call to **ungetc** without a call to **getc** will force the previous character to be forgotten. **fseek** erases all memory of a pushed-back character.

fgetc behaves exactly like **getc**, except that it is a true function while **getc** is a macro.

fgetchar is a function that is the same as **fgetc**(*stdin*).

getch is a function that reads a single character directly from the console, without echoing.

getche is a function that reads and echoes a single character from the console.

ungetch pushes the character *c* back to the console, causing *c* to be the next character read. The **ungetch** function fails if it is called more than once before the next **read**.

getw returns the next integer in the named input *stream*. **getw** assumes no special alignment in the file.

Return value
On success, **getc**, **getchar**, **fgetc**, and **fgetchar** return the character read, after converting it to an `int` without sign extension. On end-of-file or error, they return EOF.

getch and **getche** return the character read. There is no error return for these two functions.

getw returns the next integer on the input *stream*. On end-of-file or error, **getw** returns EOF. Because EOF is a legitimate value for **getw** to return, **feof** or **ferror** should be used to detect end-of-file or error.

ungetc always returns the character pushed back.

ungetch returns the character *c* if it is successful. A return value of EOF indicates an error.

Portability
getch, **getche**, and **ungetche** are MS-DOS specific. **fgetc**, **fgetchar**, **getc**, **getchar**, **getw**, and **ungetc** are available on UNIX systems. **getc** and **getchar** are defined in Kernighan and Ritchie.

See also
ferror, **fopen**, **fread**, **fseek**, **gets**, **putc**, **read**, **scanf**

getcbrk

Name	**getcbrk** – gets control-break setting
Usage	int getcbrk(void);
Related functions usage	int setcbrk(int *value*);
Prototype in	dos.h
Description	**getcbrk** uses the MS-DOS system call 0x33 to return the current setting of control-break checking.
	setcbrk uses the MS-DOS system call 0x33 to set control-break checking *on* or *off*.

value = 0 Turns checking *off* (check only during I/O to console, printer, or communications devices)

value = 1 Turns checking *on* (check at every system call)

Return value	**getcbrk** returns 0 if control-break checking is *off* and returns 1 if checking is *on*.
	setcbrk returns *value*.
Portability	Unique to MS-DOS.

getch

Name	**getch** – gets character from console, no echoing
Usage	int getch(void);
Prototype in	conio.h
Description	see **getc**

getchar

Name	**getchar** – gets character from stream
Usage	#include <stdio.h> int getchar(void);
Prototype in	stdio.h
Description	see **getc**

getche

Name	**getche** – gets character from the console, with echoing
Usage	int getche(void);
Prototype in	conio.h
Description	see **getc**

getcurdir

Name	**getcurdir** – gets current directory for specified drive
Usage	int getcurdir(int *drive*, char *direc*);
Prototype in	dir.h
Description	**getcurdir** gets the name of the current working directory for the named *drive*. *drive* contains a drive number (0 = default, 1 = A, etc.). *direc* points to an area of memory of length MAXDIR where the directory name will be placed. The null-

terminated name does not contain the drive specification and does not begin with a backslash.

Return value   **getcurdir** returns 0 on success or –1 in the event of error.

Portability   Unique to MS-DOS.

See also   **free, getcwd**

Example

```
#include <dir.h>
#include <stdio.h>

char *current_directory(char *path)
{
   strcpy(path, "X:\\");
   path[0] = 'A' + getdisk();
   getcurdir(0, path+3);
   return(path);
}

main()
{
   char curdir[MAXPATH];

   current_directory(curdir);
   printf("The current directory is %s\n", curdir);
}
```

Program output

```
The current directory is C:\TURBOC
```

getcwd

Name   **getcwd** – gets current working directory

Usage   char *getcwd(char *buf, int n);

Prototype in   dir.h

Description   **getcwd** gets the full path name of the *cwd* (current working directory, including the drive), up to *n* bytes long, and stores it in *buf*. If the full path name length (including the null-terminator) is longer than *n*, an error occurs.

If *buf* is NULL, a buffer *n* bytes long will be allocated for you with **malloc**. You can later free the allocated buffer by passing the **getcwd** return value to the function **free**.

Return value   **getcwd** returns *buf*; on error, it returns NULL.

In the event of an error return, the global variable *errno* is set to one of the following:

ENODEV	No such device
ENOMEM	Not enough core
ERANGE	Result out of range

Portability   Unique to MS-DOS.

See also   **free, getcurdir, malloc**

---

getdate

Name   **getdate** – gets MS-DOS date

Usage   #include <dos.h>
void getdate(struct date *dateblk);

Related functions usage   void gettime(struct time *timep);
void setdate(struct date *dateblk);
void settime(struct time *timep);

Prototype in   dos.h

Description   **getdate** fills in the **date** structure (pointed to by *dateblk*) with the system's current date.

gettime fills in the **time** structure pointed to by *timep* with the system's current time.

setdate sets the system date (month, day, and year) to that in the **date** structure pointed to by *dateblk*.

settime sets the system time to the values in the **time** structure pointed to by *timep*.

The **date** structure is defined as follows:

```
struct date {
    int da_year;                    /* Current year */
    char da_day;                    /* Day of the month */
    char da_mon;                    /* Month (1 = Jan) */
};
```

The **time** structure is defined as follows:

```
struct time {
    unsigned char ti_min;                    /* Minutes */
    unsigned char ti_hour;                   /* Hours */
    unsigned char ti_hund;         /* Hundredths of seconds */
    unsigned char ti_sec;                    /* Seconds */
};
```

Return value   These functions do not return any value.

Portability   Unique to MS-DOS.

See also   **ctime**

Example

```
#include <stdio.h>
#include <dos.h>

main()
{
    struct date today;
    struct time now;

    getdate(&today);
    printf("Today's date is %d/%d/%d\n", today.da_mon, today.da_day,
            today.da_year);

    gettime(&now);
    printf("The time is %02d:%02d:%02d.%02d\n", now.ti_hour,
            now.ti_min, now.ti_sec, now.ti_hund);
}
```

Program output

```
Today's date is 1/1/1980
The time is 17:08:22.42
```

getdfree

Name	**getdfree** – gets disk free space
Usage	#include <dos.h> void getdfree(int *drive*, struct dfree **dfreep*);
Prototype in	dos.h
Description	**getdfree** accepts a *drive* specifier in drive (0 = default, 1 = A, etc.) and fills in the **dfree** structure pointed to by *dfreep* with disk characteristics.

The **dfree** structure is defined as follows:

```
struct dfree {
    unsigned df_avail;               /* Available clusters */
    unsigned df_total;                  /* Total clusters */
    unsigned df_bsec;                /* Bytes per sector */
    unsigned df_sclus;             /* Sectors per cluster */
};
```

Return value	**getdfree** returns no value. In the event of an error, *df_sclus* in the **dfree** structure is set to −1.
Portability	Unique to MS-DOS.
See also	**getfat**

getdisk

Name	**getdisk** – gets current drive
Usage	int getdisk(void);
Related functions usage	int setdisk(int *drive*);
Prototype in	dir.h

Description	**getdisk** gets the current drive and returns an integer: 0 = A:, 1 = B:, 2 = C:; etc. (Equivalent to DOS function 0x19.) For an example that demonstrates how to use **getdisk**, refer to **getcurdir**.
	setdisk sets the current drive to the one associated with *drive*: 0 = A:, 1 = B:, 2 = C:; etc. (Equivalent to DOS function 0x0E.)
Return value	**getdisk** returns the current drive.
	setdisk returns the total number of drives available.
Portability	Unique to MS-DOS.
See also	**getcurdir**

getdta

Name	**getdta** – gets disk transfer address
Usage	char far *getdta(void);
Related functions usage	void setdta(char far *dta);
Prototype in	dos.h
Description	**getdta** returns the current setting of the disk transfer address (DTA).
	In the small and medium memory models, it is assumed that the segment is the current data segment. If C is used exclusively, this will be the case, but assembly routines may set the disk transfer address to any hardware address.
	In the compact, large, or huge memory models, the address returned by **getdta** is the correct hardware address and may be located outside the program.
	setdta changes the current setting of DTA to the value pointed to by *dta*.

Return value	**getdta** returns a pointer to the current disk transfer address.
	setdta returns nothing.
Portability	Unique to MS-DOS.

getenv

Name	**getenv** – gets string from environment
Usage	char *getenv(char *envvar);
Related functions usage	int putenv(char *envvar);
Prototype in	stdlib.h
Description	The MS-DOS environment consists of a series of entries that are of the form

> envvar = varvalue

getenv searches the environment for the entry corresponding to *envvar*, then returns a pointer to *varvalue*.

putenv accepts the string *envvar* and adds it to the current environment.

putenv can also be used to modify or delete an existing *envvar*. Delete an existing entry by making *varvalue* empty; for example, "MYVAR=".

Return value	On success, **getenv** returns a pointer to the value associated with *envvar*. The pointer is overwritten on subsequent calls. If the specified *envvar* is not defined in the environment, **getenv** returns 0.
	On success, **putenv** returns 0; on failure, –1.
Portability	Available on UNIX systems.
See also	*environ* (variable), **getdfree**

Example

```
#include <stdio.h>
#include <stdlib.h>


main()
{
   char *path, *dummy;

   path = getenv("PATH");
   dummy = getenv("DUMMY");

   printf("PATH = %s\n", path);
   printf("old value of DUMMY: %s\n",
          (dummy == NULL) ? "*none*" : dummy);
   putenv("DUMMY=TURBOC");
   dummy = getenv("DUMMY");
   printf("new value of DUMMY: %s\n", dummy);
}
```

Program output

```
PATH = C:\BIN;C:\BIN\DOS;C:\
old value of DUMMY: *none*
new value of DUMMY: TURBOC
```

getfat

Name	**getfat** – gets file-allocation table information
Usage	#include <dos.h> void getfat(int *drive*, struct fatinfo **fatblkp*);
Related functions usage	void getfatd(struct fatinfo **fatblkp*);
Prototype in	dos.h
Description	**getfat** returns information from the file-allocation table for the drive specified by *drive* (0 = default, 1 = A:, 2 = B:, etc.). *fatblkp* points to the **fatinfo** structure to be filled in.
	getfatd performs the same function as **getfat** except that the default drive (0) is always used.

The **fatinfo** structure filled in by **getfat** and **getfatd** is defined as follows:

```
struct fatinfo {
    char fi_sclus;              /* Sectors per cluster */
    char fi_fatid;             /* The FAT id byte */
    int fi_nclus;          /* Number of clusters */
    int fi_bysec;           /* Bytes per sector */
};
```

Return value	None
Portability	Unique to MS-DOS.
See also	**getdfree**

getfatd

Name	**getfatd** – gets file-allocation table information
Usage	#include <dos.h> void getfatd(struct fatinfo *fatblkp);
Prototype in	dos.h
Description	see **getfat**

getftime

Name	**getftime** – gets file date and time
Usage	#include <dos.h> int getftime(int handle, struct ftime *ftimep);
Related functions usage	int setftime(int handle, struct ftime *ftimep);
Prototype in	dos.h
Description	**getftime** retrieves the file time and date for the disk file associated with the open handle. The **ftime** structure

pointed to by *ftimep* is filled in with the file's time and date.

setftime sets the file date and time of the disk file associated with the open *handle* to the date and time in the **ftime** structure pointed to by *ftimep*.

The **ftime** structure is defined as follows:

```
struct ftime {
    unsigned ft_tsec: 5;                    /* Two seconds */
    unsigned ft_min: 6;                     /* Minutes */
    unsigned ft_hour: 5;                    /* Hours */
    unsigned ft_day: 5;                     /* Days */
    unsigned ft_month: 4;                   /* Months */
    unsigned ft_year: 7;                    /* Year - 1980*/
};
```

Return value   Both functions return 0 on success.

In the event of an error return, –1 is returned and the global variable *errno* is set to one of the following:

EINVFNC   Invalid function number
EBADF   Bad file number

Portability   Unique to MS-DOS.

See also   **fread**

---

getpass

Name   **getpass** – reads a password

Usage   char *getpass(char *prompt);

Prototype in   conio.h

Description   **getpass** reads a password from the system console after prompting with the null-terminated string *prompt* and disabling the echo. A pointer is returned to a null-terminated string of up to eight characters at most (not counting the null-terminator).

Return value	The return value is a pointer to a static string which is overwritten with each call.
Portability	Available on UNIX systems.

getpsp

Name	**getpsp** – gets the program segment prefix
Usage	unsigned getpsp(*void*);
Prototype in	dos.h
Description	**getpsp** gets the segment address of the program segment prefix (the PSP) using DOS call 0x62.
	This call only exists in DOS 3.x. For versions of MS-DOS 2.x and 3.x, the global variable *_psp* set by the start-up code may be used instead.
Return value	**getpsp** returns the segment value of the PSP.
Portability	Unique to MS-DOS 3.0; not available under earlier versions of MS-DOS.
See also	*_psp* (variable)

gets

Name	**gets** – gets a string from a stream
Usage	char *gets(char *string);
Related functions usage	char *cgets(char *string); char *fgets(char *string, int n, FILE *stream);
Prototype in	stdio.h **(fgets, gets)** conio.h **(cgets)**

Description	**gets** reads a string into *string* from the standard input stream *stdin*. The string is terminated by a newline character, which is replaced in *string* by a null character (\0).
	cgets reads a string of characters from the console, storing the string (and the string length) in the location pointed to by *string*.
	cgets reads characters until it encounters a CR/LF combination or until the maximum allowable number of characters have been read. If **cgets** reads a CR/LF combination, it replaces the combination with a \0 (null-terminator) before storing it.
	Before **cgets** is called, *string*[0] should be set to the maximum length of the string to be read. On return, *string*[1] is set to the number of characters actually read. The characters read start at *string*[2] and end with a null-terminator. Thus, *string* must be at least *string*[0] + 2 bytes long.
	fgets reads characters from *stream* into the string *string*: The function stops reading when it either reads $n - 1$ characters or reads a newline character (whichever comes first). **fgets** retains the newline character. The last character read into *string* is followed by a null character.
Return value	**gets** and **fgets**, on success, return the string argument *string*; each returns NULL on end-of-file or error.
	cgets returns &*string*[2], a pointer to the string of characters that were read. There is no error return.
Portability	Available on UNIX systems. **fgets** is also defined in Kernighan and Ritchie.
See also	**ferror, fopen, fread, getc, puts, scanf**

Example

```
#include <stdio.h>
#include <conio.h>


main()
{
        char buffer[82];
        char *p;
```

```
buffer[0] = 80;         /* there's space for 80 characters */
p = cgets(buffer);
printf("\ncgets got %d chars: \"%s\"\n", buffer[1],p);
printf("the returned pointer is %p, buffer[2] is at %p\n",
        p, &buffer[2]);

buffer[0] = 5;          /* leave space for 5 chars only */
p = cgets(buffer);
printf("\ncgets got %d chars: \"%s\"\n", buffer[1],p);
printf("the returned pointer is %p, buffer[2] is at %p\n",
        p, &buffer[2]);
}
```

Program output

```
abcdfghijklm
cgets got 12 chars: "abcdfghijklm"
the returned pointer is FEF6, buffer[2] is at FEF6
abcd
cgets got 4 chars: "abcd"
the returned pointer is FEF6, buffer[2] is at FEF6
```

gettime

Name	**gettime** – gets system time
Usage	#include <dos.h> void gettime(struct time *timep);
Prototype in	dos.h
Description	see **getdate**

getvect

Name	**getvect** – gets interrupt vector entry
Usage	void interrupt(*getvect(int *intr_num*)) ( );
Related functions usage	void setvect(int *intr_num*, void interrupt (**isr*) ( ));
Prototype in	dos.h
Description	MS-DOS includes a set of "hard-wired" interrupt vectors, numbered 0 to 255. The 4-byte value in each vector is actually an address, which is the location of an interrupt function.

getvect reads the value of the vector named by *intr_num* and interprets that value read as a (far) pointer to some interrupt function.

setvect sets the value of the vector named by *intr_num* to a new value, *vector*, which is a far pointer containing the address of a new interrupt function. The address of a C routine may only be passed to *vector* if that routine is declared to be an **interrupt** routine.

Note: If you use the prototypes declared in dos.h, you can simply pass the address of an interrupt function to **setvect** in any memory model.

Return value	**getvect** returns the current 4-byte value stored in the interrupt vector named by *intr_num*. **setvect** returns nothing.
Portability	Unique to MS-DOS.
See also	**disable**

getverify

Name	**getverify** – gets verify state
Usage	int getverify(void);
Related functions usage	void setverify(int *value*);
Prototype in	dos.h
Description	**getverify** gets the current state of the verify flag.

setverify sets the current state of the verify flag to *value*.

A *value* of 0 = verify flag *off*.
A *value* of 1 = verify flag *on*.

The verify flag controls output to the disk. When verify is *off*, writes are not verified; when verify is *on*, all disk writes are verified to insure proper writing of the data.

Return value	**getverify** returns the current state of the verify flag, either 0 or 1.

A return of 0 = verify flag *off*.
A return of 1 = verify flag *on*.

setverify returns nothing.

Portability	Unique to MS-DOS.

getw

Name	**getw** – gets integer from stream
Usage	#include <stdio.h> int getw(FILE * *stream*);
Prototype in	stdio.h
Description	see **getc**

gmtime

Name	**gmtime** – converts date and time to Greenwich Mean Time
Usage	#include <time.h> struct tm * gmtime(long * *clock*);
Prototype in	time.h
Description	see **ctime**

gsignal

Name	**gsignal** – software signals
Usage	int gsignal(int *sig*);
Prototype in	signal.h
Description	see **ssignal**

harderr

Name	**harderr** – establishes a hardware error handler
Usage	void harderr(int (*fptr*)());
Related functions usage	void hardresume(int *rescode*); void hardretn(int *errcode*);
Prototype in	dos.h

Description   harderr establishes a hardware error handler for the current program. This handler is invoked whenever an interrupt 0x24 occurs. (See the *MS-DOS Programmer's Reference Manual* for a discussion of the interrupt.)

The function pointed to by *fptr* will be called when such an interrupt occurs. The handler function will be called with the following arguments:

```
handler(int errval, int ax, int bp, int si);
```

errval is the error code set in the DI register by MS-DOS. *ax*, *bp*, and *si* are the values MS-DOS sets for the AX, BP, and SI registers, respectively.

- *ax* indicates whether a disk error or other device error was encountered. If *ax* is non-negative, a disk error was encountered; otherwise, the error was a device error. For a disk error, *ax* ANDed with 0x00FF will give the failing drive number (1 = A, 2 = B, etc.).

- *bp* and *si* together point to the device driver header of the failing driver.

The named function is not called directly. **harderr** establishes a DOS interrupt handler that calls the function.

peek and **peekb** can be used to retrieve device information from this driver header. *bp* is the segment address, and *si* is the offset.

The handler may issue **bdos** calls 1 through 0xC, but any other **bdos** call will corrupt MS-DOS. In particular, any of the C standard I/O or UNIX-emulation I/O calls may *not* be used.

The driver header may not be altered via **poke** or **pokeb**.

The error handler may return or call **hardresume** to return to MS-DOS. The return value of the handler or *rescode* (result code) of **hardresume** contains an abort (2), retry (1), or ignore (0) indicator. The abort is accomplished by invoking DOS interrupt 0x23, the control-break interrupt.

The error handler may return directly to the application program by calling **hardretn**.

Return value	The handler must return 0 for ignore, 1 for retry, and 2 for abort.
Portability	Unique to MS-DOS.
See also	**peek, poke, setjmp**

Example

```c
#include <stdio.h>
#include <dos.h>

#define DISPLAY_STRING   0x09
#define IGNORE 0
#define RETRY  1
#define ABORT  2


int handler(int errval, int ax, int bp, int si)
{
   char msg[25];  int drive;

   if (ax < 0) {      /* device error */
     /* can only use dos functions 0 - 0x0C */
     bdosptr(DISPLAY_STRING, "device error$", 0);
     hardretn(-1);  /* return to calling program */
   }
   drive = (ax & 0x00FF);
   sprintf(msg, "disk error on drive %c$", 'A' + drive);
   bdosptr(DISPLAY_STRING, msg, 0);
   return(ABORT);     /* abort calling program */
}

main()
{
   harderr(handler);

   printf("Make sure there is no disk in drive A:\n");
   printf("Press a key when ready...\n");
   getch();

   printf("Attempting to access A:\n");
   fopen("A:ANY.FIL","r");
}
```

Program output

```
Make sure there is no disk in drive A:
Press a key when ready...
Attempting to access A:
disk error on drive A
```

hardresume

Name	**hardresume** – hardware error handler function
Usage	void hardresume(int *rescode*);
Prototype in	dos.h
Description	see **harderr**

hardretn

Name	**hardretn** – hardware error handler function
Usage	void hardretn(int *errcode*);
Prototype in	dos.h
Description	see **harderr**

hyperb

Name	**hyperb** – hyperbolic functions

Related functions usage	double sinh(double *x*);
	double cosh(double *x*);
	double tanh(double *x*);

Prototype in	math.h
Description	These functions compute the designated hyperbolic functions for real arguments.
Return value	These functions return their computed results.

When the correct value would overflow, **sinh** and **cosh** return the value HUGE_VAL of appropriate sign.

Error handling for these routines can be modified through the function **matherr**.

Portability	Available on UNIX systems.
See also	**exp**

hypot

Name	**hypot** – calculates hypotenuse of right triangle
Usage	double hypot(double x, double y);
Prototype in	math.h
Description	**hypot** calculates the value z where

$$z^2 = x^2 + y^2$$

(This is equivalent to the length of the hypotenuse of a right triangle, if the lengths of the two sides are x and y.)

Return value	On success, **hypot** returns z, a double. On error (such as an overflow), **hypot** sets *errno* to

ERANGE   Result out of range

and returns the value HUGE_VAL.

Error handling for **hypot** can be modified through the function **matherr**.

Portability	Available on UNIX systems.
See also	**trig**

inport

Name	**inport** – inputs from hardware port
Usage	#include <dos.h> int inport(int *port*);

Related
 functions usage
	int inportb(int *port*);
	 void outport(int *port*, int *word*);
	 void outportb(int *port*, char *byte*);

Prototype in	dos.h
Description	**inport** reads a word from the input port specified by *port*.
	inportb is a macro that reads a byte from the input port specified by *port*.
	outport writes the word given by *word* to the output port specified by *port*.
	outportb is a macro that writes the byte given by *byte* to the output port specified by *port*.
	If **inportb** or **outportb** is called when dos.h has been included, they will be treated as macros that expand to in-line code.
	If you don't include dos.h, or if you do include dos.h and #undef the macros **inportb** and **outportb**, you will get the **inportb** and **outportb** functions.
Return value	**inport** and **inportb** return the value read.
	outport and **outportb** return nothing.
Portability	Unique to the 8086 family.

inportb

Name	**inportb** – inputs from hardware port
Usage	int inportb(int *port*);
Prototype in	dos.h
Description	see **inport**

int86

Name	**int86** – general 8086 software interrupt interface
Usage	#include <dos.h> int int86(int *intr_num*, union REGS **inregs*, union REGS **outregs*);
Related functions usage	int int86x(int *intr_num*, union REGS **inregs*, union REGS **outregs*, struct SREGS **segregs*);
Prototype in	dos.h
Description	Both of these functions execute an 8086 software interrupt specified by the argument *intr_num*.

Before executing the software interrupt, both functions copy register values from *inregs* into the registers.

In addition, **int86x** copies the *segregs→x.ds* and *segregs→x.es* values into the corresponding registers before executing the software interrupt. This feature allows programs that use far pointers, or that use a large data memory model, to specify which segment is to be used during the software interrupt.

After the software interrupt returns, both functions copy the current register values to *outregs*, copy the status of the system carry flag to the *x.cflag* field in *outregs*, and copy the value of the 8086 flags register to the x.flags field in *outregs*. In addition, **int86x** restores DS, and sets the *segregs→es* and *segregs→ds* fields to the values of the corresponding segment registers.

If the carry flag is set, it indicates that an error occurred.

int86x allows you to invoke an 8086 software interrupt that takes a value of DS different from the default data segment, and/or that takes an argument in ES.

Note that *inregs* can point to the same structure that *outregs* points to.

Return value   **int86** and **int86x** return the value of AX after completion of the software interrupt. If the carry flag is set (*outregs→x.cflag* != 0), indicating an error, these functions set *_doserrno* to the error code.

Portability   Unique to MS-DOS. **int86** and **int86x** will work on 8086 family processors.

See also   see **intdos**

Example

```
#include <dos.h>

#define VIDEO 0x10

/* positions cursor at line y, column x */

void gotoxy(int x, int y)
{
   union REGS regs;

   regs.h.ah = 2; /* set cursor position */
   regs.h.dh = y;
   regs.h.dl = x;
   regs.h.bh = 0; /* video page 0 */
   int86(VIDEO, &regs, &regs);
}
```

int86x

Name	**int86x** – general 8086 software interrupt interface
Usage	#include <dos.h>
	int int86x(int *intr_num*, union REGS **inregs*,
	union REGS **outregs*, struct SREGS **segregs*);
Prototype in	dos.h
Description	see **int86**

intdos

Name	**intdos** – general MS-DOS interrupt interface
Usage	#include <dos.h>
	int intdos(union REGS * *inregs*, union REGS * *outregs*);
Related	
functions usage	int intdosx(union REGS **inregs*, union REGS **outregs*,
	struct SREGS **segregs*);
Prototype in	dos.h
Description	Both of these functions execute DOS interrupt 0x21 to invoke a specified DOS function. The value of *inregs→h.al* specifies the DOS function to be invoked.
	In addition, **intdosx** copies the *segregs→x.ds* and *segregs→x.es* values into the corresponding registers before invoking the DOS function. This feature allows programs that use far pointers, or that use a large data memory model, to specify which segment is to be used during the function execution.

After the interrupt 0x21 returns, both functions copy the current register values to *outregs*, copy the status of the system carry flag to the *x.cflag* field in *outregs*, and copy the value of the 8086 flags register to the x.flags field in *outregs*. In addition, **intdosx** restores DS, and sets the *segregs→es* and *segregs→ds* fields to the values of the corresponding segment registers.

If the carry flag is set, it indicates that an error occurred.

intdosx allows you to invoke a DOS function that takes a value of DS different from the default data segment, and/or that takes an argument in ES.

Note that *inregs* can point to the same structure that *outregs* points to.

Return value   **intdos** and **intdosx** return the value of AX after completion of the DOS function call. If the carry flag is set (*outregs→x.cflag* != 0), indicating an error, these functions set _*doserrno* to the error code.

Portability   Unique to MS-DOS.

See also   **segread**

Example

```
#include <stdio.h>
#include <dos.h>

/* deletes filename; returns 0 on success, non-zero error code on
   failure */

int delete_file(char near *filename)
{
    union REGS regs; struct SREGS sregs;
    int ret;

    regs.h.ah = 0x41; /* delete file */
    regs.x.dx = (unsigned) filename;
    sregs.ds = _DS;
    ret = intdosx(&regs, &regs, &sregs);
    /* if carry flag is set, there was an error */
    return(regs.x.cflag ? ret : 0);
}

main()
{
    int err;
```

```
err = delete_file("NOTEXIST.$$$");
printf("Able to delete NOTEXIST.$$$: %s\n",
       (!err) ? "YES" : "NO");
}
```

Program output

```
Able to delete NOTEXIST.$$$: NO
```

intdosx

Name	**intdosx** – general MS-DOS interrupt interface
Usage	#include <dos.h> int intdosx(union REGS *inregs*, union REGS *outregs*, struct SREGS *segregs*);
Prototype in	dos.h
Description	see **intdos**

intr

Name	**intr** – alternate 8086 software interrupt interface
Usage	#include <dos.h> void *intr*(int *intr_num*, struct REGPACK * *preg*);
Prototype in	dos.h
Description	The **intr** function is an alternate interface for executing software interrupts. It generates an 8086 software interrupt specified by the argument *intr_num*. **intr** copies register values from the REGPACK structure *preg* into the registers before executing the software interrupt. After the software interrupt completes, **intr** copies the current register values into preg. The flags are preserved.

The arguments passed to **intr** are as follows:

intr_num   the interrupt number to be executed

preg   the address of a structure containing
(a) the input registers before the call
(b) the value of the registers after the interrupt call.

The REGPACK structure *preg* (described in dos.h) has the following format :

```
struct  REGPACK
        {
        unsigned  r_ax, r_bx, r_cx, r_dx;
        unsigned  r_bp, r_si, r_di, r_ds, r_es, r_flags;
        };
```

Return value   No value is returned. The REGPACK structure *preg* contains the value of the registers after the interrupt call.

Portability   Unique to MS-DOS; will work on 8086-family processors.

See also   **int86, intdos**

ioctl

Name   **ioctl** – controls I/0 device

Usage   int ioctl(int *handle*, int *cmd*[, int * *argdx*, int *argcx*]);

Prototype in   io.h

Description   This is a direct interface to the MS-DOS call 0x44 (IOCTL).

The exact function depends on the value of *cmd* as follows:

0   Get device information
1   Set device information (in *argdx*)
2   Read *argcx* bytes into the address pointed to by *argdx*

3   Write *argcx* bytes from the address pointed to by *argdx*

4   Same as 2, except *handle* is treated as a drive number (0 = default, 1 = A, *etc.*)

5   Same as 3, except *handle* is a drive number (0 = default, 1 = A, *etc.*)

6   Get input status

7   Get output status

8   Test removability; DOS 3.x only

11 Set sharing conflict retry count; DOS 3.x only

ioctl can be used to get information about device channels. Regular files can also be used, but only *cmd* values 0, 6, and 7 are defined for them. All other calls return an EINVAL error for files.

See the documentation for system call 0x44 in the *MS-DOS Programmer's Reference Manual* for detailed information on argument or return values.

The arguments *argdx* and *argcx* are optional.

ioctl provides a direct interface to DOS 2.0 device drivers for special functions. As a result, the exact behavior of this function will vary across different vendors' hardware and in different devices. Also, several vendors do not follow the interfaces described here. Refer to the vendor BIOS documentation for exact use of **ioctl**.

Return value

For *cmd* 0 or 1, the return value is the device information (DX of the IOCTL call).

For *cmd* values of 2 through 5, the return value is the number of bytes actually transferred.

For *cmd* values of 6 or 7, the return value is the device status.

In any event, if an error is detected, a value of –1 is returned, and *errno* is set to one of the following:

EINVAL	Invalid argument
EBADF	Bad file number
EINVDAT	Invalid data

Portability

ioctl is available on UNIX systems, but not with these parameters or functionality. UNIX version 7 and System

III differ from each other in their use of **ioctl**. **ioctl** calls are not portable to UNIX and are rarely portable across MS-DOS machines.

DOS 3.0 extends **ioctl** with *cmd* values of 8 and 11.

Example

```
#include <stdio.h>
#include <io.h>
#include <dir.h>

main()
{
   int stat;

   /* use function 8 to determine if the default drive is removable */
   stat = ioctl(0, 8, 0, 0);

   printf("Drive %c %s changeable\n", getdisk() + 'A',
          (stat == 0) ? "is" : "is not");
}
```

Program output

```
Drive C is not changeable
```

is...

Name	**is...** – character classification macros

Usage	#include <ctype.h>
	int isalpha(int *ch*);
	
	int isalnum(int *ch*);
	int isascii(int *ch*);
	
	int iscntrl(int *ch*);
	int isdigit(int *ch*);
	
	int isgraph(int *ch*);
	int islower(int *ch*);
	
	int isprint(int *ch*);
	int ispunct(int *ch*);

```
int isspace(int ch);
int isupper(int ch);
int isxdigit(int ch);
```

Prototype in   io.h

Description   These are macros that classify ASCII-coded integer values by table lookup. Each is a predicate returning non-zero for *true* and 0 for *false*.

isascii is defined on all integer values; the rest of the macros are defined only when **isascii** is *true*, or when *ch* is EOF.

Return value
isalpha	Non-zero if *ch* is a letter. ('A'-'Z', 'a'-'z')
isalnum	Non-zero if *ch* is a letter or a digit. ('A'-'Z', 'a'-'z', '0'-'9')
isascii	Non-zero if *ch* is in the range 0-127. (0x00 – 0x7F)
iscntrl	Non-zero if *ch* is a delete character or ordinary control character. (0x7F, or 0x00 – 0x1F)
isdigit	Non-zero if *ch* is a digit. ('0' – '9')
isgraph	Non-zero if *ch* is a printing character, like **isprint**, except that a space character is excluded. (0x21 – 0x7E)
islower	Non-zero if *ch* is a lowercase letter. ('a'-'z')
isprint	Non-zero if *ch* is a printing character. (0x20 – 0x7E)
ispunct	Non-zero if *ch* is a punctuation character. (**iscntrl** or **isspace**)
isspace	Non-zero if *ch* is a space, tab, carriage return, newline, vertical tab, or form-feed. (0x09 – 0x0D, 0x20)
isupper	Non-zero if *ch* is an uppercase letter. ('A'-'Z')
isxdigit	Non-zero if *ch* is a hexadecimal digit. ('0'-'9', 'A'-'F', 'a'-'f')

Portability   All these macros are available on UNIX machines. **isalpha**, **isdigit**, **islower**, **isspace**, and **isupper** are defined in Kernighan and Ritchie.

isatty

Name	**isatty** – checks for device type
Usage	int isatty(int *handle*);
Prototype in	io.h
Description	**isatty** is a function that determines whether *handle* represents any one of the following character devices:

- a terminal
- a console
- a printer
- a serial port

Return value	If the device is a character device, **isatty** returns a non-zero integer. If it is not such a device, **isatty** returns 0.

itoa

Name	**itoa** – converts an integer to a string
Usage	char *itoa(int *value*, char *string*, int *radix*);
Related functions usage	char *ltoa(long *value*, char *string*, int *radix*); char *ultoa(unsigned long *value*, char *string*, int *radix*);
Prototype in	stdlib.h
Description	These functions convert *value* to a null-terminated string and store the result in *string*. With **itoa**, *value* is an integer; with **ltoa** it is a long; with **ultoa** it is an unsigned long.

radix specifies the base to be used in converting *value*; it must be between 2 and 36 (inclusive). With **itoa** and **ltoa**, if *value* is negative, and *radix* is 10, the first character of *string* is the minus sign (-). This does not occur with **ultoa**. Also, **ultoa** performs no overflow checking.

Note: The space allocated for *string* must be large enough to hold the returned string including the terminating null character (\0). **itoa** can return up to 17 bytes; **ltoa** and **ultoa**, up to 33 bytes.

Return value   All these functions return a pointer to *string*. There is no error return.

kbhit

Name	**kbhit** – checks for recent keystrokes
Usage	int kbhit(void);
Prototype in	conio.h
Description	**kbhit** checks to see if a keystroke is currently available. Any available keystrokes can be retrieved with **getch** or **getche**.
Return value	If a keystroke is available, **kbhit** returns a non-zero integer. If not, it returns 0.
See also	**getc**

keep

Name	**keep** – exits and remains resident
Usage	void keep(int *status*, int *size*);
Prototype in	dos.h
Description	**keep** returns to MS-DOS with the exit status in *status*. The current program remains resident, however. The program is set to *size* paragraphs in length, and the remainder of the memory of the program is freed.

keep can be used when installing a TSR program. **keep** uses DOS function 0x31.

Return value	None
Portability	Unique to MS-DOS.

labs

Name	**labs** – gives long absolute value
Usage	long labs(long *n*);
Prototype in	stdlib.h
Description	see **abs**

ldexp

Name	**ldexp** – calculates $value \times 2^{exp}$
Usage	double ldexp(double *value*, int *exp*);
Prototype in	math.h
Description	see **exp**

lfind

Name	**lfind** – performs a linear search
Usage	void *lfind(void *key*, void *base*, int *nelem*, int *width*, int (*fcmp)( ));
Prototype in	stdlib.h
Description	see **bsearch**

localtime

Name	**localtime** – converts date and time to a structure
Usage	#include <time.h> struct tm *localtime(long *clock);
Prototype in	time.h
Description	see **ctime**

lock

Name	**lock** – sets file sharing locks
Usage	int lock(int *handle*, long *offset*, long *length*);
Related **functions usage**	int unlock(int *handle*, long *offset*, long *length*);
Prototype in	io.h
Description	**lock** and **unlock** provide an interface to the MS-DOS 3.x file-sharing mechanism.
	lock can be placed on arbitrary, non-overlapping regions of any file. A program attempting to read or write into a locked region will retry the operation three times. If all three retries fail, the call fails with an error.
	unlock removes **lock**; to avoid error, **lock** must be removed before a file is closed. A program must release all lock(s) before completing.
Return value	Both functions return 0 on success, –1 on error.
Portability	Unique to MS-DOS 3.x. Older versions of MS-DOS do not support these calls.
See also	**open**

log

Name	**log** – logarithm function ln(x)
Usage	double log(double x);
Prototype in	math.h
Description	see **exp**

log10

Name	**log10** – logarithm function log $_{10}$(X)
Usage	double log10(double x);
Prototype in	math.h
Description	see **exp**

longjmp

Name	**longjmp** – performs nonlocal goto
Usage	#include <setjmp.h> void longjmp(jmp_buf *env*, int *val*);
Related functions usage	int setjmp(jmp_buf *env*);
Prototype in	setjmp.h
Description	**setjmp** captures the complete *task state* in *env* and returns 0.

A later call to **longjmp** with that *env* restores the captured task state and returns in such a way that it appears that **setjmp** returned with the value *val*.

setjmp must first be called before **longjmp**. The routine that called **setjmp** and set up *env* must still be active and cannot have returned before the **longjmp** is called. If this happens, the results are unpredictable.

A task state is:

- all segment registers (CS, DS, ES, SS)
- register variables (SI, DI)
- stack pointer (SP)
- frame pointer (FP)
- flags

A task state is complete enough that **setjmp** and **longjmp** can be used to implement co-routines.

These routines are useful for dealing with errors and exceptions encountered in a low-level subroutine of a program.

Return value **setjmp** returns 0 when it is initially called.

longjmp cannot return the value 0; if passed 0 in *val*, **longjmp** will return 1.

Portability Available on UNIX systems.

See also **ctrlbrk**, **ssignal**

Example

```
#include <stdio.h>
#include <setjmp.h>

int value;
jmp_buf jumper;

main()
{
    value = setjmp(jumper);
    if (value != 0) {
        printf("Longjmp with value %d\n", value);
        exit(value);
    }
    printf("About to call subroutine ... \n");
    subroutine();
}
```

```
subroutine()
{
    longjmp(jumper,1);
}
```

Program output

```
About to call subroutine ...
Longjmp with value 1
```

lsearch

Name	**lsearch** – searches and updates a table
Usage	void *lsearch(void *key, void *base, int *nelem, int width, int (*fcmp)( ));
Prototype in	stdlib.h
Description	see **bsearch**

lseek

Name	**lseek** – moves read/write file pointer
Usage	#include <io.h> long lseek(int handle, long offset, int fromwhere);
Related functions usage	long tell(int handle);
Prototype in	io.h
Description	**lseek** sets the file pointer associated with handle to a new position that is offset bytes beyond the file location given by fromwhere. fromwhere must be one of the values 0, 1 or 2, which represent three symbolic constants (defined in stdio.h) as follows:

fromwhere		File Location
SEEK_SET	(0)	file beginning
SEEK_CUR	(1)	current file pointer position
SEEK_END	(2)	end-of-file

tell gets the current position of the file pointer associated with _handle_ and expresses it as the number of bytes from the beginning of the file.

Return value

lseek returns the offset of the pointer's new position, measured in bytes from the file beginning. **lseek** returns –1L on error, and _errno_ is set to one of the following:

EBADF	Bad file number
EINVAL	Invalid argument

On devices incapable of seeking (such as terminals and printers), the return value is undefined.

tell returns the current file pointer position. A return of –1 (long) indicates an error, and _errno_ is set to:

EBADF	Bad file number

Portability

These functions are available on all UNIX systems.

See also

fopen, fseek, ftell, getc, setbuf, ungetc

ltoa

Name	**ltoa** – converts a long to a string
Usage	char *ltoa(long *value*, char *string*, int *radix*);
Prototype in	stdlib.h
Description	see **itoa**

malloc

Name	**malloc** – allocates main memory
Usage	void *malloc(unsigned *size*);
Related functions usage	void *calloc(unsigned *nelem*, unsigned *elsize*);
	In the tiny, small, and medium models unsigned coreleft(void);
	In the compact, large, and huge models unsigned long coreleft(void);
	void free(void *ptr*);
	void *realloc(void *ptr*, unsigned *newsize*);
Prototype in	stdlib.h and alloc.h
Description	These functions provide access to the C memory heap. The heap is available for dynamic allocation of creating variable-sized blocks of memory. Many data structures such as trees and lists naturally employ heap memory allocation.
	All the space between the end of the data segment and the top of the program stack is available for use in the small data models, except for a 256-byte margin

immediately before the top of the stack. This margin is intended to allow the application some room to grow the stack plus a small amount needed by MS-DOS.

In the large data models, all the space beyond the program stack to the end of physical memory is available for the heap.

malloc returns a pointer to a memory block of length *size*. If not enough memory is available to allocate the block, **malloc** returns NULL. The contents of the block are left unchanged.

calloc allocates a block like **malloc**, except the block is of size *nelem* times *elsize*. The block is cleared to 0.

coreleft returns a measure of the unused memory. It gives different values of measurement, depending on whether the memory model is small data group or large data group.

free deallocates a previously allocated block. *ptr* must contain the address of the first byte of the block.

realloc adjusts the size of the allocated block to *newsize*, copying the contents to a new location if necessary.

Return value	**malloc** and **calloc** return a pointer to the newly allocated block, or NULL if not enough space exists for the new block.
	realloc returns the address of the reallocated block. This may be different than the address of the original block. If the block cannot be reallocated, **realloc** returns NULL.
	In the large data models, **coreleft** returns the amount of unused memory between the heap and the stack.
	In the small data memory models, **coreleft** returns the amount of unused memory between the stack and the data segment, minus 256 bytes.
Portability	**calloc**, **free**, **malloc**, and **realloc** are available on UNIX systems. **calloc** is defined in Kernighan and Ritchie.
See also	**allocmem, farmalloc, setbuf**

Example

```
#include <stdio.h>
#include <stdlib.h>


typedef struct {
   /* ... */
} OBJECT;

OBJECT *NewObject()
{
   return ((OBJECT *) malloc(sizeof(OBJECT)));
}

void FreeObject(OBJECT *obj)
{
   free(obj);
}

main()
{
   OBJECT *obj;

   obj = NewObject();
   if (obj == NULL) {
      printf("failed to create a new object\n");
      exit(1);
   }
   /* ... */
   free(obj);
}
```

_matherr

Name	**_matherr** – floating-point error handling routine
Usage	#include <math.h> double _matherr(_mexcep *why*, char **fun*, double **arg1p*, double **arg2p*, double *retval*);

**Related
functions usage**
	#include <math.h>
	matherr();

Prototype in	math.h

Description	_matherr serves as a focal point for error handling in all math library functions; it calls **matherr** and processes the return value from **matherr**. _matherr should never be called directly by user programs.

Whenever an error occurs in one of the math library routines **_matherr** is called with several arguments.

_matherr does four things;

- It uses its arguments to fill out an **exception** structure.

- It calls **matherr** with *e*, a pointer to the **exception** structure, to see if **matherr** can resolve the error.

- It examines the return value from **matherr** as follows:

    If **matherr** returned 0, (indicating that **matherr** was not able to resolve the error) **_matherr** sets *errno* (see following) and prints an error message.

    If **matherr** returns non-zero, (indicating that **matherr** was able to resolve the error) **_matherr** is silent; it does not set *errno* or print any messages.

- It returns *e→retval* to the original caller. Note that **matherr** might modify *e→retval* to specify the value it wants propagated back to the original caller.

When **_matherr** sets *errno* (based on a 0 return from **matherr**), it maps the kind of error that occurred (from the *type* field in the **exception** structure) onto an *errno* value of either EDOM or ERANGE.

Return value   **_matherr** returns the value, *e→retval*. This value is initially the value of the input parameter *retval* passed to **_matherr**, and might be modified by **matherr**.

For math function results with a magnitude greater than MAXDOUBLE, *retval* defaults to the macro HUGE_VAL of appropriate sign before being passed to **_matherr**. For math function results with a magnitude less than MINDOUBLE, *retval* is set to 0, then passed to **_matherr**. In both of these extremes, if **matherr** does not modify *e→retval*, **_matherr** sets *errno* to

    ERANGE   Result out of range

See also   matherr

matherr

Name   **matherr** – user-modifiable math error handler

Usage   #include <math.h>
int matherr(struct exception *e);

Prototype in   math.h

Description   The default version of Turbo C's **matherr** routine simply returns 0; it serves as a hook that you can replace when writing your own math error-handling routine—see the following example of a user-defined **matherr** implementation.

You can modify **matherr** to be a custom error-handling routine (such as one that catches and resolves certain types of errors); the modified **matherr** should return 0 if it failed to resolve the error, or non-zero if the error was resolved. When **matherr** returns non-zero, no error message is printed, and *errno* is not changed.

This is the **exception** structure (defined in math.h):

```
struct exception {
    int    type;
    char   *name;
    double arg1, arg2, retval;
};
```

The members of the **exception** structure are shown in the following table.

Member	What It Is (or Represents)
type	the type of mathematical error that occurred; an **enum** type defined in the **typedef** *_mexcep* (see definition after this list)
name	a pointer to a null-terminated string holding the name of the math library function that resulted in an error
arg1, *arg2*	the arguments (passed to the function *name* points to) that caused the error; if only one argument was passed to the function, it is stored in *arg1*
retval	the default return value for **matherr**; you can modify this value

The **typedef** *_mexcep*, also defined in math.h, enumerates the following symbolic constants representing possible mathematical errors:

Symbolic Constant	Mathematical Error
DOMAIN	argument was not in domain of function (such as **log**(-1))
SING	arguments would result in a singularity (such as **pow**(0, -2))
OVERFLOW	argument would produce a function result greater than MAXDOUBLE (such as **exp**(1000))
UNDERFLOW	argument would produce a function result less than MINDOUBLE (such as **exp**(-1000))
TLOSS	arguments would produce function result with total loss of significant digits (such as **sin**(10 e 70))

The symbolic constants MAXDOUBLE and MINDOUBLE are defined in values.h.

Note that **_matherr** is not meant to be modified. The **matherr** function is more widely found in C run-time libraries and thus is recommended for portable programming.

The UNIX-style **matherr** default behavior (printing a message and terminating) is not ANSI compatible. If you desire a UNIX-style version of **matherr**, use matherr.c provided on the Turbo C distribution diskettes.

Return value The default return value for **matherr** is simply 0. **matherr** can also modify $e{\rightarrow}retval$, which propagates through **_matherr** back to the original caller.

When **matherr** returns 0, (indicating that it was not able to resolve the error) **_matherr** sets *errno* and prints an error message. (See **_matherr** for details.)

When **matherr** returns non-zero (indicating that it was able to resolve the error) *errno* is not set and no messages are printed.

Example

```
/*
   This is a user-defined matherr function that catches negative
   arguments passed to sqrt and converts them to non-negative
   values before sqrt processes them.
*/

#include<math.h>
#include<string.h>

int matherr(struct exception *a);
{
   if (a -> type == DOMAIN) {
      if(strcmp(a -> name, "sqrt") == 0) {
         a -> retval = sqrt (-(a -> arg1));
         return (1);
      }
   }
   return (0);
}
```

mem...

Name	**mem...** – manipulates memory arrays
Related functions usage	void *memccpy(void *destin, void *source, unsigned char ch, unsigned n);
	void *memchr(void *s, char ch, unsigned n); void *memcmp(void *s1, void *s2, unsigned n);
	int memicmp(void *s1, void *s2, unsigned n); void *memmove(void *destin, void *source, unsigned n);
	void *memcpy(void *destin, void *source, unsigned n); void *memset(void *s, char ch, unsigned n);
Prototype in	string.h mem.h
Description	These functions, all members of the **mem...** family, manipulate memory arrays. In all of these functions, arrays are *n* bytes in length.

memcpy	copies a block of *n* bytes from *source* to *destin*. If the source and destination blocks overlap, the copy direction is chosen so that overlapping bytes are copied correctly.
memmove	identical to **memcpy**.
memset	sets all of the bytes of *s* to the byte *ch*. The size of the *s* array is given by *n*.
memcmp	compares two strings, *s1* and *s2*, for a length of exactly *n* bytes. This function compares bytes as **unsigned chars**, so `memcmp ("\xFF", "\x7F", 1)` returns a value > 0.
memicmp	compares the first *n* bytes of *s1* and *s2*, ignoring character case (upper or lower).

memccpy	copies bytes from *source* to *destin*. The copying stops as soon as either of the following occurs:

■ The character *ch* is first copied into *destin*.

■ *n* bytes have been copied in.

memchr	searches the first *n* bytes of array *s* for character *ch*.

Return value   **memmove** and **memcpy** return *destin*.

memset returns the value of *s*.

memcmp and **memicmp** return a value

< 0	if *s1* is less than *s2*
= 0	if *s1* is the same as *s2*
> 0	if *s1* is greater than *s2*

memccpy returns a pointer to the byte in *destin* immediately following *ch*, if *ch* was copied; otherwise, **memccpy** returns NULL.

memchr returns a pointer to the first occurrence of *ch* in *s*; it returns NULL if *ch* does not occur in the *s* array.

Portability   Available on UNIX System V systems.

See also   **str...**

MK_FP

Name	**MK_FP** – makes a far pointer
Usage	#include <dos.h> void far * MK_FP(unsigned *seg*, unsigned *off*);
Prototype in	dos.h
Description	see **FP_OFF**

mkdir

Name	**mkdir** – creates a directory
Usage	int mkdir(char *pathname*);
Related functions usage	int rmdir(char *pathname*);
Prototype in	dir.h
Description	**mkdir** takes the given *pathname* and creates a new directory with that name.
	rmdir deletes the directory given by *pathname*. The directory named by *pathname*
	▪ must be empty
	▪ must not be the current working directory
	▪ must not be the root directory
Return value	**mkdir** returns the value 0 if the new directory was created.
	rmdir returns 0 if the directory is successfully deleted.
	With either function, a return value of –1 indicates an error, and *errno* is set to one of the following values:
	EACCES Permission denied
	ENOENT Path or file name not found
See also	**chdir**

mktemp

Name	**mktemp** – makes a unique file name
Usage	char *mktemp(char *template*);
Prototype in	dir.h

Description	**mktemp** replaces *template* by a unique file name and returns the address of *template*.
	The *template* should be a null-terminated string with six trailing *X*'s. These *X*'s are replaced with a unique collection of letters plus a dot, so that there are two letters, a dot, and three suffix letters in the new file name.
	Starting with AA.AAA, the new file name is assigned by looking up the names on the disk and avoiding pre-existing names of the same format.
Return value	If *template* is well-formed, **mktemp** returns the address of the *template* string. Otherwise, it does not create or open the file.
Portability	Available on UNIX systems.

modf

Name	**modf** – splits into mantissa and exponent
Usage	double modf(double *value*, double **iptr*);
Prototype in	math.h
Description	see **fmod**

movedata

Name	**movedata** – copies bytes
Usage	void movedata(int *segsrc*, int *offsrc*, int *segdest*, int *offdest*, unsigned *numbytes*);
Prototype in	mem.h string.h
Description	**movedata** copies *numbytes* bytes from the source address (*segsrc:offsrc*) to the destination address (*segdest:offdest*).

movedata is useful for moving **far** data in tiny, small, and medium model programs, where data segment addresses are not known implicitly. **memcpy** can be used in compact, large, and huge model programs, since segment addresses are known implicitly.

Return value   There is no return value.

See also   **FP_OFF, memcpy, segread**

Example

```
#include <mem.h>

#define MONO_BASE 0xB000

/* saves the contents of the monochrome screen in buffer */

void save_mono_screen(char near *buffer)
{
   movedata(MONO_BASE, 0, _DS, (unsigned)buffer, 80*25*2);
}

main()
{
   char buf[80*25*2];

   save_mono_screen(buf);
}
```

movmem

Name	**movmem** – moves a block of bytes
Usage	void movmem(void *source*, void *destin*, unsigned *len*);
Related functions usage	void setmem(void *addr*, int *len*, char *value*);
Prototype in	mem.h
Description	**movmem** copies a block of *len* bytes from *source* to *destin*. If the source and destination strings overlap, the copy direction is chosen so that the data is always copied correctly.

setmem sets the first bytes of the block pointed to by *addr* to the byte *value*.

Return value	**movmem** and **setmem** return nothing.
Portability	Unique to the 8086 family.
See also	**mem…, str…**

_open

Name	**_open** – opens a file for reading or writing
Usage	#include <fcntl.h> int _open(char *pathname*, int *access*);
Prototype in	io.h
Description	see **open**

open

Name	**open** – opens a file for reading or writing
Usage	#include <fcntl.h> #include<sys\stat.h> int open(char *pathname*, int *access* [,int *permiss*]);
Related functions usage	int _open(char *pathname*, int *access*); int sopen(char *pathname*, int *access*, int *shflag*, int *permiss*);
Prototype in	io.h
Description	**open** opens the file specified by *pathname*, then prepares it for reading and/or writing as determined by the value of *access*. For **open**, *access* is constructed by bitwise ORing flags from the following two lists. Only one flag from the first

list may be used; the remaining flags may be used in any logical combination.

List 1: Read/Write flags

O_RDONLY	Open for reading only.
O_WRONLY	Open for writing only.
O_RDWR	Open for reading and writing.

List 2: Other access flags

O_NDELAY	Not used; for UNIX compatibility.
O_APPEND	If set, the file pointer will be set to the end of the file prior to each write.
O_CREAT	If the file exists, this flag has no effect. If the file does not exist, the file is created, and the bits of *permiss* are used to set the file attribute bits, as in **chmod**.
O_TRUNC	If the file exists, its length is truncated to 0. The file attributes remain unchanged.
O_EXCL	Used only with O_CREAT. If the file already exists, an error is returned.
O_BINARY	This flag can be given to explicitly open the file in binary mode.
O_TEXT	This flag can be given to explicitly open the file in text mode.

These O_... symbolic constants are defined in fcntl.h.

If neither O_BINARY nor O_TEXT is given, the file is opened in the translation mode set by the global variable *_fmode*.

If the O_CREAT flag is used in constructing *access*, you need to supply the *permiss* argument to **open**, from the following symbolic constants defined in sys\stat.h.

Value of *permiss*	Access Permission
S_IWRITE	Permission to write
S_IREAD	Permission to read
S_IREAD I S_IWRITE	Permission to read and write

For **_open**, the value of *access* in MS-DOS 2.x is limited to O_RDONLY, O_WRONLY, and O_RDWR. For MS-DOS 3.x, the following additional values can also be used:

O_NOINHERIT	Included if the file is not to be passed to child programs.
O_DENYALL	Allows only the current handle to have access to the file.
O_DENYWRITE	Allows only reads from any other open to the file.
O_DENYREAD	Allows only writes from any other open to the file.
O_DENYNONE	Allows other shared opens to the file.

Only one of the O_DENYxxx values may be included in a single **_open** under DOS 3.x. These file-sharing attributes are in addition to any locking performed on the files.

The maximum number of simultaneously open files is a system configuration parameter.

sopen is a macro defined as

```
open(pathname, (access | shflag), permiss)
```

where *pathname, access,* and *permiss* are the same as for **open**, and *shflag* is a flag specifying the type of file-sharing allowed on the file *pathname*. Symbolic constants for *shflag* are defined in share.h.

Return value
On successful completion, these routines return a non-negative integer (the file handle), and the file pointer (that marks the current position in the file) is set to the beginning of the file. On error, they return –1 and *errno* is set to one of the following:

ENOENT	Path or file name not found
EMFILE	Too many open files
EACCES	Permission denied
EINVACC	Invalid access code

Portability
open and **sopen** are available on UNIX systems. On UNIX version 7, the O_type mnemonics are not defined.

UNIX System III uses all of the O_type mnemonics except O_BINARY.

_open is unique to MS-DOS.

See also   **chmod, close, creat, dup, ferror,** *_fmode* (variable),
fopen, lock, lseek, read, searchpath, setmode, write

outport

Name   **outport** – output to a hardware port

Usage   void outport(int *port*, int *word*);

Prototype in dos.h

Description   see **inport**

outportb

Name   **outportb** – output to a hardware port

Usage   #include <dos.h>
                  void outportb(int *port*, char *byte*);

Prototype in dos.h

Description   see **inport**

parsfnm

Name   **parsfnm** – parses file name

Usage   #include <dos.h>
                  char *parsfnm(char *cmdline*, struct fcb *fcbptr*, int *option*);

Prototype in dos.h

Description	**parsfnm** parses a string, normally a command line, pointed to by **cmdline* for a file name. The file name is placed in an FCB as a drive, file name, and extension. The FCB is pointed to by *fcbptr*.
	The *option* parameter is the value documented for AL in the DOS parse system call. See the *MS-DOS Programmer's Reference Manual* under system call 0x29 for a description of the parsing operations performed on the file name.
Return value	On successfully completing the parse of a file name, **parsfnm** returns a pointer to the next byte after the end of the file name. If there is any error in parsing the file name, **parsfnm** returns 0.
Portability	Unique to MS-DOS.

peek

Name	**peek** – examines memory location
Usage	int peek(int *segment*, unsigned *offset*);
Related functions usage	char peekb(int *segment*, unsigned *offset*);
Prototype in	dos.h
Description	**peek** and **peekb** examine the memory location addressed by *segment:offset*.
	If these routines are called when dos.h has been included, they will be treated as macros that expand to in-line code. If you don't include dos.h (or if you do include it and #undef the routines) you will get the functions rather than the macros.
Return value	**peek** and **peekb** return the value stored at the memory location *segment:offset*. **peek** returns a word, and **peekb** returns a byte.
Portability	Unique to the 8086 family.
See also	**harderr, poke**

peekb

Name	**peekb** – examines memory location
Usage	#include <dos.h> char peekb(int *segment*, unsigned *offset*);
Prototype in	dos.h
Description	see **peek**

perror

Name	**perror** – system error messages
Usage	void perror(char **string*);
Prototype in	stdio.h
Description	**perror** prints an error message to *stderr*, describing the most recent error encountered in a system call from the current program.

First the argument *string* is printed, then a colon, then the message corresponding to the current value of *errno*, and finally a newline. The convention is to pass the name of the program as the argument string.

To provide more control over message formatting, the array of message strings is provided in *sys_errlist*. *errno* can be used as an index into the array to find the string corresponding to the error number. The string does not include any newline character.

sys_nerr contains the number of entries in the array.

Refer to *errno*, *sys_errlist*, and *sys_nerr* in the "Variables" section of this chapter for more information.

Return value	None

| Portability | Available on UNIX systems. |
| See also | eof |

poke

Name	**poke** – stores value at a given memory location
Usage	void poke(int *segment*, int *offset*, int *value*);
Related functions usage	void pokeb(int *segment*, int *offset*, char *value*);
Prototype in	dos.h
Description	**poke** stores the integer *value* at the memory location *segment:offset*.

If these routines are called when dos.h has been included, they will be treated as macros that expand to in-line code. If you don't include dos.h (or if you do include it and #undef the routines) you will get the functions rather than the macros.

pokeb is the same as **poke**, except that a byte *value* is deposited instead of an integer.

Return value	None
Portability	Unique to the 8086 family.
See also	**peek**

pokeb

Name	**pokeb** – value at memory location
Usage	#include <dos.h> void pokeb(int *segment*, int *offset*, char *value*);
Prototype in	dos.h
Description	see **poke**

poly

Name	**poly** – generates a polynomial from arguments
Usage	double poly(double *x*, int *n*, double *c[]*);
Prototype in	math.h
Description	**poly** generates a polynomial in *x*, of degree *n*, with coefficients *c[0]*, *c[1]*, ..., *c[n]*. For example, if *n* = 4, the generated polynomial is

$$c[4]x^4 + c[3]x^3 + c[2]x^2 + c[1]x + c[0]$$

Return value	**poly** returns the value of the polynomial as evaluated for the given *x*.
Portability	Available on UNIX systems.

pow

Name	**pow** – power function, x^y
Usage	double pow(double x, double y);
Prototype in	math.h
Description	see **exp**

pow10

Name	pow10 – power function, 10^p
Usage	double pow10(int p);
Prototype in	math.h
Description	see **exp**

...printf

Name	**...printf** – functions that send formatted output
Usage	int printf(char *format, ...);

Related functions usage	int cprintf(char *format[, argument, ...]);
	int fprintf(FILE *stream, char *format[, argument, ...]);
	
	int sprintf(char *string, char *format[, argument, ...]);
	int vfprintf(FILE *stream, char *format, va_list param);

int vprintf(char *format, va_list param);
int vsprintf(char *string, char *format, va_list param);

Prototype in   stdio.h

Description   The ...**printf** family of functions all "print" formatted output; they all:

■ accept a *format string* that determines how the output will be formatted (this is given as *format* in the Usage)

■ apply the format string to a variable number of values to produce formatted output (the values are given as either *"argument, ..."* or va_list *param* in the Usage)

The output location is implicit in three of the ...**printf** functions.

printf places its output on *stdout*; so does **vprintf**.

cprintf sends its output directly to the console.

The other four ...**printf** functions also accept another argument (the first in the list of parameters). This additional argument designates where the output goes.

fprintf and **vfprintf** place output in a named stream.

sprintf and **vsprintf** place output in a string in memory.

Four of the ...**printf** functions accept the arguments to be formatted from the function call (**printf**, **cprintf**, **fprintf**, and **sprintf**).

The other three (**vprintf**, **vfprintf**, and **vsprintf**) accept the arguments to be formatted from a variable argument list. The **v**...**printf** functions are known as *alternate entry points* for the ...**printf** functions.

See the definition of **va_**... for more information.

Here is a summary of each of the ...**printf** functions.

printf   places its output on *stdout*.

cprintf   sends its output directly to the console: it does not translate line-feed characters into CR/LF combinations.

fprintf   places its output on the named *stream*.

sprintf	places its output as a null-terminated string starting at *string*. With **sprintf**, it is the user's responsibility to ensure there is enough space in *string* to hold the string.
vprintf	behaves exactly like **printf**, except that it accepts arguments from the **va_arg** array **va_list** *param*.
vfprintf	behaves exactly like **fprintf**, except that it accepts arguments from the **va_arg** array **va_list** *param*.
vsprintf	behaves exactly like **sprintf**, except that it accepts arguments from the **va_arg** array **va_list** *param*.

For an example of how to use **vprintf**, refer to **va....**

The Format String

The format string, present in each of the **...printf** function calls, controls how each function will convert, format, and print its arguments. There must be enough arguments for the format; if not, the results are unpredictable and likely disastrous. Excess arguments (more than required by the format) are merely ignored.

The format string is a character string that contains two types of objects—*plain characters* and *conversion specifications*:

The plain characters are simply copied verbatim to the output stream.

The conversion specifications fetch arguments from the argument list and apply formatting to them.

Format Specifications

...printf format specifications have the following form:

```
% [flags] [width] [.prec] [F|N|h|l] type
```

Each conversion specification begins with the percent character (%). After the % come the following, in this order:

- an optional sequence of flag characters   [flags]
- an optional width specifier   [width]
- an optional precision specifier   [.prec]
- an optional input size modifier   [F | N | h | l]
- the conversion type character   [*type*]

Optional Format String Components

These are the general aspects of output formatting controlled by the optional characters, specifiers, and modifiers in the format string:

Character or Specifier	What It Controls or Specifies
flags	output justification, numeric signs, decimal points, trailing zeroes, octal and hex prefixes
width	minimum number of characters to print, padding with blanks or zeroes
precision	maximum number of characters to print; for integers, minimum number of digits to print
size	override default size of argument (**N** = near pointer, **F** = far pointer **h** = short int, **l** = long)

...printf Conversion Type Characters

The following table lists the **...printf** conversion type characters, the type of input argument accepted by each, and in what format the output will appear.

The information in this table of type characters is based on the assumption that no flag characters, width specifiers, precision specifiers, or input-size modifiers were included in the format specification. To see how the addition of the optional characters and specifiers affects the ...**printf** output, refer to the tables following this one.

Type Character	Input Argument	Format of Output
	Numerics	
d	integer	signed decimal int
i	integer	signed decimal int
o	integer	unsigned octal int
u	integer	unsigned decimal int
x	integer	unsigned hexadecimal int (with a, b, c, d, e, f)
X	integer	unsigned hexadecimal int (with A, B, C, D, E, F)
f	floating point	signed value of the form [-]dddd.dddd
e	floating point	signed value of the form [-]d.dddd e [+/-]ddd
g	floating point	signed value in either **e** or **f** form, based on given value and precision. Trailing zeroes and the decimal point are printed only if necessary.

Type Character	Input Argument	Format of Output
	Numerics (continued)	
E	floating point	same as **e**, but with **E** for exponent
G	floating point	same as **g**, but with **E** for exponent if **e** format used
	Characters	
c	character	single character
s	string pointer	prints characters until a null-terminator is hit or precision is reached
%	none	the **%** character is printed
	Pointers	
n	pointer to int	stores (in the location pointed to by the input argument) a count of the characters written so far
p	pointer	prints the input argument as a pointer
		far pointers are printed as XXXX:YYYY. near pointers are printed as YYYY (offset only)

Conventions

Certain conventions accompany some of these specifications, as summarized in the following table.

Characters	Conventions
e or **E**	The argument is converted to match the style [-] d.ddd...e[+/-]ddd where: • one digit precedes the decimal point • the number of digits after the decimal point is equal to the precision • the exponent always contains three digits
f	The argument is converted to decimal notation in the style [-] ddd.ddd... where the number of digits after the decimal point is equal to the precision (if a non-zero precision was given).
g or **G**	The argument is printed in style **e**, **E** or **f**, with the precision specifying the number of significant digits. Trailing zeroes are removed from the result, and a decimal point appears only if necessary. The argument is printed in style **e** or **f** (with some restraints) if **g** is the conversion character, and in style **E** if the character is **G**. Style **e** is used only if the exponent that results from the conversion is either (a) greater than the precision or (b) less than -4.
x or **X**	For **x** conversions, the letters a, b, c, d, e, and f will appear in the output; for **X** conversions, the letters A, B, C, D, E, and F will appear.

Flag Characters

The flag characters are minus (-), plus (+), sharp (#) and blank ( ): They can appear in any order and combination.

Flag	What It Specifies
-	Left-justifies the result, pads on the right with blanks. If not given, right-justifies result, pads on left with zeroes or blanks.
+	Signed conversion results always begin with a plus (+) or minus (-) sign.
blank	If value is non-negative, the output begins with a blank instead of a plus; negative values still begin with minus.
#	Specifies that arg is to be converted using an "alternate form." See the following table.

Note: Plus takes precedence over blank if both given.

Alternate Forms

If the # flag is used with a conversion character, it has the following effect on the argument (*arg*) being converted:

Conversion Character	How # Affects *arg*
`c,s,d,i,u`	No effect
`o`	0 will be prepended to a non-zero *arg*.
`x` or `X`	0x (or 0X) will be prepended to *arg*.
`e, E` or `f`	The result will always contain a decimal point even if no digits follow the point. Normally, decimal point appears in these results only if a digit follows it.
`g` or `G`	Same as `e` and `E`, with the addition that trailing zeroes will not be removed.

Width Specifiers

The width specifier sets the minimum field width for an output value.

Width is specified in one of two ways; directly, through a decimal digit string, or indirectly, through an asterisk (*). If you use an asterisk for the width specifier, the next argument in the call (which must be an int) specifies the minimum output field width.

In no case does a non-existent or small field width cause truncation of a field. If the result of a conversion is wider than the field width, the field is simply expanded to contain the conversion result.

Width Specifier	How Output Width Is Affected
n	At least **n** characters are printed. If the output value has less than **n** characters, the output is padded with blanks (right-padded if "-" flag given, left-padded otherwise).
0n	At least **n** characters are printed. If the output value has less than **n** characters, it is filled on the left with zeroes.
*	The argument list supplies the width specifier, which must precede the actual argument being formatted.

Precision Specifiers

Precision specification always begins with a dot (.), to separate it from any preceding width specifier. Then, like width, precision is specified either directly, through a decimal digit string, or indirectly, through an asterisk (*). If you use an asterisk for the precision specifier, the next argument in the call (treated as an int) specifies the precision.

If you use asterisks for the width or the precision, or for both, the width argument must immediately follow the specifiers, followed by the precision argument, then the argument for the data to be converted.

Precision Specifier	How Output Precision Is Affected
(none given)	Precision set to default (default = 1 for **d, i, o, u, x, X** types; default = 6 for **e, E, f** types; default = all significant digits for **g, G** types; default = print to first null character for **s** types; no effect on **c** types.)
.0	for **d, i, o, u, x** types, precision set to default for **e, E, f** types, no decimal point is printed
.n	**n** characters or **n** decimal places are printed. If the output value has more than **n** characters, the output might be truncated or rounded. (Whether or not this happens depends on the type character.)
*	The argument list supplies the precision specifier, which must precede the actual argument being formatted.

Conversion Character	How Precision Specification (.n) Affects Conversion
d i o u x X	.n specifies that at least n digits will be printed. If the input argument has less than n digits, the output value is left-padded with zeroes. If the input argument has more than n digits, the output value is not truncated.
e E f	.n specifies that n characters will be be printed after the decimal point, and the last digit printed is rounded.
g G	.n specifies that at most n significant digits will be printed.
c	.n has no effect on the output.
s	.n specifies that no more than n characters will be printed.

Input Size Modifier

The input-size modifier character (**F**, **N**, **h** or **l**) gives the size of the subsequent input argument:

F = far pointer
N = near pointer
h = short int
l = long

The input-size modifiers (**F**, **N**, **h**, and **l**) affect how the **...printf** functions interpret the data-type of the corresponding input argument *arg*. **F** and **N** apply only to input *args* that are pointers (%**p**, %**s**, and %**n**). **h** and **l** apply to input *args* that are numeric (integers and floating-point).

Both **F** and **N** reinterpret the input *arg*. Normally, the *arg* for a %**p**, %**s**, or %**n** conversion is a pointer of the default size for the memory model. **F** says "interpret *arg* as a far pointer". **N** says "interpret *arg* as a near pointer".

Both **h** and **l** override the default size of the numeric data input args: **l** applies to integer (**d**, **i**, **o**, **u**, **x**, **X**) and floating-point (**e**, **E**, **f**, **g**, and **G**) types, while **h** applies to integer types only. Neither **h** nor **l** affect character (**c, s**) or pointer (**p, n**) types.

Input-Size Modifier	How *arg* Is Interpreted
F	*arg* is read as a far pointer
N	*arg* is read as a near pointer
	N cannot be used with any conversion in huge model.
h	*arg* is interpreted as a short int for **d, i, o, u, x,** or **X.**
l	*arg* is interpreted as a long int for **d, i, o, u, x, or X;** *arg* is interpreted as a double for **e, E, f, g,** or **G.**

Return value Each function returns the number of bytes output. **sprintf** does not include the null byte in the count. In the event of error, these functions return EOF.

Portability The functions **printf, cprintf, fprintf,** and **sprintf** are available on UNIX systems and are defined in Kernighan and Ritchie.

vprintf, vfprintf, and **vsprintf** are available on UNIX System V but are not defined in Kernighan and Ritchie.

See also **ecvt, fread, putc, puts, scanf, va...**

Example

```
#define I 555
#define R 5.5

main()
{
    int i,j,k,l;
    char buf[7];
    char *prefix = &buf;
    char tp[20];
```

```
      printf("prefix     6d       6o        8x       10.2e      10.2f\n");
      strcpy(prefix,"%");
      for (i=0;i<2;i++){
        for (j=0;j<2;j++)
         for (k=0;k<2;k++)
          for (l=0;l<2;l++){
             if (i==0)  strcat(prefix,"-");
             if (j==0)  strcat(prefix,"+");
             if (k==0)  strcat(prefix,"#");
             if (l==0)  strcat(prefix,"0");
             printf("%5s |",prefix);
             strcpy(tp,prefix);
             strcat(tp,"6d |");
             printf(tp,I);
             strcpy(tp,"");
             strcpy(tp,prefix);
             strcat(tp,"6o |");
             printf(tp,I);
             strcpy(tp,"");
             strcpy(tp,prefix);
             strcat(tp,"8x |");
             printf(tp,I);
             strcpy(tp,"");
             strcpy(tp,prefix);
             strcat(tp,"10.2e |");
             printf(tp,R);
             strcpy(tp,prefix);
             strcat(tp,"10.2f |");
             printf(tp,R);
             printf("  \n");
             strcpy(prefix,"%");
          }
      }
}
```

Program output

```
 prefix  6d       6o        8x       10.2e          10.2f
 %-+#0  |+555   |01053  |0x22b    |+5.50e+000  |+5.50        |
 %-+#   |+555   |01053  |0x22b    |+5.50e+000  |+5.50        |
 %-+0   |+555   |1053   |22b      |+5.50e+000  |+5.50        |
 %-+    |+555   |1053   |22b      |+5.50e+000  |+5.50        |
 %-#0   |555    |01053  |0x22b    |5.50e+000   |5.50         |
 %-#    |555    |01053  |0x22b    |5.50e+000   |5.50         |
 %-0    |555    |1053   |22b      |5.50e+000   |5.50         |
 %-     |555    |1053   |22b      |5.50e+000   |5.50         |
 %+#0   |+00555 |001053 |0x00022b |+5.50e+000  |+000005.50 |
 %+#    |  +555 | 01053 |   0x22b |+5.50e+000  |      +5.50 |
 %+0    |+00555 |001053 |0000022b |+5.50e+000  |+000005.50 |
 %+     |  +555 |  1053 |     22b |+5.50e+000  |      +5.50 |
 %#0    |000555 |001053 |0x00022b |05.50e+000  |0000005.50 |
 %#     |   555 | 01053 |   0x22b | 5.50e+000  |       5.50 |
 %0     |000555 |001053 |0000022b |05.50e+000  |0000005.50 |
 %      |   555 |  1053 |     22b | 5.50e+000  |       5.50 |
```

putc

Name
putc – outputs a character to a stream

Usage
#include <stdio.h>
int putc(int *ch*, FILE *stream*);

**Related
functions usage**
int fputc(int *ch*, FILE *stream*);
int fputchar(char *ch*);
int putch(int *ch*);

int putchar(int *ch*);
int putw(int *w*, FILE *stream*);

Prototype in
stdio.h

Description
putc is a macro that outputs the character *ch* to the named output *stream*.

putchar(*ch*) is a macro defined to be **putc**(*ch*, *stdout*).

fputc is like **putc** but it is a true function that outputs *ch* to the named *stream*.

fputchar outputs *ch* to *stdout*. **fputchar**(char *ch*) is the same as **fputc**(char *ch*, *stdout*).

putch outputs the character *ch* to the console.

putw outputs the integer *w* to the output *stream*. **putw** neither expects nor causes special alignment in the file.

Return value
On success **putc**, **fputc**, **fputchar**, and **putchar** return the character *ch*, while **putw** returns the integer *w*, and **putch** returns nothing.

On error, all the functions except **putch** return EOF. **putch** returns nothing.

Since EOF is a legitimate integer, **ferror** should be used to detect errors with **putw**.

Portability	All these functions are available on UNIX systems. **putc** and **putchar** and are defined in Kernighan and Ritchie.
See also	**ferror, fopen, fread, getc, printf, puts, setbuf**

putch

Name	**putch** – puts character on console
Usage	int putch(int *ch*);
Prototype in	conio.h
Description	see **putc**

putchar

Name	**putchar** – puts character on a stream
Usage	#include <stdio.h> int putchar(int *ch*);
Prototype in	stdio.h
Description	see **putc**

putenv

Name	**putenv** – adds string to current environment
Usage	int putenv(char *envvar*);
Prototype in	stdlib.h
Description	see **getenv**

puts

Name	**puts** – puts a string on a stream
Usage	int puts(char *string);
Related functions usage	void cputs(char *string); int fputs(char *string, FILE *stream);
Prototype in	stdio.h (**fputs** and **puts**) conio.h (**cputs**)
Description	**puts** copies the null-terminated string *string* to the standard output stream *stdout* and appends a newline character. **cputs** writes the null-terminated string *string* to the console; it does not append a newline character. **fputs** copies the null-terminated string *string* to the named output *stream*; it does not append a newline character.
Return value	On successful completion, **puts** and **fputs** return the last character written. Otherwise, a value of EOF is returned. **cputs** returns no value.
Portability	These functions are available on UNIX systems. Kernighan and Ritchie also define **fputs**.
See also	**ferror, fopen, fread, gets, open, printf, putc**

putw

Name	**putw** – puts character or word on a stream
Usage	#include <stdio.h> int putw(int *w*, FILE **stream*);
Prototype in	stdio.h
Description	see **putc**

qsort

Name	**qsort** – sorts using the quick sort routine
Usage	void qsort(void **base*, int *nelem*, int *width*, int (**fcmp*)());
Prototype in	stdlib.h
Description	**qsort** is an implementation of the "median of three" variant of the quicksort algorithm. **qsort** sorts the entries in a table into order by repeatedly calling the user-defined comparison function pointed to by *fcmp*.

- *base* points to the base (0th element) of the table to be sorted.
- *nelem* is the number of entries in the table.
- *width* is the size of each entry in the table, in bytes.

*fcmp, the comparison function, accepts two arguments, *elem1* and *elem2*, each a pointer to an entry in the table. The comparison function compares each of the pointed-to items (**elem1* and **elem2*), and returns an integer based on the result of the comparison.

If the items			*fcmp* returns
elem1	<	*elem2*	an integer < 0
elem1	==	*elem2*	0
elem1	>	*elem2*	an integer > 0

In the comparison, the *less than* symbol (<) means that the left element should appear before the right element in the final, sorted sequence. Similarly, the *greater than* (>) symbol means that the left element should appear after the right element in the final, sorted sequence.

Return value   **qsort** does not return a value.

Portability   Available on UNIX systems.

See also   **bsearch**, **lsearch**

---

rand

Name   **rand** – random number generator

Usage   int rand(void);

Related functions usage   void srand(unsigned *seed*);

Prototype in   stdlib.h

Description   **rand** uses a multiplicative congruential random-number generator with period 2^{32} to return successive pseudo-random numbers in the range from 0 to $2^{15}-1$.

The generator is reinitialized by calling **srand** with an argument value of 1. It can be set to a new starting point by calling **srand** with a given *seed* number.

Portability   Available on UNIX systems.

Example

```
#include <time.h>
#include <stdio.h>
#include <stdlib.h>
```

```
main()    /* Prints 5 random numbers from 0 to 32767 */
{
   int i; long now;

   srand(time(&now) % 37);    /* start at a random place */
   for (i=0; i<5; i++)
      printf("%d\n", rand());
}
```

Program output

```
9680
7414
22510
13860
6005
```

randbrd

Name	**randbrd** – random block read
Usage	#include <dos.h> int randbrd(struct fcb *fcbptr, int reccnt);
Related functions usage	int randbwr(struct fcb *fcbptr, int reccnt);
Prototype in	dos.h
Description	**randbrd** reads *reccnt* number of records using the open FCB pointed to by *fcbptr*. The records are read into memory at the current disk transfer address. They are read from the disk record indicated in the *random record* field of the FCB. This is accomplished by calling DOS system call 0x27.

randbwr performs essentially the same function as **randbrd**, except that data is written to disk instead of read from disk. This is accomplished using DOS system call DOS 0x28. If *reccnt* is 0, the file is truncated to the length indicated by the *random record* field.

The actual number of records read or written can be determined by examining the *random record* field of the

FCB. The random record field will be advanced by the number of records actually read or written.

Return value   The following values are returned, depending upon the result of the **randbrd** or **randbwr** operation:

  0 All records are read or written.

  1 End-of-file is reached and the last record read is complete.

  2 Reading records would have wrapped around address 0xFFFF (as many records as possible are read).

  3 End-of-file is reached with the last record incomplete.

randbwr returns 1 if there is not enough disk space to write the records (no records are written).

Portability   Unique to MS-DOS.

randbwr

Name   **randbwr** – random block write

Usage   #include <dos.h>
                  int randbwr(struct fcb *fcbptr*, int *reccnt*);

Prototype in   dos.h

Description   see **randbrd**

_read

Name	**_read** – reads from file
Usage	int _read(int *handle*, void *buf*, int *nbyte*);
Prototype in	io.h
Description	see **read**

read

Name	**read** – reads from file
Usage	int read(int *handle*, void *buf*, int *nbyte*);
Related functions usage	int _read(int *handle*, void *buf*, int *nbyte*);
Prototype in	io.h
Description	**read** and **_read** attempt to read *nbyte* bytes from the file associated with *handle* into the buffer pointed to by *buf*. **_read** is a direct call to the MS-DOS read system call.
	For a file opened in text mode, **read** removes carriage returns and reports end-of-file when a *Ctrl-Z* character is read. No such removal or reporting is performed by **_read**.
	handle is a file handle obtained from a **creat**, **open**, **dup**, **dup2**, or **fcntl** call.
	On disk files, these functions begin reading at the current file pointer. When the reading is complete, they increment the file pointer by the number of bytes read. On devices, the bytes are read directly from the device.
Return value	Upon successful completion, a positive integer is returned indicating the number of bytes placed in the

buffer; if the file was opened in text mode, **read** does not count carriage returns or *Ctrl-Z* characters in the number of bytes read.

On end-of-file, both functions return zero. On error, both functions return –1 and *errno* is set to one of the following:

EACCES	Permission denied
EBADF	Bad file number

Portability   **read** is available on UNIX systems.
_read is unique to MS-DOS.

See also   **creat, dup, fread, getc, open**

---

realloc

Name   **realloc** – reallocates memory

Usage   void *realloc(void *ptr, unsigned newsize);

Prototype in   stdlib.h and alloc.h

Description   see **malloc**

---

remove

Name   **remove** – removes a file

Usage   int remove(char *filename);

Prototype in   stdio.h

Description   see **unlink**

rename

Name	**rename** – renames a file
Usage	int rename(char *oldname*, char *newname*);
Prototype in	stdio.h
Description	**rename** changes the name of a file from *oldname* to *newname*. If a drive specifier is given in *newname*, the specifier must be the same as that given in *oldname*.
	Directories in a path need not be the same, so **rename** can be used to move a file from one directory to another. Wildcards are not allowed.
Return value	On successfully renaming the file, **rename** returns 0. In the event of error, –1 is returned, and *errno* is set to one of the following:

ENOENT	Path or file name not found
EACCES	Permission denied
ENOTSAM	Not same device

Portability	Unique to MS-DOS.

rewind

Name	**rewind** – repositions a stream
Usage	#include <stdio.h> int rewind(FILE *stream*);
Prototype in	stdio.h
Description	see **fseek**

rmdir

Name	**rmdir** – removes directory
Usage	int rmdir(char *pathname*);
Prototype in	dir.h
Description	see **mkdir**

sbrk

Name	**sbrk** – changes data segment space allocation
Usage	char *sbrk(int *incr*);
Prototype in	alloc.h
Description	see **brk**

...scanf

Name	**...scanf** – performs formatted input
Usage	int scanf(char *format*[, *argument* ...]);

Related functions usage	int cscanf(char *format*[, *argument*, ...]);
	int fscanf(FILE *stream*, char *format*[, *argument*, ...]);
	
	int sscanf(char *string*, char *format*[, *argument*, ...]);
	int vfscanf(FILE *stream*, char *format*, va_list *argp*);
	
	int vscanf(char *format*, va_list *argp*);
	int vsscanf(char *string*, char *format*, va_list *argp*);

Include files	#include <stdio.h>
Description	The **...scanf** family of functions all scan input fields, one character at a time, and convert them according to a given format; these functions all:

- accept a format string that determines how the input fields are to be interpreted (this is given as *format* in the Usage)

- apply the format string to a variable number of input fields in order to format the input

- store the formatted input in the addresses given as arguments after the format string (these addresses are given as either *"argument, ..."* or va_list *param* in the Usage)

When a **...scanf** function encounters its first format specification in the format string, it scans and converts the first input field according to that specification, then stores the result in the location given by the first address argument; it then scans, converts and stores the second input field, then the third, etc.

The input source is implicit in three of the **...scanf** functions.

scanf accepts its input from *stdin*; so does **vscanf**.

cscanf accepts its input directly from the console.

The other four **...scanf** functions also take an other argument (the first in the list of parameters). This additional argument designates the input source.

fscanf and **vfscanf** accept their input from a stream (pointed to by *stream*).

sscanf and **vsscanf** accept their input from a string in memory (pointed to by *string*).

Four of the **...scanf** functions take the set of address arguments directly from the function call (**scanf, cscanf, fscanf, sscanf**).

The other three (**vscanf, vfscanf, vsscanf**) take their address arguments from a variable argument list . The **v...scanf** functions are known as *alternate entry points* for the **...scanf** functions.

See the definition of **va_...** for more information about variable argument lists.

Here is a summary of each of the **...scanf** functions.

scanf	reads data from *stdin* and stores it in the locations given by the address arguments *&arg1, ..., &argn*.
cscanf	reads data directly from the console and stores it in the locations given by the address arguments *&arg1, ..., &argn*.
fscanf	reads data from the named input stream into the locations given by the address arguments *&arg1, ..., &argn*.
sscanf	reads data (stored in character string *string*) into the locations given by the address arguments *&arg1, ..., &ar gn*. **sscanf** does not change the source string *string*.
vscanf	behaves exactly like **scanf** except that it accepts address arguments from the **va_arg** array **va_list** *param*.
vfscanf	behaves exactly like **fscanf** except that it accepts address arguments from the **va_arg** array **va_list** *param*.
vsscanf	behaves exactly like **sscanf** except that it accepts address arguments from the **va_arg** array **va_list** *param*.

The Format String

The format string, present in each of the **...scanf** function calls, controls how each function will scan, convert and store its input fields. There must be enough address arguments for the given format specifications; if not, the results are unpredictable, and likely disastrous. Excess address arguments (more than required by the format) are merely ignored.

The format string is a character string that contains three types of objects: *whitespace characters, non-whitespace characters,* and *format specifications.*

- The whitespace characters are blank ( ), tab (\t) or newline (\n). If a **...scanf** function encounters a whitespace character in the format string, it will read, but not store, all consecutive whitespace characters up to the next non-whitespace character in the input.

- The non-whitespace characters are all other ASCII characters except the percent sign (%). If a **...scanf** function encounters a non-whitespace character in the format string, it will read, but not store, a matching non-whitespace character.

- The format specifications direct the **...scanf** functions to read and convert characters from the input field into specific types of values, then store them in the locations given by the address arguments.

Trailing white space is left unread (including a newline), unless explicitly matched in the format string.

Format Specifications

...scanf format specifications have the following form:

```
 % [*] [width] [F|N] [h|l] type_character
```

Each format specification begins with the percent character (%). After the % come the following, in this order:

- an optional assignment-suppression character   [*]
- an optional width-specifier   [width]
- an optional pointer size-specifier   [F|N]
- an optional argument-type modifier   [h|l]
- the type character

Optional Format String Components

These are the general aspects of input formatting controlled by the optional characters and specifiers in the **...scanf** format string:

Character or Specifier	What It Controls or Specifies
*	suppresses assignment of the next input field
width	maximum number of characters to read; fewer characters might be read if the **...scanf** function encounters a white-space or non-convertible character
size	overrides default size of address argument (**N** = near pointer, **F** = far pointer)
argument type	overrides default type of address argument (**h** = pointer to short int, **l** = pointer to long int)

...scanf Type Characters

The following table lists the **...scanf** type characters, the type of input expected by each, and in what format the input will be stored.

The information in this table is based on the assumption that no optional characters, specifiers or modifiers (*, width, or size) were included in the format specification. To see how the addition of the optional elements affects the **...scanf** input, refer to the tables following this one.

Type Character	Input	Type of Argument
Numerics		
d	Decimal integer	Pointer to int (int *arg)
D	Decimal integer	Pointer to long (long *arg)
o	Octal integer	Pointer to int (int *arg)
O	Octal integer	Pointer to long (long *arg)
i	Decimal, octal or hexadecimal integer	Pointer to int (int *arg)
I	Decimal, octal or hexadecimal integer	Pointer to long (long *arg)
u	Unsigned decimal integer	Pointer to unsigned int (unsigned int *arg)
U	Unsigned decimal integer	Pointer to unsigned long (unsigned long *arg)
x	Hexadecimal integer	Pointer to int (int *arg)
X	Hexadecimal integer	Pointer to long (long *arg)

Type Character	Input	Type of Argument
Numerics (continued)		
e	Floating	Pointer to float (float *arg)
E	Floating	Pointer to double (double *arg)
f	Floating	Pointer to float (float *arg)
g	Floating	Pointer to float (float *arg)
G	Floating	Pointer to double (double *arg)
Characters		
s	Character string	Pointer to array of characters (char arg[])
c	Character	Pointer to character (char *arg) If a field width W is given along with the **c** type character (such as %5c): Pointer to array of W characters (char arg[W])
%	% character	No conversion is done; the % character is stored.
Pointers		
n	(none)	Pointer to int (int *arg) The number of characters read successfully, up to the **%n**, is stored in this pointer.
p	Hexadecimal number in the form YYYY:ZZZZ or ZZZZ	Pointer to an object (far * or near *) **%p** conversions default to the pointer size native to the memory model

Input Fields

Any one of the following is an input field:

- all characters up to (but not including) the next whitespace character
- all characters up to the first one that cannot be converted under the current format specification (such as an 8 or 9 under octal format)
- up to *n* characters, where *n* is the specified field width

Conventions

Certain conventions accompany some of these format specifications, as summarized here.

%c conversion

This specification reads the next character, including a whitespace character. To skip one whitespace character and read the next non-whitespace character, use %1s.

%Wc conversion (W = width specification)

The address argument is a pointer to an array of characters; the array consists of W elements (char arg[W]).

%s conversion

The address argument is a pointer to an array of characters (char *arg[]*).

The array size, must be *at least* (n+1) bytes, where *n*=length of string *s* (in characters). A space or newline terminates the input field. A null-terminator is automatically appended to the string and stored as the last element in the array.

%[search_set] conversion

The set of characters surrounded by square brackets can be substituted for the **s** type character. The address argument is a pointer to an array of characters (char arg[]).

These square brackets surround a set of characters that define a *search set* of possible characters making up the string (the input field).

If the first character in the brackets is a caret (^), the search set is inverted to include all ASCII characters except those between the square brackets. (Normally, a caret will be included in the inverted search set unless explicitly listed somewhere after the first caret.)

The input field is a string not delimited by whitespace. The **...scanf** function reads the corresponding input field up to the first character it reaches that does not appear in the search set (or in the inverted search set). Two examples of this type of conversion are

`%[abcd]`	which will search for any of the characters *a*, *b*, *c*, and *d* in the input field
`%[^abcd]`	which will search for any characters except *a*, *b*, *c*, and *d* in the input field.

You can also use a "range facility" shortcut to define a range of characters (numerics or letters) in the search set. For example, to catch all decimal digits, you could define the search set by using

`%[0123456789]`

or you could use the shortcut to define the same search set by using

`%[0-9]`

To catch alphanumerics, you could use the following shortcuts:

`%[A-Z]`	catches all uppercase letters
`%[0-9A-Za-z]`	catches all decimal digits and all letters (uppercase and lowercase)
`%[A-FT-Z]`	catches all uppercase letters from *A* through *F* and from *T* through *Z*

The rules covering these search set ranges are straightforward.

- The character prior to the dash (-) must be lexically less than the one after it.

- The dash must not be the first nor the last character in the set. (If it is first or last, it is considered to just be the dash character, not a range definer.)

- The characters on either side of the dash must be the ends of the range, and not part of some other range.

Here are some examples where the dash just means the dash character, not a range between two ends:

`%[-+*/]`	the four arithmetic operations
`%[z-a]`	the characters 'z', '-', and 'a'
`%[+0-9-A-F]`	the characters '+' and '-', and the ranges 0 through 9 and A through Z
`%[+0-9A-F-]`	also the characters '+' and '-', and the ranges 0 through 9 and A through Z

`%[^-0-9+A-F]`   all characters except '+' and '-', and those in the ranges 0 through 9 and A through Z

%e, %E. %f, %g and %G (floating-point) conversions

Floating-point numbers in the input field must conform to the following generic format:

```
[+/-] dddddddd [.] dddd [E | e] [+/-] ddd
```

where [item] indicates that item is optional and ddd represents decimal, octal or hexadecimal digits.

%d, %i, %o, %x, %D, %I, %O, %X, %c, %n conversions

A pointer to unsigned character, unsigned integer, or unsigned long can be used in any conversion where a pointer to a character, integer, or long is allowed.

Assignment-Suppression Character

The assignment-suppression character is an asterisk (*); it is not to be confused with the C indirection (pointer) operator (also an asterisk).

If this character (*) follows the % in a format specification, the next input field will be scanned but will not be assigned to the next address argument. The suppressed input data is assumed to be of the type specified by the type character that follows the * character.

The success of literal matches and suppressed assignments is not directly determinable.

Width Specifiers

The width specifier (n), a decimal integer, controls the maximum number of characters that will be read from the current input field.

If the input field contains less than n characters, the ...scanf function reads all the characters in the field, then proceeds with the next field and format specification.

If a whitespace or non-convertible character occurs before width characters are read, the characters up to that character are read, converted and stored, then the function attends to the next format specification.

A non-convertible character is one that cannot be converted according to the given format (such as an 8 or 9 when the format is octal, or a *J* or *K* when the format is hexadecimal or decimal).

Width Specifier	How Width of Stored Input Is Affected
n	up to **n** characters will be read, converted, and stored in the current address argument.

Input-Size and Argument-Type Modifiers

The input-size modifiers (**N** and **F**) and argument-type modifiers (**h** and **l**) affect how the **...scanf** functions interpret the corresponding address argument *arg*.

F and **N** override the default or declared size of *arg*.

h and **l** indicate which type (version) of the following input data is to be used (**h** = short, **l** = long). The input data will be converted to the specified version, and the *arg* for that input data should point to an object of the corresponding size (short object for %**h**, long or double object for %**l**).

Modifier	How Conversion Is Affected
F	overrides default or declared size; *arg* interpreted as far pointer
N	overrides default or declared size; *arg* interpreted as near pointer Cannot be used with any conversion in huge model.
h	for **d**, **i**, **o**, **u**, **x** types: convert input to short int, store in short object for **D**, **I**, **O**, **U**, **X** types: has no effect for **e**, **f**, **c**, **s**, **n**, **p** types: has no effect
l	for **d**, **i**, **o**, **u**, **x** types: convert input to long int, store in long object for **e**, **f** types: convert input to double, store in double object for **D**, **I**, **O**, **U**, **X** types: has no effect for **c**, **s**, **n**, **p** types: has no effect

When ...scanf Functions Stop Scanning

The **...scanf** functions may stop scanning a particular field before reaching the normal field-end character (whitespace), or may terminate entirely, for a variety of reasons.

The **...scanf** function will stop scanning and storing the current field and proceed to the next input field if any of the following occurs:

- An assignment-suppression character (*) appears after the percent character in the format specification; the current input field is scanned but not stored.

- *width* characters have been read (*width* = width specification, a positive decimal integer in the format specification).

- The next character read cannot be converted under the current format (for example, an *A* when the format is decimal).

- The next character in the input field does not appear in the search set (or does appear in an inverted search set).

When the **...scanf** function stops scanning the current input field for one of these reasons, the next character is assumed to be unread and to be the first character of the following input field, or the first character in a subsequent read operation on the input.

The **...scanf** function will terminate under the following circumstances:

- The next character in the input field conflicts with a corresponding non-whitespace character in the format string.
- The next character in the input field is EOF.
- The format string has been exhausted.

If a character sequence that is not part of a format specification occurs in the format string, it must match the current sequence of characters in the input field; the **...scanf** function will scan, but not store, the matched characters. When a conflicting character occurs, it remains in the input field as if it were never read.

Return value   All the **...scanf** functions return the number of input fields successfully scanned, converted and stored; the return value does not include scanned fields that were not stored.

If one of these functions attempts to read at end-of-file (or end-of-string for **sscanf** and **vsscanf**), the return value is EOF.

If no fields were stored, the return value is 0.

Portability   The functions **scanf**, **fscanf**, **sscanf**, and **cscanf** are available on UNIX systems and are defined in Kernighan and Ritchie.

vscanf, **vfscanf**, and **vsscanf** are available on UNIX System V but are not defined in Kernighan and Ritchie.

See also   **atof, getc, printf**

searchpath

Name   **searchpath** – searches the DOS path

Usage   char *searchpath(char *filename);

Prototype in   dir.h

Description	**searchpath** attempts to locate a file, given by *filename*, using the MS-DOS path. A pointer to the complete path-name string is returned as the function value.

searchpath attempts to locate a file, given by *filename*, using the MS-DOS path. A pointer to the complete path-name string is returned as the function value.

The current directory of the current drive is checked first. If the file is not found there, the PATH environment variable is fetched, and each directory in the path is searched in turn until the file is found or the path is exhausted.

When the file is located, a string is returned containing the full path name. This string can be used in a call to **open** or **exec...** to access the file.

The string returned is located in a static buffer and is destroyed on each subsequent call to **searchpath**.

Return value   A pointer to a *filename* string is returned if the file is successfully located; otherwise, **searchpath** returns NULL.

Portability   Unique to MS-DOS.

See also   **exec...**, **open**, **system**

Example

```
#include <stdio.h>
#include <dir.h>

main()
{
   char *p;

   p = searchpath("TLINK.EXE");
   printf("Search for TLINK.EXE : %s\n", p);
   p = searchpath("NOTEXIST.FIL");
   printf("Search for NOTEXIST.FIL : %s\n", p);
}
```

Program output

```
Search for TLINK.EXE : C:\BIN\TLINK.EXE
Search for NOTEXIST.FIL : (null)
```

segread

Name	**segread** – reads segment registers
Usage	#include <dos.h> void segread(struct SREGS *segtbl);
Prototype in	dos.h
Description	**segread** places the current values of the segment registers (stored in SEGREGS) into the structure pointed to by *segtbl*. This call is intended for use with **intdosx** and **int86x**.
Return value	None
Portability	Unique to MS-DOS.
See also	**FP_OFF, intdos, int86**

setblock

Name	**setblock** – modifies the size of a previously allocated DOS memory segment
Usage	int setblock(int *seg*, int *newsize*);
Prototype in	dos.h
Description	see **allocmem**

setbuf

Name	**setbuf** – assigns buffering to a stream
Usage	#include <stdio.h> void setbuf(FILE *stream*, char *buf*);
Related **functions usage**	int setvbuf(FILE *stream*, char *buf*, int *type*, unsigned *size*);
Prototype in	stdio.h
Description	**setbuf** and **setvbuf** cause the buffer *buf* to be used for I/O buffering instead of an automatically allocated buffer. They are used after the given *stream* is opened.

In **setbuf**, if *buf* is NULL, I/O will be unbuffered; otherwise, it will be fully buffered. The buffer must be BUFSIZ bytes long (specified in stdio.h). In **setvbuf**, if *buf* is NULL, a buffer will be allocated using **malloc**; the buffer will use *size* as the amount allocated. The *size* parameter specifies the buffer size and must be greater than zero.

stdin and *stdout* are unbuffered if they are not redirected; otherwise, they are fully buffered. **setbuf** may be used to change the buffering style being used.

Unbuffered means that characters written to a stream are immediately output to the file or device, while *buffered* means that the characters are accumulated and written as a block.

In **setvbuf**, the *type* parameter is one of the following:

 _IOFBF The file is *fully buffered*. When a buffer is empty, the next input operation will attempt to fill the entire buffer. On output the buffer will be completely filled before any data is written to the file.

_IOLBF   The file is *line buffered*. When a buffer is empty, the next input operation will still attempt to fill the entire buffer. On output, however, the buffer will be flushed whenever a newline character is written to the file.

_IONBF   The file is *unbuffered*. The *buf* and *size* parameters are ignored. Each input operation will read directly from the file, and each output operation will immediately write the data to the file.

setbuf will produce unpredictable results if it is called for a *stream*, except immediately after opening the *stream* or any call to **fseek**. Calling **setbuf** after a *stream* has been unbuffered is legal and will not cause problems.

A common cause for error is to allocate the buffer as an automatic (local) variable and then fail to close the file before returning from the function where the buffer was declared.

Return value   **setbuf** returns nothing.

setvbuf returns 0 on success. It returns non-zero if an invalid value is given for *type* or *size*, if *buf* is NULL, or if there is not enough space to allocate a buffer.

setvbuf returns 0 on success.

Portability   Available on UNIX systems.

See also   **fopen, fclose, fseek, malloc, open**

Example

```
#include <stdio.h>

main ()
{
    FILE *input, *output;
    char bufr[512];

    input = fopen("file.in", "r");
    output = fopen("file.out", "w");

    /* Set up the input stream for minimal disk access,
       using our own character buffer */
```

```
if (setvbuf(input, bufr, _IOFBF, 512) != 0)
    printf("failed to set up buffer for input file\n");
else
    printf("buffer set up for input file\n");

/* Set up the output stream for line buffering using space that
   will  be obtained through an indirect call to malloc */
if (setvbuf(output, NULL, _IOLBF, 132) != 0)
    printf("failed to set up buffer for output file\n");
else
    printf("buffer set up for output file\n");

/* Perform file I/O here */

/* Close files */

fclose(input);
fclose(output);

}
```

setcbrk

Name	**setcbrk** – gets control-break setting
Usage	int setcbrk(int *value*);
Prototype in	dos.h
Description	see **getcbrk**

setdate

Name	**setdate** – sets MS-DOS date
Usage	#include <dos.h> void setdate(struct date **dateblk*);
Prototype in	dos.h
Description	see **getdate**

setdisk

Name	**setdisk** – sets current disk drive
Usage	int setdisk(int *drive*);
Prototype in	dir.h
Description	see **getdisk**

setdta

Name	**setdta** – sets disk transfer address
Usage	void setdta(char far *dta*);
Prototype in	dos.h
Description	see **getdta**

setftime

Name	**setftime** – gets file date and time
Usage	#include <io.h> int setftime(int *handle*, struct ftime *ftimep*);
Prototype in	io.h
Description	see **getftime**

setjmp

Name	**setjmp** – nonlocal goto
Usage	#include <setjmp.h> int setjmp(jmp_buf *env*);
Prototype in	setjmp.h
Description	see **longjmp**

setmem

Name	**setmem** – assigns a value to memory
Usage	void setmem(void *addr*, int *len*, char *value*);
Prototype in	mem.h
Description	see **movmem**

setmode

Name	**setmode** – sets mode of open file
Usage	int setmode(int *handle*, unsigned *mode*);
Prototype in	io.h
Description	**setmode** sets the mode of the open file associated with *handle* to either binary or text. The argument *mode* must have a value of either O_BINARY or O_TEXT, never both.
Return value	**setmode** returns 0 if successful; on error it returns –1 and sets *errno* to

EINVAL   Invalid argument

Portability **setmode** is available on UNIX systems.

See also **fread**, **read**, *_fmode* (variable),

---

settime

Name **settime** – sets system time

Usage #include <dos.h>
void settime(struct time *timep*);

Prototype in dos.h

Description see **gettime**

---

setvbuf

Name **setvbuf** – assigns buffering to a stream

Usage #include <stdio.h>
int setvbuf(FILE *stream*, char *buf*, int *type*,
        unsigned *size*);

Prototype in stdio.h

Description see **setbuf**

setvect

Name	**setvect** – sets interrupt vector entry
Usage	void setvect(int *intr_num*, void interrupt (**isr*) ( ));
Prototype in	dos.h
Description	see **getvect**

setverify

Name	**setverify** – sets verify state
Usage	void setverify(int *value*);
Prototype in	dos.h
Description	see **getverify**

sin

Name	**sin** – trigonometric sine function
Usage	double sin(double *x*);
Prototype in	math.h
Description	see **trig**

sinh

Name	**sinh** – hyperbolic sine function
Usage	double sinh(double *x*);
Prototype in	math.h
Description	see **hyperb**

sleep

Name	**sleep** – suspends execution for interval
Usage	unsigned sleep(unsigned *seconds*);
Prototype in	dos.h
Description	With a call to **sleep**, the current program is suspended from execution for the number of seconds specified by the argument *seconds*. The interval is only accurate to the nearest hundredth of a second, or the accuracy of the MS-DOS clock, whichever is less accurate.
Return value	None
Portability	Available on UNIX systems.

sopen

Name	**sopen** – opens a shared file
Usage	#include <fcntl.h> #include <sys\stat.h> #include <share.h> #include <io.h> int sopen(char * *pathname*, int *access*, int *shflag*, int *permiss*);
Prototype in	io.h
Description	see **open**

spawn...

Name	**spawn...** – creates and runs child processes

Usage	#include <process.h>
	int spawnl(int *mode*, char **pathname*, char **arg0*, *arg1*,
	       ..., *argn*, NULL);
	int spawnle(int *mode*, char **pathname*, char **arg0*, *arg1*,
	       ..., *argn*, NULL, char **envp[]*);
	
	int spawnlp(int *mode*, char **pathname*, char **arg0*, *arg1*,
	       ..., *argn*, NULL);
	int spawnlpe(int *mode*, char **pathname*, char **arg0*, *arg1*,
	       ..., *argn*, NULL, char **envp[]*);
	
	int spawnv(int *mode*, char **pathname*, char **argv[]*);
	int spawnve(int *mode*, char **pathname*, char **argv[]*,
	       char **envp[]*);
	
	int spawnvp(int *mode*, char **pathname*, char **argv[]*);
	int spawnvpe(int *mode*, char **pathname*, char **argv[]*,
	       char **envp[]*);

Prototype in	process.h
Description	The functions in the **spawn...** family create and run (execute) other files, known as *child processes*. There must be sufficient memory available for loading and executing the child process.

The value of *mode* determines what action the calling function (the *parent process*) will take after the spawn call. The possible values of *mode* are:

P_WAIT	Puts parent process "on hold" until child process completes execution.
P_NOWAIT	Continues to run parent process while child process runs.
P_OVERLAY	Overlays child process in memory location formerly occupied by parent. Same as an **exec...** call.

Note: P_NOWAIT is currently not available; using it will generate an error value.

pathname is the file name of the called child process. The **spawn...** function calls search for *pathname* using the standard MS-DOS search algorithm:

■ No extension or no period: Search for exact file name; if not successful, add .EXE and search again.

■ Extension given: Search only for exact file name.

■ Period given: Search only for file name with no extension.

The suffixes *l*, *v*, *p*, and *e* added to the **spawn...** "family name" specify that the named function will operate with certain capabilities.

p Specifies that the function will search for the child in those directories specified by the DOS PATH environment variable. Without the *p* suffix, the function will only search the root and current working directory.

l Specifies that the argument pointers *arg0*, *arg1*, ..., *argn* are passed as separate arguments. Typically, the *l* suffix is used when you know in advance the number of arguments to be passed.

v Specifies that the argument pointers *argv[0], ..., arg[n]* are passed as an array of pointers. Typically, the *v* suffix is used when a variable number of arguments is to be passed.

e Specifies that the argument *envp* may be passed to the child process, allowing you to alter the environment for the child process. Without the *e* suffix, child processes inherit the environment of the parent process.

Each function in the **spawn...** family *must* have one of the two argument-specifying suffixes (either *l* or *v*). The *path search* and *environment inheritance* suffixes (*p* and *e*) are optional.

For example:

- **spawnl** is a **spawn...** function that takes separate arguments, searches only the root or current directory for the child, and passes on the parent's environment to the child.

- **spawnvpe** is a **spawn...** function that takes an array of argument pointers, incorporates PATH in its search for the child process, and accepts the *envp* argument for altering the child's environment.

The **spawn...** functions must pass at least one argument to the child process (*arg0* or *argv[0]*): This argument is, by convention, a copy of *pathname*. (Using a different value for this zeroth argument won't produce an error.)

Under MS-DOS 3.0 and later, *pathname* is available for the child process; under earlier versions, the child process cannot use the passed value of the zeroth argument (*arg0* or *argv[0]*).

When the *l* suffix is used, *arg0* usually points to *pathname*, and *arg1, ..., argn* point to character strings that form the new list of arguments. A mandatory NULL following *argn* marks the end of the list.

When the *e* suffix is used, you pass a list of new environment settings through the argument *envp*. This environment argument is an array of **char***. Each element points to a null-terminated character string of the form

envvar = value

where *envvar* is the name of an environment variable, and *value* is the string value to which *envvar* is set. The last element in *envp[]* is NULL. When *envp[0]* is NULL, the child inherits the parents' environment settings.

The combined length of *arg0 + arg1 + ... + argn* (or of *argv[0] + argv[1] + ... + argv[n]*), including space characters that separate the arguments, must be < 128 bytes. Null-terminators are not counted.

When a **spawn...** function call is made, any open files remain open in the child process.

Return value   On a successful execution, the return value is the child process's exit status (0 for a normal termination). If the child specifically calls **exit** with a non-zero argument, its exit status can be set to a non-zero value.

On error, the **spawn...** functions return –1, and *errno* is set to one of the following:

E2BIG	Arg list too long
EINVAL	Invalid argument
ENOENT	Path or file name not found
ENOEXEC	Exec format error
ENOMEM	Not enough core

See also   **abort, atexit, exit, exec..., system**

Example

```
/*
   This program is SPAWNFAM.C

   To run this example, you must first compile CHILD.C to an EXE
   file.
*/

#include <stdio.h>
#include <process.h>


status(int val)
{
    if (val == -1)
        printf("failed to start child process\n");
```

```
        else
            if (val > 0)  printf("child terminated abnormally\n");

} /* status */


main()
{

/*
   ** NOTE: These environment strings should be changed
      to work on your machine. **
*/

        /* create an environment string */
        char *envp[] =  { "PATH=C:\\",
                          "DUMMY=YES",
                        };

        /* create a pathname */
        char *pathname = "C:\\CHILDREN\\CHILD.EXE";

        /* create an argument string */
        char *args[] =  { "CHILD.EXE",
                          "1st",
                          "2nd",
                           NULL
                        };

        printf("SPAWNL:\n");
        status(spawnl(P_WAIT, pathname,args[0], args[1], NULL));

        printf("\nSPAWNV:\n");
        status(spawnv(P_WAIT, pathname, args));

        printf("\nSPAWNLE:\n");
        status(spawnle(P_WAIT, pathname, args[0], args[1], NULL, envp));

        printf("\nSPAWNVPE:\n");
        status(spawnvpe(P_WAIT, pathname, args, envp));

}
/* main */

/*
   This is CHILD.C --- the child process for SPAWNFAM.C
*/

#include <stdio.h>
#include <stdlib.h>

main(int argc, char *argv[])
{
        int i;
        char *path, *dummy;
```

```
    path = getenv("PATH");
    dummy = getenv("DUMMY");

    for (i = 0; i < argc; i++)
        printf("argv[%d] %s\n", i, argv[i]);


    if (path)
        printf("PATH = %s\n", path);

    if (dummy)
        printf("DUMMY = %s\n", dummy);

    exit(0);   /* return to parent with error code 0 */
} /* main */
```

sprintf

Name	**sprintf** – sends formatted output to a string
Usage	int sprintf(char *string*, char *format*[, *argument*, ...]);
Prototype in	stdio.h
Description	see **printf**

sqrt

Name	**sqrt** – calculates square root
Usage	double sqrt(double *x*);
Prototype in	math.h
Description	see **exp**

srand

Name	**srand** – initializes random number generator
Usage	void srand(unsigned *seed*);
Prototype in	stdlib.h
Description	see **rand**

sscanf

Name	**sscanf** – performs formatted input from a string
Usage	int sscanf(char *string*, char *format*[, *argument*, ...]);
Prototype in	stdio.h
Description	see **scanf**

ssignal

Name	**ssignal** – implements software signals
Usage	int (*ssignal(int *sig*, int (*action*)( ))( );
Related functions usage	int gsignal(int *sig*);
Prototype in	signal.h
Description	**ssignal** and **gsignal** implement a software-signalling facility. Software signals are associated with integers in the range from 1 to 15.

gsignal raises the signal given by *sig* and executes the action routine.

ssignal is used to establish an action routine for servicing a signal. The first argument to **ssignal**, *sig*, is a number identifying the type of signal for which an action is established.

The second argument, *action*, defines the action; it is either the name of a user-defined action function or one of the constants SIG_DFL (default) or SIG_IGN (ignore). These constants are defined in signal.h.

If an action function has been established for *sig*, then that action is reset to SIG_DFL, and the action function is entered with argument *sig*.

Return value   **ssignal** returns the action previously established or, if the signal number is illegal, returns SIG_DFL.

gsignal returns the value returned to it by the *action* function. **gsignal**'s return values for actions assigned to *sig* are listed in the following:

Action	Return
SIG_IGN	1
SIG_DFL	0
Illegal value or no action specified	0

In all cases, **gsignal** takes no action other than returning a value.

Portability   Available on UNIX systems.

stat

Name	**stat** – gets information about open file
Usage	#include <sys\stat.h> int stat(char *pathname*, struct stat *buff*)
Related functions usage	int fstat(char *handle*, struct stat *buff*)
Prototype in	sys\stat.h
Description	**stat** and **fstat** store information about a given open file (or directory) in the **stat** structure.

stat gets information about the open file or directory given by *pathname*.

fstat gets information about the open file associated with *handle*.

In both functions, *buff* points to the **stat** structure (defined in sys\stat.h). That structure contains the following fields:

st_mode	bit mask giving information about the open file's mode
st_dev	drive number of disk containing the file, or file handle if the file is on a device
st_rdev	same as *st_dev*
st_nlink	set to the integer constant 1
st_size	size of the open file, in bytes
st_atime	most recent time the open file was modified
st_mtime	same as *st_atime*
st_ctime	same as *st_atime*

The **stat** structure contains three more fields not mentioned here: they contain values that are not meaningful under MS-DOS.

The bit mask that gives information about the mode of the open file includes the following bits:

One of the following bits will be set:

S_IFCHR   set if *handle* refers to a device (**fstat**)

S_IFREG   set if an ordinary file is referred to by *handle* (**fstat**), or specified by *pathname* (**stat**)

S_IFDIR   set if *pathname* specifies a directory (**stat**)

One or both of the following bits will be set:

S_IWRITE   set if user has permission to write to file

S_IREAD   set if user has permission to read to file

For **stat**, the bit mask also contains user-execute bits; these are set according to the open file's extension.

The bit mask also includes the read/write bits; these are set according to the file's permission mode.

Return value   Both functions return 0 if they successfully retrieved the information about the open file. On error (failure to get the information), each function returns –1 and sets *errno*.

On failure, **stat** sets *errno* to

ENOENT   File or path not found

On failure, **fstat** sets *errno* to

EBADF   Bad file handle

_status87

Name	**_status87** – gets floating-point status
Usage	unsigned int _status87();
Prototype in	float.h

Description	_status87 gets the floating-point status word, which is a combination of the 8087/80287 status word and other conditions detected by the 8087/80287 exception handler.
Return value	The bits in the return value give the floating-point status. See float.h for a complete definition of the bits returned by **_status87**.
See also	**_clear87, _control87, _fpreset**

stime

Name	**stime** – sets time
Usage	int stime(long *tp*);
Prototype in	time.h
Description	see **time**

stpcpy

Name	**stpcpy** – copies one string into another
Usage	char *stpcpy(char *destin*, char *source*);
Prototype in	string.h
Description	see **str...**

str...

Name	**str...** – family of string manipulation functions
Usage	char * stpcpy(char *destin, char *source);

```
char    *    stpcpy(char *destin, char *source);
char    *    strcat(char *destin, char *source);

char    *    strchr(char *str, char c);
int          strcmp(char *str1, char *str2);

char    *    strcpy(char *destin, char *source);
int          strcspn(char *str1, char *str2);

char    *    strdup(char *str);
int          stricmp(char *str1, char *str2);

int          strcmpi(char *str1, char *str2);
unsigned strlen(char *str);

char    *    strlwr(char *str);
char    *    strncat(char *destin, char *source, int maxlen);

int          strncmp(char *str1, char *str2, int maxlen);
char    *    strncpy(char *destin, char *source, int maxlen);

int          strnicmp(char *str1, char *str2,
                        unsigned maxlen);
int          strncmpi(char *str1, char *str2,
                        unsigned maxlen);

char    *    strnset(char *str, char ch, unsigned n);
char    *    strpbrk(char *str1, char *str2);

char    *    strrchr(char *str, char c);
char    *    strrev(char * str);

char    *    strset(char *str, char ch);
int          strspn(char *str1, char *str2);

char    *    strstr(char *str1, char *str2);
double       strtod(char *str, char **endptr);

long         strtol(char *str, char **endptr, int base);
char    *    strtok(char *str1, char *str2);
char    *    strupr(char *str);
```

Prototype in	string.h
Description	Here is an alphabetical summary of the **str...** functions. Following this list are detailed explanations of these *string manipulation* functions, organized by the types or categories of tasks they perform. The category is listed in parentheses after each entry.

strcat   appends one string to another (binding)

strchr   scans a string for the first occurrence of a given character (searching)

strcmp   compares one string to another (comparing)

strcpy   copies one string into another (copying)

strcspn   scans a string for the first segment not containing any subset of a given set of characters (searching)

strdup   copies a string into a newly-created location (copying)

stricmp   compares one string to another, without case sensitivity (comparing)

strcmpi   compares one string to another, without case sensitivity (comparing)

strlen   calculates the length of a string (searching)

strlwr   converts uppercase letters in a string to lowercase (changing)

strncat   appends a portion of one string to another (binding)

strncmp   compares a portion of one string to a portion of another (comparing)

strncpy   copies a given number of bytes from one string into another, truncating or padding as necessary (copying)

strncmpi   compares a portion of one string to a portion of another, without case sensitivity (comparing)

strnicmp	compares a portion of one string to a portion of another, without case sensitivity (comparing)
strnset	sets a specified number of characters in a string to a given character (changing)
strpbrk	scans a string for the first occurrence of any character from a given set (searching)
strrchr	scans a string for the last occurrence of a given character (searching)
strrev	reverses a string (changing)
strset	sets all characters in a string to a given character (changing)
strspn	scans a string for the first segment that is a subset of a given set of characters (searching)
strstr	scans a string for the occurrence of a given substring (searching)
strtod	converts a string to a double value (converting)
strtok	searches one string for tokens, which are separated by delimiters defined in a second string (searching)
strtol	converts a string to a long value (converting)
strupr	converts lowercase letters in a string to uppercase (changing)

These 27 **str...** (*string manipulation*) functions perform a variety of tasks. These can be broken down into six general categories:

- binding
- changing
- comparing
- converting
- copying
- searching

Here is a more complete explanation of what each **str...** function does; these are organized by the type (or category) of task the functions perform.

Binding (concatenation)

strcat	appends a copy of *source* to the end of *destin*. The length of the resulting string is **strlen**(*destin*) + **strlen**(*source*).
strncat	copies at most *maxlen* characters of *source* to the end of *destin* and then appends a null character. The maximum length of the resulting string is **strlen**(*destin*) + *maxlen*.

Changing

strlwr	converts uppercase letters in string *str* to lowercase. No other changes occur.
strupr	converts lowercase letters in string *str* to uppercase. No other changes occur.
strset	sets all characters in the string *str* to the character *ch*.
strnset	sets up to the first *n* bytes of the string *str* to the character *ch*. If *n* > **strlen**(*str*), then **strlen**(*str*) replaces *n*.
strrev	reverses all characters in a string (except the terminating null character).

Comparing

strcmp	compares *str1* to *str2*.
stricmp	compares *str1* to *str2*, without case sensitivity.
strcmpi	compares *str1* to *str2*, without case sensitivity (same as **stricmp**—implemented as a macro).
strncmp	makes the same comparison as **strcmp**, but looks at no more than *maxlen* characters.
strnicmp	compares *str1* to *str2*, for a maximum length of *maxlen* bytes, without case sensitivity.

strncmpi compares *str1* to *str2*, for a maximum length of *maxlen* bytes, without case sensitivity (same as **strnicmp**—implemented as a macro).

All these comparing functions return a value (<0, 0 or >0) based on the result of comparing *str1* (or part of it) to *str2* (or part of it).

The routines **strcmpi** and **strncmpi** are the same, respectively, as **stricmp** and **strnicmp**. They (**strcmpi** and **strncmpi**) are implemented via macros in string.h. These macros translate calls from **strcmpi** to **stricmp**, and calls from **strncmpi** to **strnicmp**. Therefore, in order to use **strcmpi** or **strncmpi**, you must #include the header file string.h for the macros to be available. These macros are provided for compatibility with other C compilers.

Converting

strtod   converts a character string, *str*, to a **double** value. *str* is a sequence of characters that can be interpreted as a double value; they must match this generic format:

```
[ws] [sn] [ddd] [.] [ddd] [fmt[sn]ddd]
```

where

```
[ws]  = optional whitespace
[sn]  = optional sign (+ or –)
[ddd] = optional digits
[fmt] = optional e or E
[.]   = optional decimal point
```

For example, here are some character strings that **strtod** can convert to double:

```
+1231.1981 e–1
502.85E2
–2010.952
```

strtod stops reading the string at the first character that cannot be interpreted as an appropriate part of a double value.

If *endptr* is not NULL, **strtod** sets *endptr* to point to the character that stopped the scan (*endptr = &stopper).

strtol converts a character string, *str*, to a long integer value. *str* is a sequence of characters that can be interpreted as a long value; they must match this generic format

```
[ws] [sn] [0] [x] [ddd]
```

where

[ws]	=	optional whitespace
[sn]	=	optional sign (+ or –)
[0]	=	optional zero (0)
[x]	=	optional x or X
[ddd]	=	optional digits

strtol stops reading the string at the first character that it doesn't recognize.

If *base* is between 2 and 36, the long integer is expressed in base *base*.

If *base* is 0, the first few characters of *str* determine the base of the value being converted.

First Character	Second Character	String Interpreted as
0	1 – 7	octal
0	x or X	hexadecimal
1 – 9	———	decimal

If *base* is 1, it is considered to be an invalid value.

If *base* is < 0, it is considered to be an invalid value.

If *base* is > 36, it is considered to be an invalid value.

Any invalid value for *base* causes the result to be 0 and sets the next character pointer to the starting string pointer.

If the value in *str* is meant to be interpreted as octal, any character other than 0 to 7 would be unrecognized.

If the value in *str* is meant to be interpreted as decimal, any character other than 0 to 9 would be unrecognized.

If the value in *str* is meant to be interpreted as a number in any other base, then only the numerals and letters used to represent numbers in that base would be recognized. (For example, if *base* = 5, only 0 to 4 would be recognized; if *base* = 20, only 0 to 9 and *A* to *J* would be recognized.)

Copying

strcpy	copies string *source* to *destin*, stopping after the terminating null character has been moved.
strncpy	copies exactly *maxlen* characters from *source* into *destin*, truncating or null-padding *destin*. The target string, *destin*, might not be null-terminated if the length of *source* is *maxlen* or more.
stpcpy	copies the bytes of *source* into *destin* and stops after copying the terminating null character of *source*. **stpcpy** (*a*, *b*) is the same as **strcpy** (*a*, *b*) except that the return values differ.
strcpy	(*a*, *b*) returns *a*, while **stpcpy** (*a*, *b*) returns *a* + **strlen** (*b*).
strdup	makes a duplicate of string *str*, obtaining space with a call to **malloc**. The allocated space is (**strlen** (*str*) + 1) bytes long.

Searching

strchr   scans a string in the forward direction, looking for a specific character. **strchr** finds the *first* occurrence of the character *ch* in the string *str*.

The null-terminator is considered to be part of the string, so that, for example

```
strchr(strs, 0)
```

returns a pointer to the terminating null character of the string *"strs"*.

strrchr   scans a string in the reverse direction, looking for a specific character. **strrchr** finds the *last* occurrence of the character *ch* in the string *str*. The null-terminator is considered to be part of the string.

strpbrk   scans a string, *str1*, for the first occurrence of any character appearing in *str2*.

strspn   returns the length of the initial segment of string *str1* that consists entirely of characters from string *str2*.

strcspn   returns the length of the initial segment of string *str1* that consists entirely of characters *not* from string *str2*.

strstr   scans *str1* for the first occurrence of the substring *str2*.

strtok   considers the string *str1* to consist of a sequence of zero or more text tokens, separated by spans of one or more characters from the separator string *str2*.

The first call to **strtok** returns a pointer to the first character of the first token in *str1* and writes a null character into *str1* immediately following the returned token. Subsequent calls with NULL for the first argument will work through the string *str1* in this way until no tokens remain.

The separator string, *str2*, may be different from call to call.

When no tokens remain in *str1*, **strtok** returns a NULL pointer.

Return value   These are the return values for the **str...** functions, arranged in alphabetical order by the function names.

stpcpy   returns *destin* + **strlen** (*source*).

strchr   returns a pointer to the first occurrence of the character *ch* in *str*; if *ch* does not occur in *str*, **strchr** returns NULL.

strcmp, stricmp, strcmpi, strncmp, strnicmp and **strncmpi**   all these routines return an `int` value that is

$$< 0 \quad \text{if } str1 \text{ is less than } str2$$
$$= 0 \quad \text{if } str1 \text{ is the same as } str2$$
$$> 0 \quad \text{if } str1 \text{ is greater than } str2$$

All six of these functions perform a signed comparison.

strcpy   returns *destin*.

strdup   returns a pointer to the storage location containing the duplicated *str*, or returns NULL if space could not be allocated.

strlen   returns the number of characters in *str*, not counting the null-terminating character.

strncpy   returns *destin*.

strpbrk   returns a pointer to the first occurrence of any of the characters in *str2*; if none of the *str2* characters occurs in *str1*, it returns NULL.

strrchr   returns a pointer to the last occurrence of the character *ch*. If *ch* does not occur in *str*, **strrchr** returns NULL.

strrev   returns a pointer to the reversed string. There is no error return.

strstr   returns a pointer to the element in *str1* that contains *str2* (points to *str2* in *str1*). If *str2* does not occur in *str1*, **strstr** returns NULL.

Portability	Available on UNIX systems. Kernighan and Ritchie define **strcat**.
See also	**malloc, mem…, movmem**

Example

```
/* strtok - This example demonstrates the use of strtok to parse dates. Note
            that in order to parse dates of varying formats (e.g., 12/3/87;
            Dec.12,1987; January 15, 1987 12-FEB-87, etc.), you must specify
            the delimiter string to contain either a period, space, comma,
            minus, or slash. Notice in the output that the delimiters are not
            returned.
*/

#include <stdio.h>
#include <string.h>


main ()
{
    char *ptr;

    ptr = strtok ("FEB.14,1987", ". ,-/" );
    printf ("ptr = %s\n", ptr);

    ptr = strtok (NULL, ". ,-/" );
    printf ("ptr = %s\n", ptr);

}
```

Program output

```
ptr = FEB
ptr = 14
```

strerror

Name	**strerror** – returns pointer to error message string
Usage	char *strerror(char *str);
Prototype in	string.h

Description	strerror allows you to generate customized error messages; it returns a pointer to a null-terminated string containing an error message.

If *str* is NULL, the return value contains the most recently generated system error message; this string is null-terminated.

If *str* is not NULL, the return value contains *str* (your customized error message), a colon, a space, the most recently generated system error message, and a newline.

The length of *str* should be 94 characters or less.

strerror is different from **perror** in that it does not print error messages.

For accurate error-handling, **strerror** should be called as soon as a library routine generates an error return.

Return value	strerror returns a pointer to a constructed error string. The error message string is constructed in a static buffer that is over-written with each call to **perror**.
Portability	Available on UNIX systems.
See also	**perror**

swab

Name	**swab** – swaps bytes
Usage	void swab(char *from, char *to, int nbytes);
Prototype in	stdlib.h
Description	**swab** copies *n bytes* from the *from* string to the *to* string. Adjacent even- and odd-byte positions are swapped. This is useful for moving data from one machine to another machine with a different byte order. *nbytes* should be even.
Return value	There is no return value.
Portability	Available on UNIX systems.

system

Name	**system** – issues an MS-DOS command
Usage	int system(char *command*);
Prototype in	stdlib.h
Description	**system** invokes the MS-DOS COMMAND.COM file to execute a command given in the string *command*, as if the command had been typed at the DOS prompt.
	The COMSPEC environment variable is used to find the COMMAND.COM file, so the file does not need to be in the current directory.
Return value	**system** returns the exit status of COMMAND.COM when the given *command* is completed.
Portability	Available on UNIX systems. Defined in Kernighan and Ritchie.
See also	**exec..., searchpath, spawn...**

tan

Name	**tan** – trigonometric tangent function
Usage	double tan(double *x*);
Prototype in	math.h
Description	see **trig**

tanh

Name	**tanh** – hyperbolic tangent function
Usage	double tanh(double *x*);
Prototype in	math.h
Description	see **hyperb**

tell

Name	**tell** – gets current position of file pointer
Usage	long tell(int *handle*);
Prototype in	io.h
Description	see **fseek**

time

Name	**time** – gets time of day
Usage	long time(long **tloc*);
Prototype in	time.h
Related functions usage	int stime(long **tp*);
Description	**time** gives the current time, in seconds, elapsed since 00:00:00 GMT, January 1, 1970, and stores that value in the location pointed to by *tloc*.

stime sets the system time and date. *tp* points to the value of the time as measured in seconds from 00:00:00 GMT, January 1, 1970

Return value   **time** returns the elapsed time, in seconds, as described.

stime returns a value of 0.

Portability   Available on UNIX systems.

toascii

Name   **toascii** – translates characters to ASCII format

Usage   int toascii(int *c*);

Related
functions usage   int tolower(int *c*);
                    int toupper(int *c*);

                    int _tolower(int *c*);
                    int _toupper(int *c*);

Prototype in   ctype.h

Description   **toascii** is a function that converts the integer *c* to ASCII by clearing all but the lower seven bits; this gives a value in the range 0 to 127. It is intended for compatibility with other systems.

                    tolower is a function that converts an integer *c* (in the range EOF to 255) to its lowercase value (*if* it was uppercase): all others are left unchanged.

                    toupper is a function that converts an integer *c* (in the range EOF to 255) to its uppercase value (*if* it was lowercase): all others are left unchanged.

                    _tolower is a macro that does the same conversion as **tolower**, except that it should be used only when *c* is known to be uppercase.

                    _toupper is a macro that does the same conversion as **toupper**, except that it should be used only when *c* is known to be lowercase.

To use **_tolower** or **_toupper**, you must include ctype.h.

Return value   Each function and macro returns the converted value of *c*, on success, and nothing on failure.

Portability   All functions are available on UNIX systems; **toupper** and **tolower** are defined in Kernighan and Ritchie.

_tolower

Name   **_tolower** – translates characters to lowercase

Usage   #include <ctype.h>
int _tolower(int *c*);

Prototype in   ctype.h

Description   see **toascii**

tolower

Name   **tolower** – translates characters to lowercase

Usage   int tolower(int *c*);

Prototype in   ctype.h

Description   see **toascii**

_toupper

Name	**_toupper** – translates characters to uppercase
Usage	#include <ctype.h>
	int _toupper(int *c*);
Prototype in	ctype.h
Description	see **toascii**

toupper

Name	**toupper** – translates characters to uppercase
Usage	int toupper(int *c*);
Prototype in	ctype.h
Description	see **toascii**

trig

Name	**trig** – trigonometric functions
Usage	double acos(double *x*);
	double asin(double *x*);
	double atan(double *x*);
	double atan2(double *y*, double *x*);
	double cos(double *x*);
	double sin(double *x*);
	double tan(double *x*);
Prototype in	math.h

Description	**sin**, **cos**, and **tan** return the corresponding trigonometric functions. Angles are specified in radians.
	asin, **acos**, and **atan** return the arc sine, arc cosine, and arc tangent, respectively, of the input value. Arguments to **asin** and **acos** must be in the range –1 to 1. Arguments outside that range will cause **asin** or **acos** to return 0 and set *errno* to:

EDOM   Domain error

atan2 returns the arc tangent of y/x and will produce correct results even when the resulting angle is near $pi/2$ or $-pi/2$ (x near 0).

Return value	**sin** and **cos** return a value in the range –1 to 1. **asin** returns a value in the range $-pi/2$ to $pi/2$.

acos returns a value in the range 0 to pi.
atan returns a value in the range $-pi/2$ to $pi/2$.

atan2 returns a value in the range $-pi$ to pi.

tan returns any value for valid angles. For angles close to $pi/2$ or $-pi/2$, **tan** returns 0 and *errno* is set to:

ERANGE   Result out of range

Error handling for these routines can be modified through the function **matherr**.

Portability	Available on UNIX systems.
See also	**_matherr, matherr, perror**

tzset

Name	**tzset** – UNIX time compatibility
Usage	void tzset(void);
Prototype in	time.h
Description	see **ctime**

ultoa

Name	**ultoa** – converts an unsigned long to a string
Usage	char *ultoa(unsigned long *value*, char **string*, int *radix*);
Prototype in	stdlib.h
Description	see **itoa**

ungetc

Name	**ungetc** – pushes a character back into input stream
Usage	#include <stdio.h> int ungetc(char *c*, FILE **stream*);
Prototype in	stdio.h
Description	see **getc**

ungetch

Name	**ungetch** – pushes a character back to the keyboard buffer
Usage	int ungetch(int *c*);
Prototype in	conio.h
Description	see **getc**

unixtodos

Name	**unixtodos** – converts date and time to DOS format
Usage	#include <dos.h> void unixtodos(long *utime*, struct date **dateptr*, struct time **timeptr*);
Prototype in	dos.h
Description	see **dostounix**

unlink

Name	**unlink** – deletes a file
Usage	int unlink(char **filename*);
Related functions usage	int remove(char **filename*);
Prototype in	dos.h
Description	**unlink** deletes a file specified by *filename*. Any MS-DOS drive, path, and file name may be used as a *filename*. Wildcards are not allowed.
	Read-only files cannot be deleted by this call. To remove read-only files, first use **chmod** or **_chmod** to change the read-only attribute.
	remove is a macro that simply translates the call to a call to **unlink**.
Return value	On successful completion, a 0 is returned. On error, a –1 is returned, and *errno* is set to one of the following values:

                         ENOENT   Path or file name not found
                         EACCES   Permission denied

Portability	Available on UNIX systems.
See also	chmod

unlock

Name	**unlock** – releases file-sharing locks
Usage	int unlock(int *handle*, long *offset*, long *length*);
Prototype in	dos.h
Description	see **lock**

va_...

Name	**va_...** – implements variable argument list

Usage	#include <stdarg.h>
	void va_start(va_list *param*, *lastfix*);
	type va_arg(va_list *param*, *type*);
	void va_end(va_list *param*);

Prototype in	stdarg.h
Description	Some C functions, such as **vfprintf** and **vprintf**, take variable argument lists in addition to taking a number of fixed (known) parameters. The **va_...** macros provide a portable way to access these argument lists. They are used for stepping through a list of arguments when the called function does not know the number and types of the arguments being passed.

The header file stdarg.h declares one type (*va_list*), and three macros (**va_start**, **va_arg**, and **va_end**).

va_list

This array holds information needed by **va_arg** and **va_end**. When a called function takes a variable argument list, it declares a variable *param* of type *va_list*.

va_start

This routine (implemented as a macro) sets *param* to point to the first of the variable arguments being passed to the function. **va_start** must be used before the first call to **va_arg** or **va_end**.

va_start takes two parameters; *param* and *lastfix*. (*param* is explained under *va_list* in the preceding paragraph; *lastfix* is the name of the last fixed parameter being passed to the called function.)

va_arg

This routine (also implemented as a macro) expands to an expression that has the same type and value as the next argument being passed (one of the variable arguments). The variable *param* to **va_arg** should be the same *param* that **va_start** initialized.

The first time **va_arg** is used, it returns the first argument in the list. Each successive time **va_arg** is used, it returns the next argument in the list. It does this by first de-referencing *param*, and then incrementing *param* to point to the following item. **va_arg** uses the *type* to both perform the de-reference and to locate the following item. Each successive time **va_arg** is invoked, it modifies *param* to point to the next argument in the list.

va_end

This macro helps the called function perform a normal return. **va_end** might modify *param* in such a way that it cannot be used unless **va_start** is re-called. **va_end** should be called after **va_arg** has read all the arguments: failure to do so might cause strange, undefined behavior in your program.

Return value   **va_start** and **va_end** return no values; **va_arg** returns the current argument in the list (the one that *param* is pointing to).

See also   ...scanf, printf

Example

```c
#include <stdio.h>
#include <stdarg.h>

/* calculate sum of a 0 terminated list */

void sum(char *msg, ...)
{
   int total = 0;
   va_list ap;
   int arg;

   va_start(ap, msg);
   while ((arg = va_arg(ap,int)) != 0) {
        total += arg;
   }
   printf(msg, total);
}

main()
{
        sum("The total of 1+2+3+4 is %d\n", 1,2,3,4,0);
}
```

Program output

```
The total of 1+2+3+4 is 10
```

Another example

```c
#include <stdio.h>
#include <stdarg.h>

void error(char *format,...)
{
   va_list argptr;

   printf("error: ");
   va_start(argptr, format);
   vprintf(format, argptr);
   va_end(argptr);
}

main()
{
   int value = -1;
```

```
    error("this is just an error message\n");
    error("invalid value %d encountered\n", value);
}
```

Program output

```
error: this is just an error message
error: invalid value -1 encountered
```

va_arg

Name	**va_arg** – accesses variable argument list
Usage	#include <stdarg.h> *type* va_arg(va_list *param*, *type*);
Prototype in	stdarg.h
Description	see **va_...**

va_end

Name	**va_end** – ends variable argument access
Usage	#include <stdarg.h> void va_end(va_list *param*);
Prototype in	stdarg.h
Description	see **va_...**

va_start

Name	**va_start** – begins variable argument access
Usage	#include <stdarg.h> void va_start(va_list *param*, *lastfix*);
Prototype in	stdarg.h
Description	see **va_...**

vfprintf

Name	**vfprintf** – sends formatted output to a stream
Usage	#include <stdio.h> #include <stdarg.h> int vfprintf(FILE **stream*, char **format*, va_list *param*);
Prototype in	stdio.h stdarg.h
Description	see **printf**

vfscanf

Name	**vfscanf** – performs formatted input from a stream
Usage	#include <stdio.h> int vfscanf(FILE **stream*, char **format*, va_list *param*);
Prototype in	stdio.h
Description	see **...scanf**

vprintf

Name	**vprintf** – send formatted output to *stdout*
Usage	int vprintf(char *format*, va_list *param*);
Prototype in	stdio.h
Description	see **printf**

vscanf

Name	**vscanf** – performs formatted input from *stdin*
Usage	int vscanf(char *format*, va_list *param*);
Prototype in	stdio.h
Description	see **...scanf**

vsprintf

Name	**vsprintf** – sends formatted output to a string
Usage	int vsprintf(char *string*, char *format*, va_list *param*);
Prototype in	stdio.h
Description	see **printf**

vsscanf

Name	**vsscanf** – performs formatted input from a stream
Usage	int vsscanf(char *s, char *format, va_list param);
Prototype in	stdio.h
Description	see ...scanf

_write

Name	**_write** – writes to a file
Usage	int _write(int handle, void *buf, int nbyte);
Prototype in	io.h
Description	see **write**

write

Name	**write** – writes to a file
Usage	int write(int handle, void *buf, int nbyte);
Related functions usage	int _write(int handle, void *buf, int nbyte);
Prototype in	io.h
Description	Both **write** and **_write** are functions that write a buffer of data to the file or device named by the given handle. handle is a file handle obtained from a **creat**, **open**, **dup**, **dup2**, or **fcntl** call.

These functions attempt to write *nbyte* bytes from the buffer pointed to by *buf* to the file associated with *handle*. Except when **write** is used to write to a text file, the number of bytes written to the file will be no more than the number requested.

On text files, when **write** sees a linefeed (LF) character, it outputs a CR-LF pair. **_write** does no such translation, since all of its files are binary files.

If the number of bytes actually written is less than that requested, the condition should be considered an error and probably indicates a full disk.

For disk or diskette files, writing always proceeds from the current file pointer (see **lseek**). For devices, bytes are directly sent to the device.

For files opened with the O_APPEND option, the file pointer is positioned to EOF by **write** (but not by **_write**) before writing the data.

Return value The number of bytes written are returned by both functions. A **write** to a text file does not count generated carriage returns. In case of error, each function returns –1 and sets the global variable *errno* to one of the following:

> EACCES   Permission denied
> EBADF   Bad file number

Portability **Write** is available on UNIX systems.
_write is unique to MS-DOS.

See also **creat, dup, lseek, open**

A

The Turbo C Interactive Editor

Introduction

Turbo C's built-in editor is specifically designed for creating program source text. If you are familiar with the Turbo Pascal or SideKick editor, or MicroPro's WordStar program, you already know how to use the Turbo C editor, since its commands are almost identical to one of these editors. A section at the end of this appendix summarizes the few differences between Turbo C's editor commands and WordStar's commands.

The Turbo C editor, unlike WordStar, has a "restore" facility that lets you take back changes if you haven't yet left the line. This command (*Ctrl-Q L*) is described in "Miscellaneous Editing Commands."

Quick In, Quick Out

To invoke the editor, choose Edit from Turbo C's main menu. The Edit window becomes the "active" window; the Edit window's title is highlighted and the cursor is positioned in the Edit window.

To enter text, type as though you were using a typewriter. To end a line, press the *Enter* key.

To invoke the main menu from within the editor, press *F10* (the data in the Edit window remains on screen).

The Edit Window Status Line

The status line in the top bar of the Edit window gives you information about the file you are editing, where in the file the cursor is located, and which editing modes are activated:

```
Line   Col  Insert    Indent  Tab   X:FILENAME.TYP
```

Line	Shows which file line number contains the cursor.
Col	Shows which file column number contains the cursor.
Insert	Tells you that the editor is in "Insert mode"; characters entered on the keyboard are inserted at the cursor position, and text in front of the cursor moves to the right.
	Use the *Ins* key or *Ctrl-V* to toggle the editor between Insert mode and Overwrite mode.
	In Overwrite mode, text entered at the keyboard overwrites characters under the cursor, instead of inserting them before existing text.
Indent	Indicates the autoindent feature is *on*. You toggle it *off* and *on* with the command *Ctrl-O I*.
Tab	Indicates whether or not you can insert tabs. Use *Ctrl-O T* to toggle this *on* or *off*.
X:FILENAME.TYP	Indicates the drive (X:), name (FILENAME), and extension (.TYP) of the file you are editing. If the file name and extension is NONAME.C, then you have not specified a file name yet. (NONAME.C is Turbo C's default file name.)

Editor Commands

The editor uses approximately 50 commands to move the cursor around, page through text, find and replace strings, and so on. These commands can be grouped into four main categories:

- cursor movement commands (basic and extended)
- insert and delete commands
- block commands
- miscellaneous commands

Table A.1 summarizes the commands. Each entry in the table consists of a command definition, followed by the default keystrokes used to activate the command. In the pages after Table A.1, we further explain the actions of each editor command.

Table A.1: Summary of Editor Commands

Basic Cursor Movement Commands

Character left	*Ctrl-S* or *Left*
Character right	*Ctrl-D* or *Right*
Word left	*Ctrl-A*
Word right	*Ctrl-F*
Line up	*Ctrl-E* or *Up*
Line down	*Ctrl-X* or *Down*
Scroll up	*Ctrl-W*
Scroll down	*Ctrl-Z*
Page up	*Ctrl-R* or *PgUp*
Page down	*Ctrl-C* or *PgDn*

Quick Cursor Movement Commands

Beginning of line	*Ctrl-Q S* or *Home*
End of line	*Ctrl-Q D* or *End*
Top of window	*Ctrl-Q E*
Bottom of window	*Ctrl-Q X*
Top of file	*Ctrl-Q R*
End of file	*Ctrl-Q C*
Beginning of block	*Ctrl-Q B*
End of block	*Ctrl-Q K*
Last cursor position	*Ctrl-Q P*

Insert and Delete Commands

Insert mode on/off	*Ctrl-V* or *Ins*
Insert line	*Ctrl-N*
Delete line	*Ctrl-Y*
Delete to end of line	*Ctrl-Q Y*
Delete character left of cursor	*Ctrl-H* or *Backspace*
Delete character under cursor	*Ctrl-G* or *Del*
Delete word right of cursor	*Ctrl-T*

Block Commands

Mark block-begin	*Ctrl-K B*
Mark block-end	*Ctrl-K K*
Mark single word	*Ctrl-K T*
Copy block	*Ctrl-K C*
Delete block	*Ctrl-K Y*
Hide/display block	*Ctrl-K H*
Move block	*Ctrl-K V*
Read block from disk	*Ctrl-K R*
Write block to disk	*Ctrl-K W*

Miscellaneous Commands

Abort operation	*Ctrl-U*
Autoindent on/off	*Ctrl-O I*
Control character prefix	*Ctrl-P*
Find	*Ctrl-Q F*
Find and replace	*Ctrl-Q A*
Find place marker	*Ctrl-Q N*
Invoke main menu	*F10*
Load file	*F3*
Quit edit, no save	*Ctrl-K D* or *Ctrl-K Q*
Repeat last find	*Ctrl-I*
Restore line	*Ctrl-Q L*
Save and edit	*Ctrl-K S* or *F2*
Set place marker	*Ctrl-K N*
Tab	*Ctrl-I* or *Tab*
Tab mode	*Ctrl-O T*

Basic Cursor Movement Commands

The editor uses control-key commands to move the cursor up, down, back, and forth on the screen. To control cursor movement in the part of your file currently on-screen, use the following sequences:

When you press	The cursor does this:
Ctrl-A	Moves to first letter in word to left of cursor
Ctrl-S	Moves to first position to left of cursor
Ctrl-D	Moves to first position to right of cursor
Ctrl-F	Moves to first letter in word to right of cursor
Ctrl-E	Moves up one line
Ctrl-R	Moves up one full screen
Ctrl-X	Moves down one line
Ctrl-C	Moves down one full screen
Ctrl-W	Scrolls screen down one line; cursor stays in line
Ctrl-Z	Scrolls screen up one line; cursor stays in line
PgUp	Scrolls screen and cursor up one screen
PgDn	Scrolls screen and cursor down one screen

Quick Cursor Movement Commands

The editor also provides six commands to move the cursor quickly to the extreme ends of lines, to the beginning and end of the file, and to the last cursor position.

When you press	The cursor does this:
Ctrl-Q S or Home	Moves to column one of the current line
Ctrl-Q D or End	Moves to the end of the current line
Ctrl-Q E	Moves to the top of the screen
Ctrl-Q X	Moves to the bottom of the screen
Ctrl-Q R	Moves to the first character in the file
Ctrl-Q C	Moves to the last character in the file

The *Ctrl-Q* prefix with a *B, K,* or *P* character allows you to jump to certain special points in a document.

Ctrl-Q B   Moves the cursor to the block-begin marker set with *Ctrl-K B.* The command works even if the block is not displayed (see "Hide/display block" under "Block Commands") or if the block-end marker is not set.

Ctrl-Q K   Moves the cursor to the block-end marker set with *Ctrl-K K.* The command works even if the block is not displayed (see "Hide/display block") or the block-begin marker is not set.

Ctrl-Q P   Moves to the last position of the cursor before the last command. This command is particularly useful after a Find or Find/Replace operation has been executed and you'd like to return to the last position before its execution.

Insert and Delete Commands

To write a program, you need to know more than just how to move the cursor around. You also need to be able to insert and delete text. The following commands insert and delete characters, words, and lines.

Insert mode on/off   *Ctrl-V* or *Ins*

When entering text, you can choose between two basic entry modes: *Insert* and *Overwrite.* You can switch between these modes with the Insert mode toggle, *Ctrl-V* or *Ins*. The current mode is displayed in the status line at the top of the screen.

Insert mode is the Turbo C editor's default; this lets you insert new characters into old text. Text to the right of the cursor simply moves to the right as you enter new text.

Use Overwrite mode to replace old text with new; any characters entered replace existing characters under the cursor.

Delete character left of cursor   *Ctrl-H* or *Backspace*

Moves one character to the left and deletes the character positioned there. Any characters to the right of the cursor move one position to the left. You can use this command to remove line breaks.

Delete character under cursor   *Ctrl-G* or *Del*

Deletes the character under the cursor and moves any characters to the right of the cursor one position to the left. This command does not work across line breaks.

Delete word right of cursor   *Ctrl-T*
   Deletes the word to the right of the cursor. A word is defined as a
   sequence of characters delimited by one of the following characters:

```
space   <      >      ,      ;      .        (      )
[       ]      ^      '      *      +        -      /      $
```

   This command works across line breaks, and may be used to remove
   them.

Insert line   *Ctrl-N*
   Inserts a line break at the cursor position.

Delete line   *Ctrl-Y*
   Deletes the line containing the cursor and moves any lines below one
   line up. There's no way to restore a deleted line, so use this command
   with care.

Delete to end of line   *Ctrl-Q Y*
   Deletes all text from the cursor position to the end of the line.

Block Commands

The block commands also require a control-character command sequence.
A block of text is any amount of text, from a single character to hundreds of
lines, that has been surrounded with special block-marker characters. There
can be only one block in a document at a time.

You mark a block by placing a block-begin marker before the first character
and a block-end marker after the last character of the desired portion of
text. Once marked, you can copy, move, or delete the block, or write it to a
file.

Mark block-begin   *Ctrl-K B*
   Marks the beginning of a block. The marker itself is not visible, and
   the block itself only becomes visible when the block-end marker is set.
   Marked text (a block) is displayed in a different intensity.

Mark block-end   *Ctrl-K K*
   Marks the end of a block. The marker itself is invisible, and the block
   itself becomes visible only when the block-begin marker is also set.

Mark single word   *Ctrl-K T*

Marks a single word as a block, replacing the block-begin/block-end sequence. If the cursor is placed within a word, then the word will be marked. If it is not within a word, then the word to the left of the cursor will be marked.

Copy block   *Ctrl-K C*

Copies a previously marked block to the current cursor position. The original block is unchanged, and the markers are placed around the new copy of the block. If no block is marked or the cursor is within the marked block, nothing happens.

Delete block   *Ctrl-K Y*

Deletes a previously marked block. There is no provision to restore a deleted block, so be careful with this command.

Hide/display block   *Ctrl-K H*

Causes the visual marking of a block to be alternately switched *off* and *on*. The block manipulation commands (copy, move, delete, and write to a file) work only when the block is displayed. Block-related cursor movements (jump to beginning/end of block) work whether the block is hidden or displayed.

Move block   *Ctrl-K V*

Moves a previously marked block from its original position to the cursor position. The block disappears from its original position, and the markers remain around the block at its new position. If no block is marked, nothing happens.

Read block from disk   *Ctrl-K R*

Reads a previously marked disk file into the current text at the cursor position, exactly as if it were a block. The text read is then marked as a block of different intensity.

When you issue this command, Turbo C's editor prompts you for the name of the file to read. You can use DOS wildcards to select a file to read; a directory appears in a small window on-screen. The file specified may be any legal file name. If you specify no file type (.C, .TXT, .BAK, etc.) the editor assumes you meant .C. To read a file that lacks an extension, append a period to the file name.

Write block to disk   *Ctrl-K W*

Writes a previously marked block to a file. The block is left unchanged in the current file, and the markers remain in place. If no block is marked, nothing happens.

When you issue this command, Turbo C's editor prompts you for the name of the file to write to. To select a file to overwrite, use DOS wildcards; a directory appears in a small window on-screen. If the file specified already exists, the editor issues a warning and prompts for verification before overwriting the existing file. You can give the file any legal name (the default extension is .C). To write a file that lacks an extension, append a period to the file name.

Miscellaneous Editing Commands

This section describes commands that do not fall into any of the categories already covered. These commands are listed in alphabetical order.

Abort operation *Ctrl-U*

Lets you abort any command in process whenever it pauses for input, such as when Find/Replace asks `Replace Y/N?`, or when you are entering a search string or a file name (Block read and write).

Autoindent on/off *Ctrl-O I*

Provides automatic indenting of successive lines. When autoindent is active, the cursor does not return to column one when you press *Enter*; instead, it returns to the starting column of the line you just terminated.

When you want to change the indentation, use the space bar and *Left* arrow key to select the new column. When autoindent is *on*, the message `Indent` shows up in the status line; when *off*, the message disappears. Autoindent is *on* by default. (When Tab is *on*, autoindent is disabled.)

Control character prefix *Ctrl-P*

Allows you to enter control characters into the file by prefixing the desired control character with a *Ctrl-P*; that is, first press *Ctrl-P*, then press the desired control character. Control characters will appear as low-intensity capital letters on the screen (or inverse, depending on your screen setup).

Find *Ctrl-Q F*

Lets you search for a string of up to 30 characters. When you enter this command, the status line is cleared, and the editor prompts you for a search string. Enter the string you are looking for and then press *Enter*.

The search string may contain any characters, including control characters. You enter control characters into the search string with the ^P prefix. For example, enter a *Ctrl-T* by holding down the *Ctrl* key as you press *P*, and then press *T*. You may include a line break in a search string by specifying *Ctrl-M J* (carriage return/line feed). Note that *Ctrl-A* has special meaning: It matches any character and may be used as a wildcard in search strings.

You may edit search strings with the character left, character right, word left, and word right commands. Word right recalls the previous search string, which you may then edit. To abort (quit) the search operation, use the abort command (*Ctrl-U*).

When you specify the search string, Turbo C's editor asks for search options. The following options are available:

B   Searches backward from the current cursor position toward the beginning of the text.

G   Globally searches the entire text, irrespective of the current cursor position. This stops only at the last occurrence of the string.

N   Finds the next occurrence of a search string, starting at the current cursor position in your file. When using both the *N* and the *G* options at the same time, the *G* option overrides the *N* option.

n   Where *n* equals a number, finds the *n*th occurrence of the search string, counted from the current cursor position.

U   Ignores uppercase/lowercase distinctions.

W   Searches for whole words only, skipping matching patterns embedded in other words.

Examples of Find Options:

W   Searches for whole words only. The search string *term* will match *term*, for example, but not *terminal*.

BU   Searches backward and ignores uppercase/lowercase differences. *Block* matches both *blockhead* and *BLOCKADE*, and so on.

125 Finds the 125th occurrence of the search string.

You can end the list of find options (if any) by pressing *Enter*; the search starts. If the text contains a target matching the search string, the editor positions the cursor on the target. The search operation may be repeated by the Repeat last find command (*Ctrl-L*).

Find and replace   *Ctrl-Q A*

This operation works identically to the Find command, except that you can replace the "found" string with any other string of up to 30 characters. Note that *Ctrl-A* only functions as a wildcard in the Find string; it has no special meaning in the Replace string.

When you specify the search string, the editor asks you to enter the string that will replace the search string. Enter up to 30 characters; control character entry and editing is performed as with the Find command. If you just press *Enter*, the editor replaces the target with nothing, effectively deleting it.

Your choice of options are the same as those in the Find command with the addition of the following:

N   Replaces without asking; does not ask for confirmation of each occurrence of the search string.

n   Replaces the next *n* cases of the search string. If the *G* option is used, the search starts at the top of the file; otherwise it starts at the current cursor position.

Examples of Find and Replace Options:

N10   Finds the next ten occurrences of the search string and replaces each without asking.

GW   Finds and replaces whole words in the entire text, ignoring uppercase/lowercase. It prompts for a replacement string.

GNU   Finds (throughout the file) uppercase and lowercase small, antelope-like creatures and replaces them without asking.

Again, you can end the option list (if any) by pressing *Enter*; the Find/Replace operation starts. When the editor finds the item (and if the *N* option is not specified), it then positions the cursor at one end of the item, and asks `Replace (Y/N)?` in the prompt line at the top of the screen. You may abort the Find/Replace operation at this point with the Abort command (*Ctrl-U*). You can repeat the Find/Replace operation with the Repeat last find command (*Ctrl-L*).

Find place marker Ctrl-Q N

Finds up to four place markers (0-3) in text. Move the cursor to any previously set marker by pressing *Ctrl-Q* and the marker number, *n*.

Load file F3

Lets you edit an existing file or create a new file.

Quit edit, no save Ctrl-K D or Ctrl-K Q

Quits the editor and returns you to the main menu. You can save the edited file on disk either explicitly with the main menu's Save option under the Files command or manually while in the editor (*Ctrl-K S* or *F2*).

Repeat last find Ctrl-L

Repeats the latest Find or Find/Replace operation as if all information had been re-entered.

Restore line Ctrl-Q L

Lets you undo changes made to a line, as long as you have not left the line. The line is restored to its original state regardless of any changes you have made.

Save file Ctrl-K S or F2

Saves the file and remains in the editor.

Set place marker Ctrl-K N

You can mark up to four places in text; press *Ctrl-K*, followed by a single digit *n* (0-3). After marking your location, you can work elsewhere in the file and then easily return to the marked location by using the *Ctrl-Q N* command.

Tab Ctrl-I or Tab

Tabs are fixed to eight columns apart in the Turbo C editor.

Tab mode Ctrl-O T

With **Tab** mode *on*, a tab is placed in the text using a fixed tab stop of 8. Toggle it *off*, and it spaces to the beginning of the first letter of each word in the previous line.

The Turbo C Editor Vs. WordStar

A few of the Turbo C editor's commands are slightly different from WordStar. Also, although the Turbo C editor contains only a subset of WordStar's commands, several features not found in WordStar have been added to enhance program source-code editing. These differences are discussed here, in alphabetical order.

Autoindent:

The Turbo C editor's *Ctrl-O I* command toggles the autoindent feature *on* and *off*.

Carriage returns:

In Turbo C, carriage returns cannot be entered at the end of a file in Overwrite mode. (If you press *Enter* at the end of a line when Insert mode is *off*, the editor will not insert a carriage return character or move the cursor to the next line.) To enter carriage returns, you can either switch to Insert mode or use *Ctrl-N* in Overwrite mode.

Cursor movement:

Turbo C's cursor movement controls—*Ctrl-S, Ctrl-D, Ctrl-E,* and *Ctrl-X*—move freely around on the screen without jumping to column one on empty lines. This does not mean that the screen is full of blanks, on the contrary, all trailing blanks are automatically removed. This way of moving the cursor is especially useful for program editing, for example, when matching indented statements.

Delete to left:

The WordStar sequence *Ctrl-Q Del*, delete from cursor position to beginning of line, is not supported.

Mark word as block:

Turbo C allows you to mark a single word as a block using *Ctrl-K T*. This is more convenient than WordStar's two-step process of separately marking the beginning and the end of the word.

Movement across line breaks:

Ctrl-S and *Ctrl-D* do not work across line breaks. To move from one line to another you must use *Ctrl-E, Ctrl-X, Ctrl-A,* or *Ctrl-F*.

Quit edit:

Turbo C's *Ctrl-K Q* does not resemble WordStar's *Ctrl-K Q* (quit edit) command. In Turbo C, the changed text is not abandoned—it is left in memory, ready to be compiled and saved.

Undo:

Turbo C's *Ctrl-Q L* command restores a line to its pre-edit contents as long as the cursor has not left the line.

Updating disk file:

Since editing in Turbo C is done entirely in memory, the *Ctrl-K D* command does not change the file on disk as it does in WordStar. You must explicitly update the disk file with the Save option within the File menu or by using *Ctrl-K S* or *F2* within the editor.

B

Compiler Error Messages

The Turbo C compiler diagnostic messages fall into three classes: Fatals, Errors, and Warnings.

Fatal errors are rare and probably indicate an internal compiler error. When a fatal error occurs, compilation immediately stops. You must take appropriate action and then restart compilation.

Errors indicate program syntax errors, disk or memory access errors, and command line errors. The compiler will complete the current phase of the compilation and then stop. The compiler attempts to find as many real errors in the source program as possible during each phase (preprocessing, parsing, optimizing and code-generating).

Warnings do not prevent the compilation from finishing. They indicate conditions which are suspicious, but which are legitimate as part of the language. Also, the compiler will produce warnings if you use machine-dependent constructs in your source files.

The compiler prints messages with the message class first, then the source file name and line number where the compiler detected the condition, and finally the text of the message itself.

In the following lists, messages are presented alphabetically within message class. With each message, a probable cause and remedy are provided.

You should be aware of one detail about line numbers in error messages: the compiler only generates messages as they are detected. Because C does not force any restrictions on placing statements on a line of text, the true cause of the error may be one or more lines before the line number mentioned. In the following message list, we have indicated those messages which often appear (to the compiler) to be on lines after the real cause.

Fatal Errors

Bad call of in-line function
You have used an in-line function taken from a macro definition, but have called it incorrectly. An in-line function is one that begins and ends with a double underbar (_ _).

Irreducible expression tree
This is a sign of some form of compiler error. Some expression on the indicated line of the source file has caused the code generator to be unable to generate code. Whatever the offending expression is, it should be avoided. You should notify Borland International if the compiler ever encounters this error.

Register allocation failure
This is a sign of some form of compiler error. Some expression on the indicated line of the source file was so complicated that the code generator could not generate code for it. You should simplify the offending expression, and if this fails to solve the problem, the expression should be avoided. Notify Borland International if the compiler encounters this error.

Errors

#operator not followed by macro argument name

In a macro definition, the # may be used to indicate stringizing a macro argument. The # must be followed by a macro argument name.

'XXXXXXX' not an argument

Your source file declared the named identifier as a function argument but the identifier was not in the function argument list.

Ambiguous symbol 'XXXXXXX'

The named structure field occurs in more than one structure with different offsets, types, or both. The variable or expression used to refer to the field is not a structure containing the field. Cast the structure to the correct type, or correct the field name if it is wrong.

Argument # missing name

A parameter name has been left out in a function prototype used to define a function. If the function is defined with a prototype, the prototype must include the parameter names.

Argument list syntax error

Arguments to a function call must be separated by spaces and closed with a right parenthesis. Your source file contained an argument followed by a character other than comma or right parenthesis.

Array bounds missing]

Your source file declared an array in which the array bounds were not terminated by a right bracket.

Array size too large

The declared array would be too large to fit in the available memory of the processor.

Assembler statement too long

In-line assembly statements may not be longer than 480 bytes.

Bad configuration file

The TURBOC.CFG file contains uncommented text that is not a proper command option. Configuration file command options must begin with a dash (-).

Bad file name format in include directive

Include file names must be surrounded by quotes ("*filename.h*") or angle brackets (*<filename.h>*). The file name was missing the opening quote or angle bracket. If a macro was used, the resulting expansion text is incorrect; that is, not surrounded by quote marks.

Bad ifdef directive syntax

An `#ifdef` directive must contain a single identifier (and nothing else) as the body of the directive.

Bad ifndef directive syntax

An `#ifndef` directive must contain a single identifier (and nothing else) as the body of the directive.

Bad undef directive syntax

An `#undef` directive must contain a single identifier (and nothing else) as the body of the directive.

Bit field size syntax

A bitfield must be defined by a constant expression between 1 and 16 bits in width.

Call of non-function

The function being called is declared as a non-function. This is commonly caused by incorrectly declaring the function or misspelling the function name.

Cannot modify a const object

This indicates an illegal operation on an object declared to be **const**, such as an assignment to the object.

Case outside of switch

The compiler encountered a **case** statement outside a **switch** statement. This is often caused by mismatched curly braces.

Case statement missing :

A **case** statement must have a constant expression followed by a colon. The expression in the **case** statement either was missing a colon or had some extra symbol before the colon.

Cast syntax error

A cast contains some incorrect symbol.

Character constant too long

Character constants may only be one or two characters long.

Compound statement missing }

The compiler reached the end of the source file and found no closing brace. This is most commonly caused by mismatched braces.

Conflicting type modifiers

This occurs when a declaration is given that includes, for example, both **near** and **far** keywords on the same pointer. Only one addressing modifier may be given for a single pointer, and only one language modifier (**cdecl**, **pascal**, or interrupt) may be given on a function.

Constant expression required

Arrays must be declared with constant size. This error is commonly caused by misspelling a #define constant.

Could not find file 'XXXXXXXX.XXX'

The compiler is unable to find the file supplied on the command line.

Declaration missing ;

Your source file contained a **struct** or **union** field declaration that was not followed by a semicolon.

Declaration needs type or storage class

A declaration must include at least a type or a storage class. This means a statement like the following is not legal:

```
i,j;
```

Declaration syntax error

Your source file contained a declaration that was missing some symbol or had some extra symbol added to it.

Default outside of switch

The compiler encountered a **default** statement outside a **switch** statement. This is most commonly caused by mismatched curly braces.

Define directive needs an identifier

The first non-whitespace character after a #define must be an identifier. The compiler found some other character.

Division by zero

Your source file contained a divide or remainder in a constant expression with a zero divisor.

Do statement must have while

Your source file contained a **do** statement that was missing the closing **while** keyword.

Do-while statement missing (

In a **do** statement, the compiler found no left parenthesis after the **while** keyword.

Do-while statement missing)

In a do statement, the compiler found no right parenthesis after the test expression.

Do-while statement missing ;

In a do statement test expression, the compiler found no semicolon after the right parenthesis.

Duplicate case

Each case of a switch statement must have a unique constant expression value.

Enum syntax error

An enum declaration did not contain a properly formed list of identifiers.

Enumeration constant syntax error

The expression given for an enum value was not a constant.

Error Directive: XXXX

This message is issued when an #error directive is processed in the source file. The text of the directive is displayed in the message.

Error writing output file

This error most often occurs when the work disk is full. It could also indicate a faulty diskette. If the diskette is full, try deleting unneeded files and restarting the compilation.

Expression syntax

This is a catch-all error message when the compiler parses an expression and encounters some serious error. This is most commonly caused by two consecutive operators, mismatched or missing parentheses, or a missing semicolon on the previous statement.

Extra parameter in call

A call to a function, via a pointer defined with a prototype, had too many arguments given.

Extra parameter in call to XXXXXXXX

A call to the named function (which was defined with a prototype) had too many arguments given in the call.

File name too long

The file name given in an #include directive was too long for the compiler to process. File names in DOS must be no more than 64 characters long.

For statement missing (

In a for statement, the compiler found no left parenthesis after the for keyword.

For statement missing)

In a `for` statement, the compiler found no right parenthesis after the control expressions.

For statement missing ;

In a `for` statement, the compiler found no semicolon after one of the expressions.

Function call missing)

The function call argument list had some sort of syntax error, such as a missing or mismatched right parenthesis.

Function definition out of place

A function definition may not be placed inside another function. Any declaration inside a function that looks like the beginning of a function with an argument list is considered a function definition.

Function doesn't take a variable number of arguments

Your source file used the **va_start** macro inside a function that does not accept a variable number of arguments.

Goto statement missing label

The `goto` keyword must be followed by an identifier.

If statement missing (

In an `if` statement, the compiler found no left parenthesis after the `if` keyword.

If statement missing)

In an `if` statement, the compiler found no right parenthesis after the test expression.

Illegal character 'C' (0xXX)

The compiler encountered some invalid character in the input file. The hexadecimal value of the offending character is printed.

Illegal initialization

Initializations must be either constant expressions, or else the address of a global **extern** or **static** variable plus or minus a constant.

Illegal octal digit

The compiler found an octal constant containing a non-octal digit (8 or 9).

Illegal pointer subtraction

This is caused by attempting to subtract a pointer from a non-pointer.

Illegal structure operation

Structures may only be used with dot (.), address-of (&) or assignment (=) operators, or be passed to or from a function as parameters. The compiler encountered a structure being used with some other operator.

Illegal use of floating point

Floating point operands are not allowed in shift, bitwise boolean, conditional (? :), indirection (*), or certain other operators. The compiler found a floating-point operand with one of these prohibited operators.

Illegal use of pointer

Pointers may only be used with addition, subtraction, assignment, comparison, indirection (*) or arrow (- >). Your source file used a pointer with some other operator.

Improper use of a typedef symbol

Your source file used a **typedef** symbol where a variable should appear in an expression. Check for the declaration of the symbol and possible misspellings.

In-line assembly not allowed

Your source file contains in-line assembly language statements and you are compiling it from within the Integrated Environment. You must use the TCC command to compile this source file.

Incompatible storage class

Your source file used the **extern** keyword on a function definition. Only **static** (or no storage class at all) is allowed.

Incompatible type conversion

Your source file attempted to convert one type to another, but the two types were not convertible. This includes converting a function to or from a non-function, converting a structure or array to or from a scalar type, or converting a floating point value to or from pointer type.

Incorrect command line argument: XXXXXXXX

The compiler did not recognize the command line parameter as legal.

Incorrect configuration file argument: XXXXXXXX

The compiler did not recognize the configuration file parameter as legal; check for a preceding dash ("-").

Incorrect number format

The compiler encountered a decimal point in a hexadecimal number.

Incorrect use of default

The compiler found no colon after the **default** keyword.

Initializer syntax error

An initializer has a missing or extra operator, mismatched parentheses, or is otherwise malformed.

Invalid indirection

The indirection operator (*) requires a non-**void** pointer as the operand.

Invalid macro argument separator

In a macro definition, arguments must be separated by commas. The compiler encountered some other character after an argument name.

Invalid pointer addition

Your source file attempted to add two pointers together.

Invalid use of arrow

An identifier must immediately follow an arrow operator (- >).

Invalid use of dot

An identifier must immediately follow a dot operator (.).

Lvalue required

The left hand side of an assignment operator must be an addressable expression. These include numeric or pointer variables, structure field references or indirection through a pointer, or a subscripted array element.

Macro argument syntax error

An argument in a macro definition must be an identifier. The compiler encountered some non-identifier character where an argument was expected.

Macro expansion too long

A macro may not expand to more than 4096 characters. This error often occurs if a macro recursively expands itself. A macro cannot legally expand to itself.

May compile only one file when an output file name is given

You have supplied an -o command line option, which allows only one output file name. The first file is compiled but the other files are ignored.

Mismatched number of parameters in definition

The parameters in a definition do not match the information supplied in the function prototype.

Misplaced break

The compiler encountered a **break** statement outside a **switch** or looping construct.

Misplaced continue

The compiler encountered a `continue` statement outside a looping construct.

Misplaced decimal point

The compiler encountered a decimal point in a floating point constant as part of the exponent.

Misplaced else

The compiler encountered an `else` statement without a matching `if` statement. Beyond just being an extra `else`, this could also be caused by an extra semicolon, missing curly braces, or some syntax error in a previous `if` statement.

Misplaced elif directive

The compiler encountered an `#elif` directive without any matching `#if`, `#ifdef` or `#ifndef` directive.

Misplaced else directive

The compiler encountered an `#else` directive without any matching `#if`, `#ifdef` or `#ifndef` directive.

Misplaced endif directive

The compiler encountered an `#endif` directive without any matching `#if`, `#ifdef` or `#ifndef` directive.

Must be addressable

An ampersand (&) has been applied to an object that is not addressable, such as a register variable.

Must take address of memory location

Your source file used the address-of operator (&) with an expression which cannot be used that way, for example a register variable.

No file name ending

The file name in an `#include` statement was missing the correct closing quote or angle bracket.

No file names given

The Turbo C compile command (TCC) contained no file names. A compile has to have something to work on.

Non-portable pointer assignment

Your source file assigned a pointer to a non-pointer, or vice versa. Assigning a constant zero to a pointer is allowed as a special case. You should use a cast to suppress this error message if the comparison is proper.

Non-portable pointer comparison

Your source file made a comparison between a pointer and a non-pointer other than the constant zero. You should use a cast to suppress this error message if the comparison is proper.

Non-portable return type conversion

The expression in a return statement was not the same type as the function declaration. With one exception, this is only triggered if the function or the return expression is a pointer. The exception to this is that a function returning a pointer may return a constant zero. The zero will be converted to an appropriate pointer value.

Not an allowed type

Your source file declared some sort of forbidden type, for example a function returning a function or array.

Out of memory

The total working storage is exhausted. Try it on a machine with more memory, or if you already have 640K, you may have to simplify the source file.

Pointer required on left side of – >

Nothing but a pointer is allowed on the left side of the arrow (- >).

Redeclaration of 'XXXXXXX'

The named identifier was previously declared.

Size of structure or array not known

Some expression (such as a `sizeof` or storage declaration) occurred with an undefined structure or an array of empty length. Structures may be referenced before they are defined as long as their size is not needed. Arrays may be declared with empty length if the declaration does not reserve storage or if the declaration is followed by an initializer giving the length.

Statement missing ;

The compiler encountered an expression statement without a semicolon following it.

Structure or union syntax error

The compiler encountered the `struct` or `union` keyword without an identifier or opening curly brace following it.

Structure size too large

Your source file declared a structure which reserved too much storage to fit in the memory available.

Subscripting missing]

The compiler encountered a subscripting expression which was missing its closing bracket. This could be caused by a missing or extra operator, or mismatched parentheses.

Switch statement missing (

In a `switch` statement, the compiler found no left parenthesis after the `switch` keyword.

Switch statement missing)

In a `switch` statement, the compiler found no right parenthesis after the test expression.

Too few parameters in call

A call to a function with a prototype (via a function pointer) had too few arguments. Prototypes require that all parameters be given.

Too few parameters in call to 'XXXXXXX'

A call to the named function (declared using a prototype) had too few arguments.

Too many cases

A switch statement is limited to 257 cases.

Too many decimal points

The compiler encountered a floating point constant with more than one decimal point.

Too many default cases

The compiler encountered more than one `default` statement in a single `switch`.

Too many exponents

The compiler encountered more than one exponent in a floating point constant.

Too many initializers

The compiler encountered more initializers than were allowed by the declaration being initialized.

Too many storage classes in declaration

A declaration may never have more than one storage class.

Too many types in declaration

A declaration may never have more than one of the basic types: `char`, `int`, `float`, `double`, `struct`, `union`, `enum` or `typedef`-*name*.

Too much auto memory in function

The current function declared more automatic storage than there is room for in the available memory.

Too much code defined in file

The combined size of the functions in the current source file exceeds 64K bytes. You may have to remove unneeded code, or split up the source file.

Too much global data defined in file

The sum of the global data declarations exceeds 64K bytes. Check the declarations for any array that may be too large. Also consider reorganizing the program if all the declarations are needed.

Two consecutive dots

Because an ellipsis contains three dots (...), and a decimal point or member selection operator uses one dot (.), there is no way two dots can legally occur in a C program.

Type mismatch in parameter

The function called, via a function pointer, was declared with a prototype; the given parameter #N (counting left-to-right from 1) could not be converted to the declared parameter type.

Type mismatch in parameter # in call to 'XXXXXXX'

Your source file declared the named function with a prototype, and the given parameter #N (counting left-to-right from 1) could not be converted to the declared parameter type.

Type mismatch in parameter 'XXXXXXX'

Your source file declared the function called via a function pointer with a prototype, and the named parameter could not be converted to the declared parameter type.

Type mismatch in parameter 'XXXXXXX' in call to 'YYYYYYY'

Your source file declared the named function with a prototype, and the named parameter could not be converted to the declared parameter type.

Type mismatch in redeclaration of 'XXX'

Your source file redeclared a variable with a different type than was originally declared for the variable. This can occur if a function is called and subsequently declared to return something other than an integer. If this has happened, you must insert an **extern** declaration of the function before the first call to it.

Unable to create output file 'XXXXXXXXX.XXX'

This error occurs if the work diskette is full or write protected. If the diskette is full, try deleting unneeded files and restarting the compilation. If the diskette is write protected, move the source files to a writable diskette and restart the compilation.

Unable to create turboc.lnk

The compiler cannot create the temporary file TURBOC.$LN because it cannot access the disk or the disk is full.

Unable to execute command 'XXXXXXXX'

TLINK or MASM cannot be found, or possibly the disk is bad.

Unable to open include file 'XXXXXXXXX.XXX'

The compiler could not find the named file. This could also be caused if an #include file included itself, or if you do not have FILES set in CONFIG.SYS on your root directory (try FILES=20). Check whether the named file exists.

Unable to open input file 'XXXXXXXXX.XXX'

This error occurs if the source file cannot be found. Check the spelling of the name and whether the file is on the proper diskette or directory.

Undefined label 'XXXXXXXX'

The named label has a goto in the function, but no label definition.

Undefined structure 'XXXXXXXX'

Your source file used the named structure on some line before where the error is indicated (probably on a pointer to a structure) but had no definition for the structure. This is probably caused by a misspelled structure name or a missing declaration.

Undefined symbol 'XXXXXXXX'

The named identifier has no declaration. This could be caused by a misspelling either at this point or at the declaration. This could also be caused if there was an error in the declaration of the identifier.

Unexpected end of file in comment started on line

The source file ended in the middle of a comment. This is normally caused by a missing close of comment (*/).

Unexpected end of file in conditional started on line

The source file ended before the compiler encountered #endif. The #endif either was missing or misspelled.

Unknown preprocessor directive: 'XXX'

The compiler encountered a # character at the beginning of a line, and the directive name following was not one of these: `define`, `undef`, `line`, `if`, `ifdef`, `ifndef`, `include`, `else` or `endif`.

Unterminated character constant

The compiler encountered an unmatched apostrophe.

Unterminated string

The compiler encountered an unmatched quote character.

Unterminated string or character constant

The compiler found no terminating quote after the beginning of a string or character constant.

User break

You typed a *Ctrl-Break* while compiling or linking in the Integrated Environment.

While statement missing (

In a `while` statement, the compiler found no left parenthesis after the `while` keyword.

While statement missing)

In a `while` statement, the compiler found no right parenthesis after the test expression.

Wrong number of arguments in call of 'XXXXXXXX'

Your source file called the named macro with an incorrect number of arguments.

Warnings

'XXXXXXX' declared but never used

Your source file declared the named variable as part of the block just ending, but the variable was never used. The warning is indicated when the the compiler encounters the closing curly brace of the compound statement or function. The declaration of the variable occurs at the beginning of the compound statement or function.

'XXXXXXX' is assigned a value which is never used

The variable appears in an assignment, but is never used anywhere else in the function just ending. The warning is indicated only when the compiler encounters the closing curly brace.

'XXXXXXX' not part of structure

The named field was not part of the structure on the left hand side of the dot (.) or arrow (- >), or else the left hand side was not a structure (for a dot) or pointer to structure (for an arrow).

Ambiguous operators need parentheses

This warning is displayed whenever two shift, relational or bitwise-boolean operators are used together without parentheses. Also, an addition or subtraction operator that appears unparenthesized with a shift operator will produce this warning. Programmers frequently confuse the precedence of these operators, since the precedence assigned to them is somewhat counter-intuitive.

Both return and return of a value used

This warning is issued when the compiler encounters a `return` statement that disagrees with some previous `return` statement in the function. It is almost certainly an error for a function to return a value in only some of the `return` statements.

Call to function with no prototype

This message is given if the "Prototypes required" warning is enabled and you call a function without first giving a prototype for that function.

Call to function 'XXXX' with no prototype

This message is given if the "Prototypes required" warning is enabled and you call function XXXX without first giving a prototype for that function.

Code has no effect

This warning is issued when the compiler encounters a statement with some operators which have no effect. For example the statement:

```
a + b;
```

has no effect on either variable. The operation is unnecessary and probably indicates a bug.

Constant is long

The compiler encountered either a decimal constant greater than 32767 or an octal (or hexadecimal) constant greater than 65535 without a letter *l* or *L* following it. The constant is treated as a `long`.

Constant out of range in comparison

Your source file includes a comparison involving a constant subexpression that was outside the range allowed by the other subexpression's type. For example, comparing an `unsigned` quantity to –1 makes no sense. To get an `unsigned` constant greater than 32767 (in decimal), you should either cast the constant to `unsigned` (e.g., (`unsigned`)65535) or append a letter *u* or *U* to the constant (e.g., 65535u).

Conversion may lose significant digits

For an assignment operator or some other circumstance, your source file requires a conversion from `long` or `unsigned long` to `int` or `unsigned int` type. On some machines, since `int` type and `long` type variables have the same size, this kind of conversion may alter the behavior of a program being ported.

Whenever this message is issued, the compiler will still generate code to do the comparison. If this code ends up always giving the same result, such as comparing a `char` expression to 4000, the code will still perform the test. This also means that comparing an `unsigned` expression to –1 will do something useful, since an `unsigned` can have the same bit pattern as a –1 on the 8086.

Function should return a value

Your source file declared the current function to return some type other than `int` or `void`, but the compiler encountered a return with no value. This is usually some sort of error. `int` functions are exempt, since in old versions of C there was no `void` type to indicate functions which return nothing.

Mixing pointers to signed and unsigned char

You converted a `char` pointer to an `unsigned char` pointer, or vice versa, without using an explicit cast. (Strictly speaking, this is incorrect, but on the 8086, it is often harmless.)

No declaration for function 'XXXXXXXX'

This message is given if the "Declaration required" warning is enabled and you call a function without first declaring that function. The declaration can be either classic or modern (prototype) style.

Non-portable pointer assignment

Your source file assigned a pointer to a non-pointer, or vice versa. Assigning a constant zero to a pointer is allowed as a special case. You should use a cast to suppress this warning if the comparison is proper.

Non-portable pointer comparison

Your source file compared a pointer to a non-pointer other than the constant zero. You should use a cast to suppress this warning if the comparison is proper.

Non-portable return type conversion

The expression in a `return` statement was not the same type as the function declaration. With one exception, this is only triggered if the function or the return expression is a pointer. The exception to this is that a function returning a pointer may return a constant zero. The zero will be converted to an appropriate pointer value.

Parameter 'XXXXXXXX' is never used

The named parameter, declared in the function, was never used in the body of the function. This may or may not be an error and is often caused by misspelling the parameter. This warning can also occur if the identifier is redeclared as an automatic (local) variable in the body of the function. The parameter is masked by the automatic variable and remains unused.

Possible use of 'XXXXXXXX' before definition

Your source file used the named variable in an expression before it was assigned a value. The compiler uses a simple-minded scan of the program to determine this condition. If the use of a variable occurs physically before any assignment, this warning will be generated. Of course, the actual flow of the program may assign the value before the program uses it.

Possibly incorrect assignment

This warning is generated when the compiler encounters an assignment operator as the main operator of a conditional expression (i.e. part of an `if`, `while` or `do-while` statement). More often than not, this is a typographical error for the equality operator. If you wish to suppress this warning, enclose the assignment in parentheses and compare the whole thing to zero explicitly. Thus:

```
if (a = b) ...
```

should be rewritten as:

```
if ((a = b) != 0) ...
```

Redefinition of 'XXXXXXXX' is not identical
Your source file redefined the named macro using text that was not exactly the same as the first definition of the macro. The new text replaces the old.

Restarting compile using assembly
The compiler encountered an **asm** with no accompanying -B command line option or #pragma inline statement. The compile restarts using assembly language capabilities.

Structure passed by value
If "Structure passed by value" warning is enabled, this warning is generated anytime a structure is passed by value as an argument. It is a frequent programming mistake to leave an address-of operator (&) off a structure when passing it as an argument. Because structures can be passed by value, this omission is acceptable. This warning provides a way for the compiler to warn you of this mistake.

Superfluous & with function or array
An address-of operator (&) is not needed with an array name or function name; any such operators are discarded.

Suspicious pointer conversion
The compiler encountered some conversion of a pointer which caused the pointer to point to a different type. You should use a cast to suppress this warning if the conversion is proper.

Undefined structure 'XXXXXXXX'
The named structure was used in the source file, probably on a pointer to a structure, but had no definition in the source file. This is probably caused by a misspelled structure name or a missing declaration.

Unknown assembler instruction
The compiler encountered an in-line assembly statement with a disallowed opcode. Check the spelling of the opcode. Also check the list of allowed opcodes to see if the instruction is acceptable.

Unreachable Code
A **break, continue, goto** or **return** statement was not followed by a label or the end of a loop or function. The compiler checks **while, do** and **for** loops with a constant test condition, and attempts to recognize loops which cannot fall through.

Void functions may not return a value

Your source file declared the current function as returning **void**, but the compiler encountered a return statement with a value. The value of the return statement will be ignored.

Zero length structure

Your source file declared a structure whose total size was zero. Any use of this structure would be an error.

C

Command-Line Options

This appendix lists each of the Turbo C compile-time command-line options in alphabetical order under option type, and describes what each option does. The options are broken down into three general types:

- compiler options
- linker options
- environment options

Within the compiler options, there are several categories of options; these specify

- memory model
- #defines (macro definitions)
- code generation options
- optimization options
- source code options
- error-reporting options
- segment-naming control

To see an on-screen listing of all the TCC (command-line Turbo C) options, type `tcc` *Enter* at the DOS prompt (when you're in the TURBOC directory). Most of the command-line options have counterparts in the Turbo C Integrated Development Environment (TC) **O**ptions menus (and a few other menus). See Table C.1 for a correlation of the TC menu selections and the TCC command-line options.

Table C.1: Correlation of Command-line Options and Menu Selections

Command-line switch		Menu Selection
–A		O/C/Source/ANSI keywords only...On
–a		O/C/Code generation/Alignment...Word
–a-	**	O/C/Code generation/Alignment...Byte
–B		(Not available)
–C		O/C/Source/Nested comments...On
–c		Compile/Compile to OBJ
–D*name*		O/C/Defines
–D*name=string*		O/C/Defines
–d		O/C/Code generation/Merge duplicate strings...On
–d-	**	O/C/Code generation/Merge duplicate strings...Off
–e*filename*		Project/Project name
–f	**	O/C/Code generation/Floating point...Emulation
–f-		O/C/Code generation/Floating point...None
–f87		O/C/Code generation/Floating point...8087
–G		O/C/Optimization/Optimize for...Speed
–g#		O/C/Errors/Warnings: stop after...#
–I*pathname*		O/E/Include directories
–i#		O/E/Identifier length...#
–j#		O/C/Errors/Errors: stop after...#
–K		O/C/Code generation/Default char type...Unsigned
–K-	**	O/C/Code generation/Default char type...Signed
–k		O/C/Code generation/Standard stack frame...On
–L*pathname*		O/E/Library directory
–M		O/L/Map file
–mc		O/C/Model...Compact
–mh		O/C/Model...Huge
–ml		O/C/Model...Large
–mm		O/C/Model...Medium
–ms	**	O/C/Model...Small
–mt		O/C/Model...Tiny
–N		O/C/Code generation/Test stack overflow...On
–n*pathname*		O/E/Output directory
–O		O/C/Optimization/Optimize for...Size
–o*filename*		(Not available)
–p		O/C/Code generation/Calling convention...Pascal
–p-	**	C/Code generation/Calling convention...C
–r	**	O/C/Optimization/Use register variables...On
–S		(Not available)
–U*name*		(Not available)
–u	**	O/C/Code generation/Generate underbars...On
–w		O/C/Errors/Display warnings...On
–w-		O/C/Errors/Display warnings...Off
–w*xxx*		O/C/Errors/Portability warnings, ANSI violations, Common errors, or Less common errors...On
–w-*xxx*		O/C/Errors/Portability warnings, ANSI violations, Common errors, or Less common errors...Off
–y		O/C/Code generation/Line numbers...On
–Z		O/C/Optimization/Register optimization...On
–zA*name*		O/C/Names/Code/Class
–zB*name*		O/C/Names/Data/Class
–zC*name*		O/C/Names/Code/Segment
–zD*name*		O/C/Names/BSS/Segment
–zG*name*		O/C/Names/Data/Group
–zP*name*		O/C/Names/Code/Group
–zR*name*		O/C/Names/Data/Segment
–zS*name*		O/C/Names/BSS/Group
–zT*name*		O/C/Names/BSS/Class
–1		O/C/Code generation...80186/80286
–1-	**	O/C/Code generation...8088/8086

O/ = Options   C/ = Compiler   E/ = Environment   ** = On by default

Turning Options On and Off

You select command-line options by entering a dash (-) immediately followed by the option letter (like this, –I). To turn an option *off*, add another dash after the option letter. For example, –A turns the ANSI keywords option *on* and –A- turns the option *off*.

This feature is useful for disabling or enabling individual switches on the command line, thereby overriding the corresponding settings in the configuration file.

Syntax

You select Turbo C compiler options through a DOS command line, with the following syntax:

```
tcc [option option ...] filename filename ...
```

Turbo C compiles files according to the following set of rules:

`filename.asm`	invoke MASM to assemble to .OBJ
`filename.obj`	include as object at link time
`filename.lib`	include as library at link time
`filename`	compile filename.c
`filename.c`	compile filename.c
`filename.xyz`	compile filename.xyz

For example, given the following command line

```
tcc -a -f -C -O -Z -emyexe oldfile1.c oldfile2 nextfile.c
```

TCC will compile OLDFILE1.C, OLDFILE2.C, and NEXTFILE.C to .OBJ, producing an executable program file named MYEXE.EXE with the word alignment (-a), floating-point emulation (-f), nested comments (-C), jump optimization (-O), and register optimization (-Z) options selected.

TCC will invoke MASM if you give it an .ASM file on the command line or if a .C file contains in-line assembly. The switches TCC gives to MASM are

```
/mx /D__mdl__
```

where *mdl* is one of: TINY, SMALL, MEDIUM, COMPACT, LARGE, or HUGE. The /mx switch tells MASM to assemble with case-sensitivity on.

Compiler Options

Turbo C's command-line compiler options can be broken down into eight logical groups. These groups, and the ties that bind them, are as follows:

- *Memory model options* allow you to specify under which memory model Turbo C will compile your program. (The models range from Tiny to Huge.)

- *#defines (macro definitions)* allow you to define macros (also known as *manifest* or *symbolic* constants) to the default (which is 1), to a numeric value, or to a string; these options also allow you to undefine previously-defined macros.

- *Code generation options* govern characteristics of the generated code to be used at run-time, such as the floating-point mode, calling convention, char type, or CPU instructions.

- *Optimization options* allow you to specify how the object code is to be optimized; for size or speed, with or without the use of register variables, and with or without redundant load operations.

- *Source code options* cause the compiler to recognize (or ignore) certain features of the source code; implementation-specific (non-ANSI) keywords, nested comments, and identifier lengths.

- *Error-reporting options* allow you to tailor which warning messages the compiler will report, and the maximum number of warnings (and errors) that can occur before the compilation stops.

- *Segment-naming control* allows you to rename segments and to reassign their groups and classes.

- *Compilation control options* allow you to direct the compiler to

  - compile to assembly code (rather than to an object module)
  - compile a source file that contains in-line assembly
  - compile without linking.

Memory Model

-mc Compile using compact memory model.

-mh Compile using huge memory model.

-ml Compile using large memory model.

-mm Compile using medium memory model.

-ms Compile using small memory model (the default).

-mt Compile using tiny memory model. Generates almost the same code as the small memory model, but uses C0T.OBJ in any link performed to produce a tiny model program.

For details about the Turbo C memory models, refer to Chapter 9 in the *Turbo C User's Guide*.

#defines

-D*xxx* Defines the named identifier *xxx* to the string consisting of the single space character ( ).

-D*xxx=string* Defines the named identifier *xxx* to the string *string* after the equal sign. *string* cannot contain any spaces or tabs.

-U*xxx* Undefines any previous definitions of the named identifier *xxx*.

Code Generation Options

-1 Causes Turbo C to generate extended 80186 instructions. This option is also used when generating 80286 programs running in the unprotected mode, such as with the IBM PC/AT under MS-DOS 3.0.

-a Forces integer size items to be aligned on a machine-word boundary. Extra bytes will be inserted in a structure to insure field alignment. Automatic and global variables will be aligned properly. **char** and **unsigned char** variables and fields may be placed at any address; all others must be placed at an even numbered address.

-d Merges literal strings when one string matches another; this produces smaller programs. (Off by default.)

–f87 Generates floating-point operations using in-line 8087 instructions rather than using calls to 8087 emulation library routines. Specifies that a floating-point processor will be available at run time, so programs compiled with this option will not run on a machine that does not have a floating-point chip.

–f Emulates 8087 calls at run time if the run-time system does not have an 8087; if it does have one, calls the 8087 for floating-point calculations (the default).

–f- Specifies that the program contains no floating-point calculations, so no floating-point libraries will be linked at the link step.

–K Causes the compiler to treat all char declarations as if they were unsigned char type. This allows for compatibility with other compilers that treat char declarations as unsigned. By default, char declarations are signed.

–k Generates a standard stack frame, which is useful when using a debugger to trace back through the stack of called subroutines.

–N Generates stack overflow logic at the entry of each function: This will cause a stack overflow message to appear when a stack overflow is detected. This is costly in both program size and speed but is provided as an option because stack overflows can be very difficult to detect. If an overflow is detected, the message "Stack overflow!" is printed and the program exits with an exit code of 1.

–p Forces the compiler to generate all subroutine calls and all functions using the Pascal parameter-passing sequence. The resulting function calls are smaller and faster. Functions must pass the correct number and type of arguments, unlike normal C usage which permits a variable number of function arguments. You can use the `cdecl` statement to override this option and specifically declare functions to be C-type.

–u With -u selected, when you declare an identifier, Turbo C automatically sticks an underscore (_) on the front before saving that identifier in the object module.

Turbo C treats pascal-type identifiers (those modified by the `pascal` keyword) differently—they are uppercased and are *not* prefixed with an underscore.

Underscores for C identifiers are optional, but *on* by default. You can turn them *off* with -u-. However, if you are using the standard Turbo C libraries, you will then encounter problems unless you rebuild the libraries. (To do this, you will need the Turbo C Run-Time Library Source Code; contact Borland International for more infromation.)

See Chapter 9, "Advanced Programming in Turbo C" in the *Turbo C User's Guide* for details about underscores.

Note: Unless you are an expert, don't use –u–.

–y   Includes line numbers in the object file for use by a symbolic debugger. This increases the size of the object file but will not affect size or speed of the executable program.

This option is only useful in concert with a symbolic debugger that can use the information.

Optimization Options

–G   Causes the compiler to bias its optimization in favor of speed over size.

–O   Optimizes by eliminating redundant jumps, and reorganizing loops and switch statements.

–r-   Suppresses the use of register variables.

When you are using the –r– option, the compiler will not use register variables, and it also will not preserve register variables (SI,DI) from any caller. For that reason, you should not have code that uses register variables call code which has been compiled with –r–.

On the other hand, if you are interfacing with existing assembly-language code that does not preserve SI,DI, the –r- option will allow you to call that code for Turbo C.

–r   Enables the use of register variables (the default).

–Z   Suppresses redundant load operations by remembering the contents of registers and reusing them as often as possible.

Note: You should exercise caution when using this option, because the compiler cannot detect if a register has been invalidated indirectly by a pointer.

For example, if a variable *A* is loaded into register DX, it is retained. If *A* is later assigned a value, the value of DX is reset to indicate that its contents are no longer current. Unfortunately, if the value of *A* is modified indirectly (by assigning through a pointer that points to *A*),

Turbo C will not catch this and will continue to remember that DX contains the (now obsolete) value of *A*.

The -z optimization is designed to suppress register loads when the value being loaded is already in a register. This can eliminate whole instructions and also convert instructions from referring to memory locations to using registers instead.

The following artificial sequence illustrates both the benefits and the drawbacks of this optimization, and demonstrates why you need to exercise caution when using -z.

```
        C Code                  Optimized Assembler

func()
{
   int    A, *P, B;

   A = 4;                       mov    A,4
   ...
   B = A;                       mov    ax,A
                                mov    B,ax
   P = &A;                      lea    bx,A
                                mov    P,bx
   *P = B + 5;                  mov    dx,ax
                                add    dx,5
                                mov    [bx],dx
   printf("%d\n", A);           push   ax
}


}
```

Note first that on the statement *P = B + 5, the code generated uses a move from ax to dx first. Without the -z optimization, the move would be from B, generating a longer and slower instruction.

Second, the assignment into *P recognizes that *P* is already in bx, so a move from *P* to bx after the add instruction has been eliminated. These improvements are harmless and generally useful.

The call to **printf**, however, is not correct. Turbo C sees that ax contains the value of *A*, and so pushes the contents of the register rather than the contents of the memory location. The **printf** will then display a value of 4 rather than the correct value of 9. The indirect assignment through *P* has hidden the change to *A*.

If the statement $*P = B + 5$ had been written as $A = B + 5$, Turbo C would recognize a change in value.

The contents of registers are forgotten whenever a function call is made or when a point is reached where a jump could go (such as a label, a case statement, or the beginning or end of a loop). Because of this limit and the small number of registers in the 8086 family of processors, most programs using this optimization will never behave incorrectly.

Source Options

–A Creates ANSI-compatible code: Any of the Turbo C extension keywords are ignored and may be used as normal identifiers. These keywords include:

near	far	huge	cdecl
asm	pascal	interrupt	
_es	_ds	_cs	_ss

and the register pseudo-variables, such as _AX, _BX, _SI, etc.

–C Allows nesting of comments. Comments may not normally be nested.

–i# Causes the compiler to recognize only the first # characters of identifiers. All identifiers, whether variables, preprocessor macro names, or structure member names, are treated as distinct only if their first # characters are distinct.

By default, Turbo C uses 32 characters per identifier. Other systems, including UNIX, ignore characters beyond the first 8. If you are porting to these other environments, you may wish to compile your code with a smaller number of significant characters. Compiling in this manner will help you see if there are any name conflicts in long identifiers when they are truncated to a shorter significant length.

Errors Options

–g# Stops compiling after # messages (warning and error messages combined).

–j# Stops compiling after # error messages.

| −w*xxx* | Enables the warning message indicated by *xxx*. The option −w-*xxx* suppresses the warning message indicated by *xxx*. The possible values for −w*xxx* are as follows: |

(ANSI Violations)

−wdup	Redefinition of 'XXXXXXXX' is not identical.
−wret	Both return and return of a value used.
−wstr	'XXXXXXXX' not part of structure.
−wstu	Undefined structure 'XXXXXXXX'.
−wsus	Suspicious pointer conversion.
−wvoi	Void functions may not return a value.
−wzst	Zero length structure.

(Common Errors)

−waus	'XXXXXXXX' is assigned a value that is never used.
−wdef	Possible use of 'XXXXXXXX' before definition.
−weff	Code has no effect.
−wpar	Parameter 'XXXXXXXX' is never used.
−wpia	Possibly incorrect assignment.
−wrch	Unreachable code.
−wrvl	Function should return a value.

(Less Common Errors)

−wamb	Ambiguous operators need parentheses.
−wamp	Superfluous & with function or array.
−wnod	No declaration for function 'XXXXXXXX'.
−wpro	Call to function with no prototype.
−wstv	Structure passed by value.
−wuse	'XXXXXXXX' declared but never used.

(Portability Warnings)

−wapt	Non-portable pointer assignment.
−wcln	Constant is long.
−wcpt	Non-portable pointer comparison.
−wdgn	Constant out of range in comparison.
−wrpt	Non-portable return type conversion.
−wsig	Conversion may lose significant digits.
−wucp	Mixing pointers to signed and unsigned char.

Segment-Naming Control

–zA*name*   Changes the name of the code segment class to *name*. By default, the code segment is assigned to class _CODE.

–zB*name*   Changes the name of the uninitialized data segments class to *name*. By default, the uninitialized data segments are assigned to class _BSS.

–zC*name*   Changes the name of the code segment to *name*. By default, the code segment is named _TEXT, except for the medium, large and huge models, where the name is *filename_TEXT*. (*filename* here is the source file name).

–zD*name*   Changes the name of the uninitialized data segment to *name*. By default, the uninitialized data segment is named _BSS, except in the huge model where no uninitialized data segment is generated.

–zG*name*   Changes the name of the uninitialized data segments group to *name*. By default, the data group is named DGROUP, except in the huge model where there is no data group. This switch is ignored in the huge model.

–zP*name*   Causes any output files to be generated with a code group for the code segment named *name*. This option should not be used with the tiny model.

–zR*name*   Sets the name of the initialized data segment to *name*. By default, the initialized data segment is named _DATA except in the huge model where the segment is named *filename_DATA*.

–zS*name*   Changes the name of the initialized data segments group to *name*. By default, the data group is named DGROUP, except in the huge model, where there is no data group. This switch is ignored in the huge model.

–zT*name*   Sets the name of the initialized data segment class to *name*. By default the initialized data class segment is named _DATA.

–zX*   Uses the default name for X: for example, –zA* assigns the default class name _CODE to the code segment.

Compilation Control Options

–B   Compiles and calls the assembler to process in-line assembly code.

Note that this option is not available in the Integrated Environment (TC.EXE).

–c   Compiles and assembles the named .C and .ASM files, but does not execute a link command.

–o*filename*   Compiles the named file to the specified *filename.OBJ*.

–S   Compiles the named source files and produces assembly language output files (.ASM), but does not assemble.

Note that this option is not available in the Integrated Environment (TC.EXE).

Linker Options

–e*filename*   Derives the executable program's name from *filename* by adding .EXE (the program name will then be FILENAME.EXE). *filename* must immediately follow the –e, with no intervening whitespace. Without this option, the linker derives the .EXE file's name from the name of the first source or object file in the file name list.

–M   Forces the linker to produce a full link map. The default is to produce no link map.

Environment Options

–I*directory*   Searches *directory*, the drive specifier or path name of a sub-directory, for include files (in addition to searching the standard places). A drive specifier is a single letter, either uppercase or lowercase, followed by a colon (:). A directory is any valid path name of a directory file. Multiple –I directory options can be given.

–L*directory*   Forces the linker to get the C0x.OBJ start-up object file and the Turbo C library files (Cx.LIB, MATHx.LIB, EMU.LIB, and

FP87.LIB) from the named directory. By default, the linker looks for them in the current directory.

−n*xx*   Places any .OBJ or .ASM files created by the compiler in the directory or drive named by the path *xxx*.

D

Turbo C Utilities

Your Turbo C package supplies much more than just two versions of the fastest C compiler available. It also provides three powerful stand-alone utilities. You can use these stand-alone utilities with your Turbo C files as well as with your other modules.

These three highly useful adjuncts to Turbo C are CPP (the Turbo C Preprocessor), MAKE, and TLINK (the Turbo Linker).

This appendix explains what each utility is and illustrates, with code and command-line examples, how to use them. The Turbo C stand-alone utilities are discussed in the following order:

CPP
MAKE
TLINK

CPP: The Turbo C Preprocessor Utility

The CPP utility is a utility that augments the Turbo C compiler. CPP is not needed for normal compilations of C programs at all; its purpose is to produce a listing file of a C source program in which include files and define macros have been expanded.

Often, when the compiler reports an error inside a macro or an include file, you can get more information about what the error is if you can see the results of the macro expansions or the include files. In many multi-pass compilers a separate pass is responsible for performing that work and the results of that pass can be examined.

Since Turbo C uses an integrated single-pass compiler, CPP supplies the first-pass functionality found in other compilers. In addition, you can use CPP as a macro preprocessor.

You use CPP like you would use TCC, the stand-alone compiler. CPP reads the same TURBOC.CFG file for default options, and accepts the same command-line options as TCC.

The TCC options that don't pertain to CPP are simply ignored by CPP. To see the list of arguments handled by CPP, type

```
cpp
```

at the DOS prompt.

With one exception, the file names listed on the CPP command line are treated like they are in TCC, with wildcards allowed. The exception to this is that all files are treated as C source files. There is no special treatment for .OBJ, .LIB, or .ASM files.

For each file processed by CPP, the output is written to a file in the current directory (or the output directory named by the –n option) with the same name as the source name but with an extension of *.i.*

This output file is a text file containing each line of the source file and any include files. Any preprocessing directive lines have been removed, along with any conditional text lines excluded from the compile. Text lines are prefixed with the file name and line number of the source or include file the line came from. Within a text line, any macros are replaced with their expansion text.

Subsequently, the resulting output of CPP cannot be compiled because of the file name and line number prefix attached to each source line.

CPP as a Macro Preprocessor

The –P option to CPP tells it to prefix each line with the source file name and line number. If –P- is given, however, CPP omits this line number information. With this option turned off, CPP can be used as a macro preprocessor; the resultant .I file can then be compiled with TC or TCC.

An Example

The following simple program illustrates how CPP preprocesses a file, first with –P selected, then with –P-.

Source file: HELLOJOE.C

```
/* This is an example of the output of CPP */
#define NAME "Joe Smith"
#define BEGIN {
#define END   }

main()
BEGIN
   printf("%s\n", NAME);
END
```

Command Line Used to Invoke CPP as a Preprocessor:

```
cpp hellojoe.c
```

Output:

```
hellojoe.c 2:
hellojoe.c 3:
hellojoe.c 4:
hellojoe.c 6: main()
hellojoe.c 7: {
hellojoe.c 8:     printf("%s\n","Joe Smith");
hellojoe.c 9: }
```

Command Line Used to Invoke CPP as a Macro Preprocessor:

```
cpp -P- hellojoe.c
```

Output:
```
main()
{
   printf("%s\n","Joe Smith");
}
```

The Stand-Alone MAKE Utility

Turbo C places a great deal of power and flexibility at your fingertips. You can use it to manage large, complex programs that are built from numerous header, source, and object files. Unfortunately, that same freedom requires that you remember which files are required to produce other files. Why? Because if you make a change in one file, you must then do all the necessary recompilation and linking. One solution, of course, is simply to recompile everything each time you make a change—but as your program grows in size, that becomes more and more time consuming. So what do you do?

The answer is simple: you use MAKE. Turbo C's MAKE is an intelligent program manager that—given the proper instructions—does all the work necessary to keep your program up-to-date. In fact, MAKE can do far more than that. It can make backups, pull files out of different subdirectories, and even automatically run your programs should the data files that they use be modified. As you use MAKE more and more, you'll see new and different ways it can help you to manage your program development.

MAKE is a stand-alone utility; it is different from Project-Make, which is part of the Integrated Environment.

In this section we describe how to use stand-alone MAKE with TCC and TLINK.

A Quick Example

Let's start off with an example to illustrate MAKE's usefulness. Suppose you're writing some programs to help you display information about nearby star systems. You have one program—GETSTARS—that reads in a text file listing star systems, does some processing on it, then produces a binary data file with the resulting information in it.

GETSTARS uses certain definitions, stored in STARDEFS.H, and certain routines, stored in STARLIB.C (and declared in STARLIB.H). In addition, the program GETSTARS itself is broken up into three files:

- GSPARSE.C
- GSCOMP.C

■ GETSTARS.C

The first two files, GSPARSE and GSCOMP, have corresponding header files (GSPARSE.H and GSCOMP.H). The third file, GETSTARS.C has the main body of the program. Of the three files, only GSCOMP.C and GETSTARS.C make use of the STARLIB routines.

Here are the custom header files (other than the Turbo C headers that declare standard run-time library routines) needed by each .C file:

```
.C File          Custom Header File(s)

STARLIB.C        none
GSPARSE.C        STARDEFS.H
GSCOMP.C         STARDEFS.H,STARLIB.H
GETSTARS.C       STARDEFS.H,STARLIB.H,GSPARSE.H,GSCOMP.H
```

To produce GETSTARS.EXE (assuming a medium data model), you would enter the following command lines:

```
tcc -c -mm -f starlib
tcc -c -mm -f gsparse
tcc -c -mm -f gscomp
tcc -c -mm -f getstars
tlink lib\c0m starlib gsparse gscomp getstars,
      getstars, getstars, lib\emu lib\mathm lib\cm
```

Note: DOS requires that the TLINK command line all fit on one line: we show it here as two lines simply because the page isn't wide enough to fit it all in one line.

Looking at the preceding information, you can see some *file dependencies.*

■ GSPARSE, GSCOMP, and GETSTARS all depend on STARDEFS.H; in other words, if you make any changes to STARDEFS.H, then you'll have to recompile all three.

■ Likewise, any changes to STARLIB.H will require GSCOMP and GETSTARS to be recompiled.

■ Changes to GSPARSE.H means GETSTARS will have to be recompiled; the same is true of GSCOMP.H.

■ Of course, any changes to any source code file (STARLIB.C, GSPARSE.C, etc.) means that file must be recompiled.

■ Finally, if any recompiling is done, then the link has to be done again.

Quite a bit to keep track of, isn't it? What happens if you make a change to STARLIB.H, recompile GETSTARS.C, but forget to recompile GSCOMP.C?

You could make a .BAT file to do the four compilations and the one linkage given above, but you'd have to do them every time you made a change. Let's see how MAKE can simplify things for you.

Creating a Makefile

A makefile is just a combination of the two lists just given: dependencies and the commands needed to satisfy them.

For example, let's take the lists given, combine them, massage them a little, and produce the following:

```
getstars.exe: getstars.obj gscomp.obj gsparse.obj starlib.obj
    tlink lib\c0m starlib gsparse gscomp getstars, getstars, \
        getstars, lib\emu lib\mathm lib\cm

getstars.obj: getstars.c stardefs.h starlib.h gscomp.h gsparse.h
    tcc -c -mm -f getstars.c

gscomp.obj: gscomp.c stardefs.h starlib.h
    tcc -c -mm -f gscomp.c

gsparse.obj: gsparse.c stardefs.h
    tcc -c -mm -f gsparse.c

starlib.obj: starlib.c
    tcc -c -mm -f starlib.c
```

This just restates what was said before, but with the order reversed somewhat. Here's how MAKE interprets this file:

- The file GETSTARS.EXE depends on four files: GETSTARS.OBJ, GSCOMP.OBJ, GSPARSE.OBJ, and STARLIB.OBJ. If any of those four change, then GETSTARS.EXE must be recompiled. How? By using the TLINK command given.

- The file GETSTARS.OBJ depends on five files: GETSTARS.C, STARDEFS.H, STARLIB.H, GSCOMP.H, and GSPARSE.H. If any of those files change, then GETSTARS.OBJ must be recompiled by using the TCC command given.

- The file GSCOMP.OBJ depends on three files—GSCOMP.C, STARDEFS.H, and STARLIB.H—and if any of those three change, GSCOMP.OBJ must be recompiled using the TCC command given.

- The file GSPARSE.OBJ depends on two files—GSPARSE.OBJ and STARDEFS.H—and, again, must be recompiled using the TCC command given if either of those files change.

- The file STARLIB.OBJ depends on only one file—STARLIB.C—and must be recompiled via TCC if STARLIB.C changes.

What do you do with this? Type it into a file, which (for now) we'll call MAKEFILE. You're then ready to use MAKE.EXE.

Using a Makefile

Assuming you've created MAKEFILE as described above—and, of course, assuming that the various source code and header files exist—then all you have to do is type the command:

```
make
```

Simple, wasn't it? MAKE looks for MAKEFILE (you can call it something else; we'll talk about that later) and reads in the first line, describing the dependencies of GETSTARS.EXE. It checks to see if GETSTARS.EXE exists and is up-to-date.

This requires that it check the same thing about each of the files upon which GETSTARS.EXE depends: GETSTARS.OBJ, GSCOMP.OBJ, GSPARSE.OBJ, and STARLIB.OBJ. Each of those files depends, in turn, on other files, which must also be checked. The various calls to TCC are made as needed to update the .OBJ files, ending with the execution of the TLINK command (if necessary) to create an up-to-date version of GETSTARS.EXE.

What if GETSTARS.EXE and all the .OBJ files *already* exist? In that case, MAKE compares the time and date of the last modification of each .OBJ file with the time and date of its dependencies. If any of the dependency files are more recent than the .OBJ file, MAKE knows that changes have been made since the last time the .OBJ file was created and executes the TCC command.

If MAKE does update any of the .OBJ files, then when it compares the time and date of GETSTARS.EXE with them, it sees that it must execute the TLINK command to make an updated version of GETSTARS.EXE.

Stepping Through

Here's a step-by-step example to help clarify the previous description. Suppose that GETSTARS.EXE and all the .OBJ files exist, and that GETSTARS.EXE is more recent than any of the .OBJ files, and, likewise, each .OBJ file is more recent than any of its dependencies.

If you then enter the command

```
make
```

nothing happens, since there is no need to update anything.

Now, suppose that you modify STARLIB.C and STARLIB.H, changing, say, the value of some constant. When you enter the command

```
make
```

MAKE sees that STARLIB.C is more recent than STARLIB.OBJ, so it issues the command

```
tcc -c -mm -f starlib.c
```

It then sees that STARLIB.H is more recent than GSCOMP.OBJ, so it issues the command

```
tcc -c -mm -f gscomp.c
```

STARLIB.H is also more recent than GETSTARS.OBJ, so the next command is

```
tcc -c -mm -f getstars.c
```

Finally, because of these three commands, the files STARLIB.OBJ, GSCOMP.OBJ, and GETSTARS.OBJ are all more recent than GETSTARS.EXE, so the final command issued by MAKE is

```
tlink lib\c0m starlib gsparse gscomp getstars, getstars,
        getstars, lib\emu lib\mathm lib\cm
```

which links everything together and creates a new version of GETSTARS.EXE. (Note that this TLINK command line must actually be one line.)

You have a good idea of the basics of MAKE: what it's for, how to create a makefile, and how MAKE interprets that file. Let's now look at MAKE in more detail.

Creating Makefiles

A makefile contains the definitions and relationships needed to help MAKE keep your program(s) up-to-date. You can create as many makefiles as you want and name them whatever you want; MAKEFILE is just the default name that MAKE looks for if you don't specify a makefile when you run MAKE.

You create a makefile with any ASCII text editor, such as Turbo C's built-in interactive editor. All rules, definitions, and directives end with a newline; if a line is too long (such as the TLINK command in the previous example), you can continue it to the next line by placing a backslash (\) as the last character on the line.

Whitespace—blanks and tabs—is used to separate adjacent identifiers (such as dependencies) and to indent commands within a rule.

Components of a Makefile

Creating a makefile is almost like writing a program, with definitions, commands, and directives. Here's a list of the constructs allowed in a makefile:

- comments
- explicit rules
- implicit rules
- macro definitions
- directives: file inclusion, conditional execution, error detection, macro undefinition

Let's look at each of these in more detail.

Comments Comments begin with a sharp (#) character; the rest of the line following the # is ignored by MAKE. Comments can be placed anywhere and never have to start in a particular column.

A backslash (\) will **not** continue a comment onto the next line; instead, you must use a # on each line. In fact, you cannot use a backslash as a continuation character in a line that has a comment. If it precedes the #, it is no longer the last character on the line; if it follows the #, then it is part of the comment itself.

Here are some examples of comments in a makefile:

```
# makefile for GETSTARS.EXE
# does complete project maintenance
getstars.exe:  getstars.obj gscomp.obj gsparse.obj starlib.obj
# can't put a comment at the end of the next line
    tlink lib\c0m starlib gsparse gscomp getstars, getstars,\
            getstars, lib\emu lib\mathm lib\cm
# legal comment
#  can't put a comment between the next two lines
getstars.obj:  getstars.c stardefs.h starlib.h gscomp.h gsparse.h
    tcc -c -mm -f getstars.c   # you can put a comment here
```

Explicit Rules

You are already familiar with explicit rules, since those are what you used in the makefile example given earlier. Explicit rules take the form

```
target [target ... ]: [source source ... ]
   [command]
   [command]
   ...
```

where *target* is the file to be updated, *source* is a file upon which *target* depends, and *command* is any valid MS-DOS command (including invocation of .BAT files and execution of .COM and .EXE files).

Explicit rules define one or more target names, zero or more source files, and an optional list of commands to be performed. Target and source file names listed in explicit rules can contain normal MS-DOS drive and directory specifications, but they cannot contain wildcards.

Syntax here is important. *target* must be at the start of a line (in column 1), whereas each *command* must be indented, (must be preceded by at least one blank or tab). As mentioned before, the backslash (\) can be used as a continuation character if the list of source files or a given command is too long for one line. Finally, both the source files and the commands are optional; it is possible to have an explicit rule consisting only of *target* [target ...] followed by a colon.

The idea behind an explicit rule is that the command or commands listed will create or update *target*, usually using the *source* files. When MAKE encounters an explicit rule, it first checks to see if any of the *source* files are themselves target files elsewhere in the makefile. If so, then those rules are evaluated first.

Once all the *source* files have been created or updated based on other explicit (or implicit) rules, MAKE checks to see if *target* exists. If not, each *command* is invoked in the order given. If *target* does exist, its time and date of last modification are compared against the time and date for each *source*. If any *source* has been modified more recently than *target*, the list of commands is executed.

A given file name can occur on the left side of an explicit rule only once in a given execution of MAKE.

Each command line in an explicit rule begins with whitespace. MAKE considers all lines following an explicit rule to be part of the command list for that rule, up to the next line that begins in column 1 (without any preceding whitespace) or to the end of the file. Blank lines are ignored.

Special Considerations

An explicit rule with no command lines following it is treated a little differently than an explicit rule with command lines.

■ If an explicit rule exists for a target with commands, the only files that the target depends on are the ones listed in the explicit rule.

■ If an explicit rule has no commands, the targets depend on the files given in the explicit rule, and they also depend on any file that matches an implicit rule for the target(s).

See the following section for a discussion of implicit rules.

Examples

Here are some examples of explicit rules:

```
myprog.obj: myprog.c
   tcc -c  myprog.c

prog2.obj : prog2.c include\stdio.h
   tcc  -c -K prog2.c

prog.exe: myprog.c prog2.c include\stdio.h
   tcc -c myprog.c
   tcc -c -K prog2.c
   tlink lib\c0s myprog prog2, prog, , lib\cs
```

■ The first explicit rule states that MYPROG.OBJ depends upon MYPROG.C, and that MYPROG.OBJ is created by executing the given TCC command.

■ Similarly, the second rule states that PROG2.OBJ depends upon PROG2.C and STDIO.H (in the INCLUDE subdirectory) and is created by the given TCC command.

- The last rule states that PROG.EXE depends on MYPROG.C, PROG2.C, and STDIO.H, and that should any of the three change, PROG.EXE can be rebuilt by the series of commands given. However, this may create unnecessary work, because, even if only MYPROG.C changes, PROG2.C will still be recompiled. This occurs because all of the commands under a rule will be executed as soon as that rule's target is out of date.

- If you place the explicit rule

```
prog.exe: myprog.obj prog2.obj
    tlink lib\c0s myprog prog2, prog, , lib\cs
```

as the first rule in a makefile and follow it with the rules given (for MYPROG.OBJ and PROG2.OBJ), only those files that need to be recompiled will be.

Implicit Rules

MAKE allows you to define **implicit** rules as well. Implicit rules are generalizations of explicit rules. What do we mean by that?

Here's an example that illustrates the relationship between the two types of rules: consider this explicit rule from the previous sample program:

```
starlib.obj: starlib.c
    tcc -c -mm -f starlib.c
```

This rule is a common one, because it follows a general principle: an .OBJ file is dependent on the .C file with the same file name and is created by executing TCC. In fact, you might have a makefile where you have several (or even several dozen) explicit rules following this same format.

By redefining the explicit rule as an implicit rule, you can eliminate all the explicit rules of the same form. As an implicit rule, it would look like this:

```
.c.obj:
    tcc -c -mm -f $<
```

This rule means, "any file ending with .OBJ depends on the file with the same name that ends in .C, and the .OBJ file is created using the command

```
tcc -c -mm -f $<
```

where $<

represents the file's name with the source (.C) extension." (The symbol $< is a special macro and is discussed in the next section.)

The syntax for an implicit rule is:

```
.source_extension.target_extension:
    {command}
    {command}
    ...
```

where, as before, the commands are optional and must be indented.

The *source_extension* (which must begin in column 1) is the extension of the source file; that is, it applies to any file having the format

```
fname.source_extension
```

Likewise, the *target_extension* refers to the the file

```
fname.target_extension
```

where *fname* is the same for both files. In other words, this implicit rule replaces all explicit rules having the format:

```
fname.target_extension: fname.source_extension
    {command}
    {command}
    ...
```

for any *fname*.

Implicit rules are used if no explicit rule for a given target can be found, or if an explicit rule with no commands exists for the target.

The extension of the file name in question is used to determine which implicit rule to use. The implicit rule is applied if a file is found with the same name as the target, but with the mentioned source extension.

For example, suppose you had a makefile (named MAKEFILE) whose contents were

```
.c.obj:
    tcc -c -ms -f $<
```

If you had a C program named RATIO.C that you wanted to compile to RATIO.OBJ, you could use the command

```
make ratio.obj
```

MAKE would take RATIO.OBJ to be the target. Since there is no explicit rule for creating RATIO.OBJ, MAKE applies the implicit rule and generates the command

```
tcc -c -ms -f ratio.c
```

which, of course, does the compile step necessary to create RATIO.OBJ.

Implicit rules are also used if an explicit rule is given with no commands. Suppose, as mentioned before, you had the following implicit rule at the start of your makefile:

```
.c.obj:
    tcc -c -mm -f $<
```

You could then rewrite the last several explicit rules as follows:

```
getstars.obj: stardefs.h starlib.h gscomp.h gsparse.h
gscomp.obj: stardefs.h starlib.h
gsparse.obj: stardefs.h
```

Since you don't have explicit information on how to create these .OBJ files, MAKE applies the implicit rule defined earlier. And since STARLIB.OBJ depends only on STARLIB.C, that rule was dropped altogether from this list; MAKE automatically applies it.

Several implicit rules can be written with the same target extension, but only one such rule can apply at a time. If more than one implicit rule exists for a given target extension, each rule is checked in the order the rules appear in the makefile, until all applicable rules are checked.

MAKE uses the first implicit rule that discovers a file with the source extension. Even if the commands of that rule fail, no more implicit rules are checked.

All lines following an implicit rule are considered to be part of the command list for the rule, up to the next line that begins without whitespace or to the end of the file. Blank lines are ignored. The syntax for a command line is provided later in this chapter.

Special Considerations

Unlike explicit rules, MAKE does not know the full file name with an implicit rule. For that reason, special macros are provided with MAKE that allow you to include the name of the file being built by the rule. (See the discussion of macro definitions in this section for details.)

Examples

Here are some examples of implicit rules:

```
.c.obj:
    tcc -c $<

.asm.obj:
    masm $* /mx;
```

In the first implicit rule example, the target files are .OBJ files and their source files are .C files. This example has one command line in the command list; command line syntax is covered later in this section.

The second example directs MAKE to assemble a given file from its .ASM source file, using MASM with the /mx option.

Command Lists

We've talked about both explicit and implicit rules, and how they can have lists of commands. Let's talk about those commands and your options in setting them up.

Commands in a command list must be indented—that is, preceded by at least one blank or tab—and take the form

```
[ prefix ... ] command_body
```

Each command line in a command list consists of an (optional) list of prefixes, followed by a single command body.

Prefix

The prefixes allowed in a command modify the treatment of these commands by MAKE. The prefix is either the at (@) symbol or a hyphen (-) followed immediately by a number.

@   Forces MAKE to not display the command before executing it. The display is hidden even if the -s option was not given on the MAKE command line. This prefix applies only to the command on which it appears.

–num   Affects how MAKE treats exit codes. If a number (*num*) is provided, then MAKE will abort processing only if the exit status exceeds the number given. In this example, MAKE will abort only if the exit status exceeds 4:

```
-4 myprog sample.x
```

If no *–num* prefix is given, MAKE checks the exit status for the command. If the status is non-zero, MAKE will stop and delete the current target file.

–   With a dash, but no number, MAKE will not check the exit status at all. Regardless of what the exit status was, MAKE will continue.

Command body

The command body is treated exactly as it would be if it were entered as a line to COMMAND.COM, with the exception that redirection and pipes are not supported.

MAKE executes the following built-in commands by invoking a copy of COMMAND.COM to perform them:

break	cd	chdir	cls	copy
ctty	date	del	dir	erase
md	mkdir	path	prompt	ren
rename	set	time	type	ver
verify	vol			

MAKE searches for any other command name using the MS-DOS search algorithm:

- The current directory is searched first, followed by each directory in the path.
- In each directory, first a file with the extension .COM is checked, then a .EXE, and finally a .BAT.
- If a .BAT file is found, a copy of COMMAND.COM is invoked to execute the batch file.

Obviously, if an extension is supplied in the command line, MAKE searches only for that extension.

Examples

This command will cause COMMAND.COM to execute the command:

```
cd c:\include
```

This command will be searched for using the full search algorithm:

```
tlink lib\c0s x y,z,z,lib\cs
```

This command will be searched for using only the .COM extension:

```
myprog.com geo.xyz
```

This command will be executed using the explicit file name provided:

```
c:\myprogs\fil.exe -r
```

Macros

Often certain commands, file names, or options are used again and again in your makefile. In the example at the start of this appendix, all of the TCC commands used the switch -mm, which means to compile to the medium memory model; likewise, the TLINK command used the files C0M.OBJ, MATHM.LIB, and CM.LIB. Suppose you wanted to switch to the large memory model; what would you do? You could go through and change all the -mm options to -ml, and rename the appropriate files in the TLINK command. Or, you could define a **macro**.

A macro is a name that represents some string of characters. A macro definition gives a macro name and the expansion text; thereafter, when MAKE encounters the macro name, it replaces the name with the expansion text.

Suppose you defined the following macro at the start of your makefile:

```
MDL=m
```

You've defined the macro MDL, which is equivalent to the string m. You could now rewrite the makefile as follows:

```
MDL=m

getstars.exe: getstars.obj gscomp.obj gsparse.obj starlib.obj
    tlink lib\c0$(MDL) starlib gsparse gscomp getstars, \
        getstars, getstars, lib\emu lib\math$(MDL) lib\c$(MDL)

getstars.obj: getstars.c stardefs.h starlib.h gscomp.h gsparse.h
    tcc -c -m$(MDL) getstars.c

gscomp.obj: gscomp.c stardefs.h starlib.h
    tcc -c -m$(MDL) gscomp.c

gsparse.obj: gsparse.c stardefs.h
    tcc -c -m$(MDL) gsparse.c

starlib.obj: starlib.c
    tcc -c -m$(MDL) starlib.c
```

Everywhere a model is specified, you use the macro invocation $(MDL). When you run MAKE, $(MDL) is replaced with its expansion text, m. The result is the same set of commands you had before.

So, what have you gained? Flexibility. By changing the first line to

```
MDL=l
```

you've changed all the commands to use the large memory model. In fact, if you leave out the first line altogether, you can specify which memory model you want each time you run MAKE, using the -D (Define) option:

```
make -DMDL=l
```

This tells MAKE to treat MDL as a macro with the expansion text l.

Defining Macros

Macro definitions take the form

```
macro_name=expansion text
```

where *macro_name* is the name of the macro: a string of letters and digits with no whitespace in it, though you can have whitespace between *macro_name* and the equals sign (=). The *expansion text* is any arbitrary string containing letters, digits, whitespace, and punctuation; it is ended by newline.

If *macro_name* has previously been defined, either by a macro definition in the makefile or by the -D option on the MAKE command line, the new definition replaces the old.

Case is significant in macros; that is, the macros names md1, Md1, and MDL are all considered different.

Using Macros

Macros are invoked in your makefile with the format

```
$(macro_name)
```

The parentheses are required for all invocations, even if the macro name is just one character long, with the exception of three special predefined macros that we'll talk about in just a minute. This construct—$(macro_name)—is known as a *macro invocation*.

When MAKE encounters a macro invocation, it replaces the invocation with the macro's expansion text. If the macro is not defined, MAKE replaces it with the null string.

Special Considerations

Macros in macros: Macro cannot be invoked on the left (*macro_name*) side of a macro definition. They can be used on the right (*expansion text*) side, but they are not expanded until the macro being defined is invoked. In other words, when a macro invocation is expanded, any macros embedded in its expansion text are also expanded.

Macros in rules: Macro invocations are expanded immediately in rule lines.

Macros in directives: Macro invocations are expanded immediately in !if and !elif directives. If the macro being invoked in an !if or !elif directive is not currently defined, it is expanded to the value 0 (FALSE).

Macros in commands: Macro invocations in commands are expanded when the command is executed.

Predefined Macros

MAKE comes with several special macros built in: $d, $*, $<, $:, $., and $&. The first is a defined test macro, used in the conditional directives !if and !elif; the others are file name macros, used in explicit and implicit rules. In addition, the current SET environment strings are automatically loaded as macros, and the macro __MAKE__ is defined to be 1 (one).

Defined Test Macro ($d) The defined test macro $d expands to 1 if the given macro name is defined, or to 0 if it is not. The content of the macro's expansion text does not matter. This special macro is allowed only in !if and !elif directives.

For example, suppose you wanted to modify your makefile so that it would use the medium memory model if you didn't specify one, you could put this at the start of your makefile:

```
!if !$d(MDL)          # if MDL is not defined
MDL=m                 # define it to m (MEDIUM)
!endif
```

If you invoke MAKE with the command line

```
make -DMDL=1
```

then MDL is defined as 1. If, however, you just invoke MAKE by itself:

```
make
```

then MDL is defined as m, your "default" memory model.

Various File Name Macros

The various file name macros work in similar ways, expanding to some variation of the full path name of the file being built:

Base File name Macro ($*)

The base file name macro is allowed in the commands for an explicit or an implicit rule. This macro ($*) expands to the file name being built, excluding any extension, like this:

File name is A:\P\TESTFILE.C
$* expands to A:\P\TESTFILE

For example, you could modify the explicit GETSTARS.EXE rule already given to look like this:

```
getstars.exe: getstars.obj gscomp.obj gsparse.obj starlib.obj
    tlink lib\c0$(MDL) starlib gsparse gscomp $*, $*, $*, \
        lib\emu lib\math$(MDL) lib\c$(MDL)
```

When the command in this rule is executed, the macro $* is replaced by the target file name (sans extension), getstars. For implicit rules, this macro is very useful.

For example, an implicit rule for TCC might look like this (assuming that the macro MDL has been or will be defined, and that you are not using floating point routines):

```
.c.obj:
    tcc -c $*
```

Full File name Macro ($<)

The full file name macro ($<) is also used in the commands for an explicit or implicit rule. In an explicit rule, $< expands to the full target file name (including extension), like this:

File name is A:\P\TESTFILE.C
$< expands to A:\P\TESTFILE.C

For example, the rule

```
starlib.obj: starlib.c
    copy $< \oldobjs
    tcc -c $*
```

will copy STARLIB.OBJ to the directory \OLDOBJS before compiling STARLIB.C.

In an implicit rule, $< takes on the file name plus the source extension. For example, the previous implicit rule

```
.obj.c:
    tcc -c $*.c
```

can be rewritten as

```
.obj.c:
    tcc -c $<
```

File Name Path Macro ($:)

This macro expands to the path name (without the file name), like this:

> File name is A:\P\TESTFILE.C
> $: expands to A:\P\

File Name and Extension Macro ($.)

This macro expands to the file name, with extension, like this:

> File name is A:\P\TESTFILE.C
> $. expands to TESTFILE.C

File Name Only Macro ($&)

This macro expands to the file name only, without path or extension, like this:

> File name is A:\P\TESTFILE.C
> $& expands to TESTFILE

Directives

Turbo C's MAKE allows something that other versions of MAKE don't: directives similiar to those allowed for C itself. You can use these directives to include other makefiles, to make the rules and commands conditional, to print out error messages, and to "undefine" macros.

Directives in a makefile begin with an exclamation point (!) as the first character of the line, unlike C, which uses the sharp character (#). Here is the complete list of MAKE directives:

```
!include
!if
!else
!elif
!endif
!error
!undef
```

File-Inclusion Directive

A file-inclusion directive (!include) specifies a file to be included into the makefile for interpretation at the point of the directive. It takes the following form:

```
!include " filename "
```

These directives can be nested arbitrarily deep. If an include directive attempts to include a file that has already been included in some outer level of nesting (so that a nesting loop is about to start), the inner include directive is rejected as an error.

How do you use this directive? Suppose you created the file MODEL.MAC which contained the following:

```
!if !$d(MDL)
MDL=m
!endif
```

You could then make use of this conditional macro definition in any makefile by including the directive

```
!include "MODEL.MAC"
```

When MAKE encounters the !include directive, it opens the specified file and reads the contents as if they were in the makefile itself.

Conditional Directives

Conditional directives (!if, !elif, !else, and !endif) give a programmer a measure of flexibility in constructing makefiles. Rules and macros can be conditionalized so that a command-line macro definition (using the -D option) can enable or disable sections of the makefile.

The format of these directives parallels that of the C preprocessor:

```
!if expression
   [ lines ]
!endif


!if expression
   [ lines ]
!else
   [ lines ]
!endif


!if expression
   [ lines ]
!elif expression
   [ lines ]
!endif
```

Note: [lines] can be any of the following:

```
macro_definition
explicit_rule
implicit_rule
include_directive
if_group
error_directive
undef_directive
```

The conditional directives form a group, with at least an !if directive beginning the group and an !endif directive closing the group.

■ One !else directive can appear in the group.

■ !elif directives can appear between the !if and any !else directives.

■ Rules, macros, and other directives can appear between the various conditional directives in any number. Note that complete rules, with their commands, cannot be split across conditional directives.

■ Conditional directive groups can be nested arbitrarily deep.

Any rules, commands, or directives must be complete within a single source file.

Any !if directives must have matching !endif directives within the same source file. Thus the following include file is illegal, regardless of what is contained in any file that might include it, because it does not have a matching !endif directive:

```
!if $(FILE_COUNT) > 5
    some rules
!else
    other rules
<end-of-file>
```

Expressions Allowed in Conditional Directives

The expression allowed in an !if or an !elif directive uses a C-like syntax. The expression is evaluated as a simple 32-bit signed integer expression.

Numbers can be entered as decimal, octal, or hexadecimal constants. For example, these are legal constants in an expression:

```
4536   # decimal constant
0677   # octal constant
0x23aF # hexadecimal constant
```

An expression can use any of the following unary operators:

- negation
~ bit complement
! logical not

An expression can use any of the following binary operators:

+ addition
- subtraction
* multiplication
/ division
% remainder
» right shift
« left shift
& bitwise and
| bitwise or
^ bitwise exclusive or
&& logical and
|| logical or
> greater than
< less than
>= greater than or equal
<= less than or equal
== equality
!= inequality

An expression can contain the following ternary operator:

? : The operand before the ? is treated as a test.

If the value of that operand is non-zero, then the second operand (the part between the ? and :) is the result. If the value of the first operand is zero, the value of the result is the value of the third operand (the part after the :).

Parentheses can be used to group operands in an expression. In the absence of parentheses, binary operators are grouped according to the same precedence given in the C language.

As in C, for operators of equal precedence, grouping is from left to right, except for the ternary operator (? :), which is right to left.

Macros can be invoked within an expression, and the special macro $d() is recognized. After all macros have been expanded, the expression must have proper syntax. Any words in the expanded expression are treated as errors.

Error Directive

The error directive (`!error`) causes MAKE to stop and print a fatal diagnostic containing the text after `!error`. It takes the format

```
!error any_text
```

This directive is designed to be included in conditional directives to allow a user-defined abortion condition. For example, you could insert the following code in front of the first explicit rule:

```
!if !$d(MDL)
# if MDL is not defined
!error MDL not defined
!endif
```

If you reach this spot without having defined MDL, then MAKE will stop with this error message:

```
Fatal makefile 5: Error directive: MDL not defined
```

Undef Directive

The undefine directive (`!undef`) causes any definition for the named macro to be forgotten. If the macro is currently undefined, this directive has no effect. The syntax is:

```
!undef macro_name
```

Using MAKE

You now know a lot about how to write makefiles; now's the time to learn how to use them with MAKE.

Command Line Syntax

The simplest way to use MAKE is to type the command

```
make
```

at the MS-DOS prompt. MAKE then looks for MAKEFILE; if it can't find it, it looks for MAKEFILE.MAK; if it can't find that, it halts with an error message.

What if you want to use a file with a name other than MAKEFILE or MAKEFILE.MAK? You give MAKE the file (-f) option, like this:

```
make -fstars.mak
```

The general syntax for MAKE is

```
make option option ... target target ...
```

where *option* is a MAKE option (discussed later) and *target* is the name of a target file to be handled by explicit rules.

Here are the syntax rules:

- The word *make* is followed by a space, then a list of make options.
- Each make option must be separated from its adjacent options by a space. Options can be placed in any order, and any number of these options can be entered (as long as there is room in the command line).
- After the list of make options comes a space, then an optional list of targets.
- Each target must also be separated from its adjacent targets by a space. MAKE evaluates the target files in the order listed, recompiling their constituents as necessary.

If the command line does not include any target names, MAKE uses the first target file mentioned in an explicit rule. If one or more targets are mentioned on the command line, they will be built as necessary.

Here are some more examples of MAKE command lines:

```
make -n -fstars.mak
make -s
make -Iinclude -DMDL=c
```

A Note About Stopping MAKE

MAKE will stop if any command it has executed is aborted via a control-break. Thus, a *Ctrl-C* will stop the currently executing command and MAKE as well.

The BUILTINS.MAK File

When using MAKE, you will often find that there are macros and rules (usually implicit ones) that you use again and again. You've got three ways of handling them. First, you can put them in each and every makefile you create. Second, you can put them all in one file and use the !include directive in each makefile you create. Third, you can put them all in a file named BUILTINS.MAK.

Each time you run MAKE, it looks for a file named BUILTINS.MAK; if it finds the file, MAKE reads in it before handling MAKEFILE (or whichever makefile you want it to process).

The BUILTINS.MAK file is intended for any rules (usually implicit rules) or macros that will be commonly used in files anywhere on your computer.

There is no requirement that any BUILTINS.MAK file exist. If MAKE finds a BUILTINS.MAK file, it interprets that file first. If MAKE cannot find a BUILTINS.MAK file, it proceeds directly to interpreting MAKEFILE (or whatever makefile you specify).

How MAKE Searches for Makefiles

MAKE will search for BUILTINS.MAK in the current directory or any directory in the path. You should place this file in the same directory as the MAKE.EXE file.

MAKE always searches for the makefile in the current directory only. This file contains the rules for the particular executable program file being built. The two files have identical syntax rules.

MAKE also searches for any !include files in the current directory. If you use the -I (Include) option, it will also search in the specified directory.

The TOUCH Utility

There are times when you want to force a particular target file to be recompiled or rebuilt, even though no changes have been made to its sources. One way to do this is to use the TOUCH utility included with Turbo C. TOUCH changes the date and time of one or more files to the current date and time, making it "newer" than the files that depend on it.

To force a target file to be rebuilt, touch one of the files that target depends on. To touch a file (or files), enter

```
touch filename [filename ... ]
```

at the DOS prompt. TOUCH will then update the file's creation date(s).

Once you do this, you can invoke MAKE to rebuild the touched target file(s). (You can use the DOS wildcards * and ? with TOUCH.)

MAKE Command Line Options

We've alluded to several of MAKE's command line options; now we'll present a complete list of them. Note that case (upper or lower) **is** significant; the option -d is not a valid substitution for -D.

–D*identifier*	Defines the named identifier to the string consisting of the single character 1.
–D*iden=string*	Defines the named identifier iden to the string after the equal sign. The string cannot contain any spaces or tabs.
–I*directory*	MAKE will search for include files in the indicated directory (as well as in the current directory).
–U*identifier*	Undefines any previous definitions of the named identifier.
–s	Normally, MAKE prints each command as it is about to be executed. With the -s option, no commands are printed before execution.
–n	Causes MAKE to print the commands, but not actually perform them. This is useful for debugging a makefile.
–f*filename*	Uses filename as the MAKE file. If filename does not exist, and no extension is given, tries filename.mak.
–? or **–h**	Print help message.

MAKE Error Messages

MAKE diagnostic messages fall into two classes: fatals and errors. When a fatal error occurs, compilation immediately stops. You must take appropriate action and then restart the compilation. Errors will indicate some sort of syntax or semantic error in the source makefile. MAKE will complete interpreting the makefile and then stop.

Fatals

Don't know how to make XXXXXXXX

This message is issued when MAKE encounters a nonexistent file name in the build sequence, and no rule exists that would allow the file name to be built.

Error directive: XXXX

This message is issued when MAKE processes an `#error` directive in the source file. The text of the directive is displayed in the message.

Incorrect command line argument: XXX

This error occurs if MAKE is executed with incorrect command-line arguments.

Not enough memory

This error occurs when the total working storage has been exhausted. You should try this on a machine with more memory. If you already have 640K in your machine, you may have to simplify the source file.

Unable to execute command

This message is issued after a command was to be executed. This could be caused because the command file could not be found, or because it was misspelled. A less likely possibility is that the command exists but is somehow corrupted.

Unable to open makefile

This message is issued when the current directory does not contain a file named MAKEFILE.

Errors

Bad file name format in include statement

Include file names must be surrounded by quotes or angle brackets. The file name was missing the opening quote or angle bracket.

Bad undef statement syntax

An `!undef` statement must contain a single identifier and nothing else as the body of the statement.

Character constant too long

Character constants can be only one or two characters long.

Command arguments too long

The arguments to a command executed by MAKE were more than 127 characters—a limit imposed by MS-DOS.

Command syntax error

This message occurs if:

- The first rule line of the makefile contained any leading whitespace.
- An implicit rule did not consist of `.ext.ext:`.
- An explicit rule did not contain a name before the : character.
- A macro definition did not contain a name before the = character.

Division by zero

A divide or remainder in an `!if` statement has a zero divisor.

Expression syntax error in `!if` statement

The expression in an `!if` statement is badly formed—it contains a mismatched parenthesis, an extra or missing operator, or a missing or extra constant.

File name too long

The file name given in an `!include` directive was too long for the compiler to process. File names in MS-DOS must be no more than 64 characters long.

Illegal character in constant expression X

MAKE encountered some character not allowed in a constant expression. If the character is a letter, this indicates a (probably) misspelled identifier.

Illegal octal digit

An octal constant was found containing a digit of 8 or 9.

Macro expansion too long

A macro cannot expand to more than 4,096 characters. This error often occurs if a macro recursively expands itself. A macro cannot legally expand to itself.

Misplaced elif statement

An `!elif` directive was encountered without any matching `!if` directive.

Misplaced else statement

An `!else` directive was encountered without any matching `!if` directive.

Misplaced endif statement

An `!endif` directive was encountered without any matching `!if` directive.

No file name ending

The file name in an include statement was missing the correct closing quote or angle bracket.

Redefinition of target XXXXXXXX

The named file occurs on the left-hand side of more than one explicit rule.

Unable to open include file XXXXXXXXX.XXX

The named file could not be found. This could also be caused if an include file included itself. Check whether the named file exists.

Unexpected end of file in conditional started on line

The source file ended before MAKE encountered an `!endif`. The `!endif` was either missing or misspelled.

Unknown preprocessor statement

A ! character was encountered at the beginning of a line, and the statement name following was not `error`, `undef`, `if`, `elif`, `include`, `else`, or `endif`.

Turbo Link

In the Turbo C Integrated Development Environment (TC) the linker is built in. For the command-line version of Turbo C (TCC), the linker is invoked as a separate program. This separate program, TLINK, can also be used as a stand-alone linker.

TLINK is lean and mean; while it lacks some of the bells and whistles of other linkers, it is extremely fast and compact.

By default, Turbo C calls TLINK when compilation is successful; TLINK then combines object modules and library files to produce the executable file.

In this appendix, we describe how to use TLINK as a stand-alone linker.

Invoking TLINK

You can invoke TLINK at the DOS command line by typing `tlink` with or without parameters.

When invoked without parameters, TLINK displays a summary of parameters and options that looks like this:

```
Turbo Link  Version 1.0 Copyright (c) 1987 Borland International
The syntax is: TLINK objfiles, exefile, mapfile, libfiles
@xxxx indicates use response file xxxx
Options: /m = map file with publics
         /x = no map file at all
         /i = initialize all segments
         /l = include source line numbers
         /s = detailed map of segments
         /n = no default libraries
         /d = warn if duplicate symbols in libraries
         /c = lower case significant in symbols
```

In TLINK's summary display, the line

```
The syntax is: TLINK objfiles, exefile, mapfile, libfiles
```

specifies that you supply file names *in the given order*, separating the file *types* with commas.

For example, if you supply the command line

```
tlink /c mainline wd ln tx,fin,mfin,lib\comm lib\support
```

TLINK will interpret it to mean that

- Case is significant during linking (/c).
- The .OBJ files to be linked are MAINLINE.OBJ, WD.OBJ, LN.OBJ, and TX.OBJ.
- The executable program name will be FIN.EXE.
- The map file is MFIN.MAP.
- The library files to be linked in are COMM.LIB and SUPPORT.LIB, both of which are in subdirectory LIB.

TLINK appends extensions to file names that have none:

- .OBJ for object files
- .EXE for executable files
- .MAP for map files
- .LIB for library files

Be aware that where no .EXE file name is specified, TLINK derives the name of the executable file by appending .EXE to the first object file name listed. If for example, you had not specified FIN as the .EXE file name in the previous example, TLINK would have created MAINLINE.EXE as your executable file.

TLINK always generates a map file, unless you explicitly direct it not to by including the /x option on the command line.

- If you give the /m option, the map file includes publics.
- If you give the /s option, the map file is a detailed segment map.

These are the rules TLINK follows when determining the name of the map file.

- If no .MAP file is specified, TLINK derives the map file name by adding a .MAP extension to the .EXE file name. (The .EXE file name can be given on the command line or in the response file; if no .EXE name is given, TLINK will derive it from the name of the first .OBJ file.)
- If a map file name is specified in the command line (or in the response file), TLINK adds the .MAP extension to the given name.

Note that even if you specify a map file name, if the /x option is specified then no map file will be created at all.

Using Response Files

TLINK lets you supply the various parameters on the command line, in a response file, or in any combination of the two.

A response file is just a text file that contains the options and/or file names that you would usually type in after the name TLINK on your command line.

Unlike the command line, however, a response file can be continued onto several lines of text. You can break a long list of object or library files into several lines by ending one line with a plus character and continuing the list on the next line.

Also, you can start each of the four components on separate lines: object files, executable file, map file, libraries. When you do this, you must leave out the comma used to separate components.

To illustrate these features, suppose that you rewrote the previous command-line example as a response file, FINRESP, like this:

```
/c mainline wd+
ln tx,fin+
mfin+
lib\comm lib\support
```

You would then enter your TLINK command as:

```
tlink @finresp
```

Note that you must precede the file name with an "at" character (@) to indicate that the next name is a response file.

Alternately, you may break your link command into multiple response files. For example, you can break the previous command line into the following two response files:

File Name	Contents
LISTOBJS	mainline+ wd+ ln tx
LISTLIBS	lib\comm+ lib\support

You would then enter the TLINK command as:

```
tlink /c @listobjs,fin,mfin,@listlibs
```

Using TLINK with Turbo C Modules

Turbo C supports six different memory models: tiny, small, compact, medium, large, and huge. When you create an executable Turbo C file using TLINK, you must include the initialization module and libraries for the memory model being used.

The general format for linking Turbo C programs with TLINK is

```
tlink C0x <myobjs>, <exe>,[map],<mylibs> [emu|fp87 mathx] Cx
```

where these *<filenames>* represent the following:

<myobjs> =	the .OBJ files you want linked
<exe> =	the name to be given the executable file
[map] =	the name to be given the map file [optional]
<mylibs> =	the library files you want included at link time

The other filenames on this general TLINK command line represent Turbo C files, as follows:

C0x	= initialization module for memory model *x*
emu|fp87	= the floating-point libraries (choose one)
mathx	= math library for memory model *x*
Cx	= run-time library for memory model *x*

Initialization Modules

The initialization modules have the name C0x.OBJ, where *x* is a single letter corresponding to the model: *t, s, c, m, l, h*. Failure to link in the appropriate initialization module usually results in a long list of error messages telling you that certain identifiers are unresolved and/or that no stack has been created.

The initialization module must also appear as the first object file in the list. The initialization module arranges the order of the various segments of the program. If it is not first, the program segments may not be placed in memory properly, causing some frustrating program bugs.

Be sure that you give an explicit .EXE file name on the TLINK command line. Otherwise, your program name will be C0x.EXE—probably not what you wanted!

Libraries

After your own libraries, the libraries of the corresponding memory model must also be included in the link command. These libraries must appear in a specific order; a floating-point library with the appropriate math library (these are optional), and the corresponding run-time library. We discuss those libraries in that order here.

If your Turbo C program uses any floating-point, you must include a floating-point library (EMU.LIB or FP87.LIB) plus a math library (MATH*x*.LIB) in the link command.

Turbo C's two floating-point libraries are independent of the program's memory model.

- If you want to include floating-point emulation logic so that the program will work both on machines with and without a math coprocessor (8087 or 80287) chip, you must use EMU.LIB.

- If you know that the program will always be run on a machine with a math coprocessor chip, the FP87.LIB library will produce a smaller and somewhat faster executable program.

The math libraries have the name MATH*x*.LIB, where *x* is a single letter corresponding to the model: *t, s, c, m, l, h*.

You can always include the emulator and math libraries in a link command line. If your program does no floating-point work, nothing from those libraries will be added to your executable program file. However, if you know there is no floating-point work in your program, you can save time in your links by excluding those libraries from the command line.

You must always include the C run-time library for the program's memory model. The C run-time libraries have the name C*x*.LIB, where *x* is a single letter corresponding to the model, as before.

Note: if you are using floating-point operations, you must include the math and emulator libraries *before* the C run-time library. Failure to do this will likely result in a failed link.

Using TLINK with TCC

You can also use TCC, the stand-alone Turbo C compiler, as a "front end" to TLINK that will invoke TLINK with the correct start-up file, libraries, and executable-program name.

To do this, you give file names on the TCC command line with explicit .OBJ and .LIB extensions. For example, given the following TCC command line

```
tcc -mx mainfile.obj sub1.obj mylib.lib
```

TCC will invoke TLINK with the files C0x.OBJ, EMU.LIB, MATHx.LIB and Cx.LIB (initialization module, default 8087 emulation library, math library and run-time library for memory model x). TLINK will link these along with your own modules MAINLINE.OBJ and SUB1.OBJ, and your own library MYLIB.LIB.

Note: When TCC invokes TLINK, it always uses the /c (case-sensitive link) option.

TLINK Options

TLINK options can occur anywhere on the command line. The options consist of a slash (/) followed by the option-specifying letter (*m, s, l, i, n, d, x*, or *c*).

If you have more than one option, spaces are not significant (/m/c is the same as /m   /c), and you can have them appear in different places on the command line. The following sections describe each of the options.

The /x, /m, /s Options

By default, TLINK always creates a map of the executable file. This default map includes only the list of the segments in the program, the program start address, and any warning or error messages produced during the link.

If you want to create a more complete map, the /m option will add a list of public symbols to the map file, sorted in increasing address order,. This kind of map file is useful in debugging. Many debuggers, such as SYMDEB, can use the list of public symbols to allow you to refer to symbolic addresses when you are debugging.

The /s option creates a map file with segments, public symbols and the program start address just like the /m option did, but also adds a detailed segment map. The following is an example of a detailed segment map:

[Detailed map of segments]

Address	Length (Bytes)	Class	Segment Name	Group	Module	Alignment/ Combining
0000:0000	0E5B	C=CODE	S=SYMB_TEXT	G=(none)	M=SYMB.C	ACBP=28
00E5:000B	2735	C=CODE	S=QUAL_TEXT	G=(none)	M=QUAL.C	ACBP=28
0359:0000	002B	C=CODE	S=SCOPY_TEXT	G=(none)	M=SCOPY	ACBP=28
035B:000B	003A	C=CODE	S=LRSH_TEXT	G=(none)	M=LRSH	ACBP=20
035F:0005	0083	C=CODE	S=PADA_TEXT	G=(none)	M=PADA	ACBP=20
0367:0008	005B	C=CODE	S=PADD_TEXT	G=(none)	M=PADD	ACBP=20
036D:0003	0025	C=CODE	S=PSBP_TEXT	G=(none)	M=PSBP	ACBP=20
036F:0008	05CE	C=CODE	S=BRK_TEXT	G=(none)	M=BRK	ACBP=28
03CC:0006	066F	C=CODE	S=FLOAT_TEXT	G=(none)	M=FLOAT	ACBP=20
0433:0006	000B	C=DATA	S=_DATA	G=DGROUP	M=SYMB.C	ACBP=48
0433:0012	00D3	C=DATA	S=_DATA	G=DGROUP	M=QUAL.C	ACBP=48
0433:00E6	000E	C=DATA	S=_DATA	G=DGROUP	M=BRK	ACBP=48
0442:0004	0004	C=BSS	S=_BSS	G=DGROUP	M=SYMB.C	ACBP=48
0442:0008	0002	C=BSS	S=_BSS	G=DGROUP	M=QUAL.C	ACBP=48
0442:000A	000E	C=BSS	S=_BSS	G=DGROUP	M=BRK	ACBP=48

For each segment in each module, this map includes the address, length in bytes, class, segment name, group, module, and ACBP information.

If the same segment appears in more than one module, each module will appear as a separate line (for example, SYMB.C). Most of the information in the detailed segment map is self-explanatory, except for the ACBP field.

The ACBP field encodes the A (*alignment*) and C (*combining*) attributes into a set of 4 bit fields, as defined by Intel. TLINK uses only two of the fields, the A and C fields. The ACBP value in the map is printed in hexadecimal: The following values of the fields must be OR'ed together to arrive at the ACBP value printed.

Field	Value	Description
The A field (alignment)	00	An Absolute segment.
	20	A byte aligned segment.
	40	A word aligned segment.
	60	A paragraph aligned segment.
	80	A page aligned segment.
	A0	An unnamed absolute portion of storage.
The C field (combination)	00	May not be combined.
	08	A public combining segment.

The /l Option

The /l option creates a section in the .MAP file for source code line numbers. To use it, you must have created the .OBJ files by compiling with the -y (Line numbers...On) option. If you tell TLINK to create no map at all (using the /x option), this option will have no effect.

The /i Option

The /i option causes trailing segments to be output into the executable file even if the segments do not contain data records. Note that this is not normally necessary.

The /n Option

The /n option causes the linker to ignore default libraries specified by some compilers. This option is necessary if the default libraries are in another directory, because TLINK does not support searching for libraries. You may want to use this option when linking modules written in another language.

The /c Option

The /c option forces the case to be significant in publics and externals. For example, by default, TLINK regards *fred*, *Fred*, and *FRED* as equal; the /c option makes them different.

The /d Option

Normally, TLINK will not warn you if a symbol appears in more than one library file. If the symbol must be included in the program, TLINK will use the copy of that symbol in the first file mentioned on the command line. Since this is a commonly used feature, TLINK does not normally warn about the duplicate symbols. The following hypothetical situation illustrates how you might want to use this feature.

Suppose you have two libraries: one called SUPPORT.LIB, and a supplemental one called DEBUGSUP.LIB. Suppose also that DEBUGSUP.LIB contains duplicates of some of the routines in SUPPORT.LIB (but the duplicate routines in DEBUGSUP.LIB include slightly different functionality, such as debugging versions of the routines). If you include DEBUGSUP.LIB *first* in the link command, you will get the debugging routines and *not* the routines in SUPPORT.LIB.

If you are not using this feature or are not sure which routines are duplicated, you may include the /d option. This will force TLINK to list all symbols duplicated in libraries, even if those symbols are not going to be used in the program.

The /d option also forces TLINK to warn about symbols that appear both in an .OBJ and a .LIB file. In this case, since the symbol that appears in the first (left-most) file listed on the command line is the one linked in, the symbol in the .OBJ file is the one that will be used.

With Turbo C, the distributed libraries you would use in any given link command do not contain any duplicated symbols. Thus while EMU.LIB and FP87.LIB (or CS.LIB and CL.LIB) obviously have duplicate symbols, they would never rightfully be used together in a single link. There are no symbols duplicated between EMU.LIB, MATHS.LIB, and CS.LIB, for example.

Restrictions

As we said earlier, TLINK is lean and mean; it does not have an excessive supply of options. Following are the only serious restrictions to TLINK:

- Overlays are not supported.
- Microsoft CodeView Debugger is not supported (but SST and SYMDEB work fine).
- Common variables are only partly supported: A public must be supplied to resolve them.

- You can have a maximum of 8182 symbols and 4000 logical segments.

- Segments that are of the same name and class should either *all* be able to be combined, or not. (Only assembler programmers might encounter this as a problem.)

- Code compiled in Microsoft C or Microsoft Fortran cannot be linked with TLINK. This is because Microsoft languages have undocumented object record formats in their OBJ files, which TLINK does not currently support.

TLINK is designed to be used with Turbo C (both the Integrated Environment and command-line versions), as well as with MASM and other compilers; however, it is not a general replacement for MS Link.

Error Messages

TLINK has three types of errors: warnings, non-fatal errors, and fatal errors.

- Warnings are just that: warnings of conditions that you probably want to fix. When warnings occur .EXE and .MAP files are still created.

- A non-fatal error does not delete .EXE or .MAP files, but you shouldn't try to execute the .EXE file.

- A fatal error causes TLINK to stop immediately; the .EXE and .MAP files are deleted.

The following generic names and values appear in the error messages listed in this section. When you get an error message, the appropriate name or value is substituted.

```
<sname>    symbol name
<mname>    module name
<fname>    file name
 XXXXh     a 4-digit hexadecimal number, followed by 'h'
```

Warnings

TLINK has only three warnings. The first two deal with duplicate definitions of symbols; the third, applicable to tiny model programs, indicates that no stack has been defined. Here are the messages:

Warning: XXX is duplicated in module YYY

The named symbol is defined twice in the named module. This could happen in Turbo C object files, for example, if two different **pascal** names were spelled using different cases in a source file.

Warning: XXX defined in module YYY is duplicated in module ZZZ

The named symbol is defined in each of the named modules. This could happen if a given object file is named twice in the command line, or if one of the two copies of the symbol were misspelled.

Warning: no stack

This warning is issued if no stack segment is defined in any of the object files or in any of the libraries included in the link. This is a normal message for the tiny memory model in Turbo C, or for any application program that will be converted to a .COM file. For other programs, this indicates an error.

If a Turbo C program produces this message for any but the tiny memory model, check the C0x start-up object files to be sure they are correct.

Non-Fatal Errors

TLINK has only two non-fatal errors. As mentioned, when a non-fatal error occurs, the .EXE and .MAP files are not deleted. However, these same errors are treated as fatal errors under the Integrated Environment. Here are the error messages:

XXX is unresolved in module YYY

The named symbol is referenced in the given module but is not defined anywhere in the set of object files and libraries included in the link. Check the spelling of the symbol for correctness. You will usually see this error from TLINK for Turbo C symbols if you did not properly match a symbol's declarations of **pascal** and **cdecl** type in different source files

Fixup overflow, frame = xxxxh, target = xxxxh, offset = xxxxh in module XXXXXXX

This indicates an incorrect data or code reference in an object file that TLINK must fix up at link time. In a *fixup*, the object file indicates the name of a memory location being referenced and the name of a segment that the memory location should be in. The *frame* value is the segment where the memory location should be according to the object file. The *target* value is the segment where the memory location actually is. The *offset* field is the offset within the target segment where the memory location is.

This message is most often caused by a mismatch of memory models. A **near** call to a function in a different code segment is the most likely cause. This error can also result if you generate a **near** call to a data variable or a data reference to a function.

To diagnose the problem, generate a map with public symbols (/m). The value of the target and offset fields in the error message should be the address of the symbol being referenced. If the target and offset fields do not match some symbol in the map, look for the symbol nearest to the address given in the message. The reference is in the named module, so look in the source file of that module for the offending reference.

If these techniques do not identify the cause of the failure, or if you are programming in assembly language or some other high-level language besides Turbo C, there may be other possible causes for this message. Even in Turbo C, this message could be generated if you are using different segment or group names than the default values for a given memory model.

Fatal Errors

When fatal errors happen, TLINK stops and deletes the .EXE and .MAP files.

XXXXXXXX.XXX: bad object file
An ill-formed object file was encountered. This is most commonly caused by naming a source file or by naming an object file that was not completely built. This can occur if the machine was rebooted during a compile, or if a compiler did not delete its output object file when a *Ctrl-brk* was struck.

XXXXXXXX.XXX: unable to open file
This occurs if the named file does not exist or is misspelled.

Bad character in parameters
One of the following characters was encountered in the command line or in a response file: " * < = > ? [ ] | or any control character other than horizontal tab, line feed, carriage return, or *Ctrl-Z.*

msdos error, ax = XXXXh
This occurs if an MS-DOS call returned an unexpected error. The *ax* value printed is the resulting error code. This could indicate a TLINK

internal error or an MS-DOS error. The only MS-DOS calls TLINK makes where this error could occur are read, write, and close.

Not enough memory

There was not enough memory to complete the link process. Try removing any terminate-and-stay-resident applications currently loaded, or reduce the size of any RAM disk currently active. Then run TLINK again.

Segment exceeds 64K

This message will occur if too much data was defined for a given data or code segment, when segments of the same name in different source files are combined. This message also occurs if a group exceeds 64K bytes when the segments of the group are combined.

Symbol limit exceeded

You can define a maximum of 8,182 public symbols, segment names, and group names in a single link. This message is issued if that limit is exceeded.

Unexpected group definition

Group definitions in an object file must appear in a particular sequence. This message will generally occur only if a compiler produced a flawed object file. If this occurs in a file created by Turbo C, try recompiling the file. If the problem persists, contact Borland International.

Unexpected segment definition

Segment definitions in an object file must appear in a particular sequence. This message will generally occur only if a compiler produced a flawed object file. If this occurs in a file created by Turbo C, try recompiling the file. If the problem persists, contact Borland International.

Unknown option

A slash character (/) was encountered on the command line or in a response file without being followed by one of the allowed options.

Write failed, disk full?

This occurs if TLINK could not write all of the data it attempted to write. This is almost certainly caused by the disk being full.

E

Language Syntax Summary

This appendix uses a modified Backus-Naur Form to summarize the syntax for Turbo C constructs. These constructs are arranged categorically, as follows:

- *Lexical Grammar*: tokens, keywords, identifiers, constants, string literals, operators and punctuators
- *Phrase Structure Grammar*: expressions, declarations, statements, external definitions
- *Preprocessing directives*

Lexical Grammar

Tokens

token:
    keyword
    identifier
    constant
    string-literal
    operator
    punctuator

Keywords

keyword: one of the following

asm	do	goto	return	union
auto	double	huge	short	unsigned
break	else	if	signed	void
case	enum	int	sizeof	volatile
cdecl	extern	interrupt	static	while
char	far	long	struct	_cs
const	float	near	switch	_ds
continue	for	pascal	typedef	_es
default		register		_ss

Identifiers

identifier:
  nondigit
  identifier nondigit
  identifier digit

nondigit: one of the following
  a b c d e f g h i j k l m n o p q r s t u v w x y z _ $
  A B C D E F G H I J K L M N O P Q R S T U V W X Y Z

digit: one of the following
  0 1 2 3 4 5 6 7 8 9

Constants

constant:
  floating-constant
  integer-constant
  enumeration-constant
  character-constant

floating-constant:
  fractional-constant exponent-part$_{opt}$ *floating-suffix*$_{opt}$
  digit-sequence exponent-part floating-suffix$_{opt}$

fractional-constant:
  digit-sequence$_{opt}$. *digit-sequence*
  digit-sequence .

exponent-part:
  e *sign*_{opt} *digit-sequence*
  E *sign*_{opt} *digit-sequence*

sign: one of the following
  + −

digit-sequence:
  digit
  digit-sequence digit

floating-suffix: one of the following
  f l F L

integer-constant:
  *decimal-constant integer-suffix*_{opt}
  *octal-constant integer-suffix*_{opt}
  *hexadecimal-constant integer-suffix*_{opt}

decimal-constant:
  nonzero-digit
  decimal-constant digit

octal-constant:
  0
  octal-constant octal-digit

hexadecimal-constant:
  0 x *hexadecimal-digit*
  0 X *hexadecimal-digit*
  hexadecimal-constant hexadecimal-digit

nonzero-digit: one of the following
  1 2 3 4 5 6 7 8 9

octal-digit: one of the following
  0 1 2 3 4 5 6 7

hexadecimal-digit: one of the following
  0 1 2 3 4 5 6 7 8 9
  a b c d e f
  A B C D E F

integer-suffix:
  *unsigned-suffix long-suffix*_{opt}
  *long-suffix unsigned-suffix*_{opt}

unsigned-suffix: one of the following
  u U

long-suffix: one of the following
  l L

enumeration-constant:
  identifier

character-constant:
  c-char-sequence

c-char-sequence:
  c-char
  c-char-sequence c-char

c-char:
    any character in the source character set except
    the single-quote ('), backslash (\), or newline ( ) character

    escape-sequence

escape-sequence: one of the following

\'	\b	\v	\xhh
\"	\f	\o	\xhhh
\?	\n	\oo	\Xh
\\	\r	\ooo	\Xhh
\a	\t	\xh	\Xhhh

String Literals

string-literal:
  " *s-char-sequence*_{opt} "

s-char-sequence:
  s-char
  s-char-sequence s-char

s-char:
    any character in the source character set except
    the double-quote ("), backslash (\), or newline ( ) character

    escape-sequence

Operators

operator: one of the following

[]	()	.	- >	++	--
&	*	+	-	˜	!
sizeof /	%	<<	>>	<
>	<=	>=	==	!	=
^	|	&&	||	? :	=
*=	/=	%=	+=	-=	<<=
>>=	&=	^=	|=	.	#
##					

Punctuators

punctuator: one of the following

[ ]	( )	{ }	*	,	:
=	;	...	#		

Phrase Structure Grammar

Expressions

primary-expression:
   identifier
   constant
   pseudo-variable
   string-literal
   (*expression*)

pseudo-variable:

_AX	_AL	_AH	_SI	_ES
_BX	_BL	_BH	_DI	_SS
_CX	_CL	_CH	_BP	_CS
_DX	_DL	_DH	_SP	_DS

postfix-expression:
    primary-expression
    postfix-expression [*expression*]
    postfix-expression (*argument-expression-list*_{opt})
    postfix-expression . *identifier*
    postfix-expression – > *identifier*
    postfix-expression ++
    postfix-expression —

argument-expression-list:
    assignment-expression
    argument-expression-list , *assignment-expression*

unary-expression:
    postfix-expression
    ++ *unary-expression*
    - - *unary-expression*
    unary-operator cast-expression
    sizeof *unary-expression*
    sizeof (*type-name*)

unary-operator: one of the following
    & * + – ~ !

cast-expression:
    unary-expression
    (*type-name*) *cast-expression*

multiplicative-expression:
    cast-expression
    multiplicative-expression * *cast-expression*
    multiplicative-expression / *cast-expression*
    multiplicative-expression % *cast-expression*

additive-expression:
    multiplicative-expression
    additive-expression + *multiplicative-expression*
    additive-expression – *multiplicative-expression*

shift-expression:
  additive-expression
  shift-expression < < *additive-expression*
  shift-expression > > *additive-expression*

relational-expression:
  shift-expression
  relational-expression < *shift-expression*
  relational-expression > *shift-expression*
  relational-expression <= *shift-expression*
  relational-expression >= *shift-expression*

equality-expression:
  relational-expression
  equality expression = = *relational-expression*
  equality expression ! = *relational-expression*

AND-expression:
  equality-expression
  AND-expression & *equality-expression*

exclusive-OR-expression:
  AND-expression
  exclusive-OR-expression ^ *AND-expression*

inclusive-OR-expression:
  exclusive-OR-expression
  inclusive-OR-expression | *exclusive-OR-expression*

logical-AND-expression:
  inclusive-OR-expression
  logical-AND-expression && *inclusive-OR-expression*

logical-OR-expression:
  logical-AND-expression
  logical-OR-expression || *logical-AND-expression*

conditional-expression:
  logical-OR-expression
  logical-OR-expression ? *expression* : *conditional-expression*

assignment-expression:
  conditional-expression
  unary-expression assignment-operator assignment-expression

assignment-operator: one of the following

    =   *=   /=   %=   +=   − =

```
<<=   >>=   &=     ^=      |=
```

expression:
   assignment-expression
   expression , assignment-expression

constant-expression:
   conditional-expression

Declarations

---

declaration:
   declaration-specifiers init-declarator-list$_{opt}$

declaration-specifiers:
   storage-class-specifier declaration-specifiers$_{opt}$
   type-specifier declaration-specifiers$_{opt}$

init-declarator-list:
   init-declarator
   init-declarator-list , init-declarator

init-declarator:
   declarator
   declarator = initializer

storage-class-specifier:
   typedef
   extern
   static
   auto
   register

type-specifier:
  void
  char
  short
  int
  long
  float
  double
  signed
  unsigned
  const
  volatile
  struct-or-union-specifier
  enum-specifier
  typedef-name

struct-or-union-specifier:
  struct-or-union identifier$_{opt}$ { *struct-declaration-list* }
  struct-or-union identifier

struct-or-union:
  struct
  union

struct-declaration-list:
  struct-declaration
  struct-declaration-list struct-declaration

struct-declaration:
  type-specifier-list struct-declarator-list;

type-specifier-list:
  type-specifier
  type-specifier-list type-specifier

struct-declarator-list:
  struct-declarator
  struct-declarator-list , *struct-declarator*

struct-declarator:
  declarator
  declarator$_{opt}$: *constant-expression*

enum-specifier:
  enum *identifier*$_{opt}$ { *enumerator-list* }
  enum *identifier*

enumerator-list:
   enumerator
   enumerator-list , enumerator

enumerator:
   enumeration-constant
   enumeration-constant = constant-expression

declarator:
   pointer$_{opt}$ *direct-declarator*
   modifier-list$_{opt}$

direct-declarator:
   identifier
   (declarator)
   direct-declarator [*constant-expression*$_{opt}$]
   direct-declarator (*parameter-type-list*)
   direct-declarator (*identifier-list*$_{opt}$)

pointer:
   * *type-specifier-list*$_{opt}$
   * *type-specifier-list*$_{opt}$ *pointer*

modifier-list:
   modifier
   modifier-list modifier

modifier:
   cdecl
   pascal
   interrupt
   near
   far
   huge

parameter-type-list:
   parameter-list
   parameter-list , ...

parameter-list:
   parameter-declaration
   parameter-list , parameter-declaration

parameter-declaration:
   declaration-specifiers declarator
   declaration-specifiers abstract-declarataor$_{opt}$

identifier-list:
  identifier
  identifier-list , *identifier*

type-name:
  type-specified-list abstract-declarator$_{opt}$

abstract-declarator:
  pointer
  pointer$_{opt}$ *direct-abstract-declarator*$_{opt}$
  modifier-list$_{opt}$

modifier-list:
  modifier
  modifier-list modifier

modifier:
  cdecl
  pascal
  interrupt
  near
  far
  huge

direct-abstract-declarator:
  (*abstract-declarator*)
  direct-abstract-declarator$_{opt}$ [*constant-expression*$_{opt}$]
  direct-abstract-declarator$_{opt}$ (*parameter-type-list*$_{opt}$)

typedef-name:
  identifier

initializer:
  assignment-expression
  { *initializer-list* }
  { *initializer-list* , }

initializer-list:
  initializer
  initializer-list , *initializer*

Statements

statement:
> labeled-statement
> compound-statement
> expression-statement
> selection-statement
> iteration-statement
> jump-statement
> asm-statement

asm-statement
> **asm** tokens newline
> **asm** tokens;

labeled-statement:
> identifier : statement
> **case** constant-expression : statement
> **default** : statement

compound-statement:
> { declaration-list$_{opt}$ statement-list$_{opt}$ }

declaration-list:
> declaration
> declaration-list declaration

statement-list:
> statement
> statement-list statement

expression-statement:
> expression$_{opt}$

selection-statement:
> **if** (expression) statement
> **if** (expression) statement **else** statement
> **switch** (expression) statement

iteration-statement:
> **while** (expression) statement
> **do** statement **while** (expression);
> **for** (expression$_{opt}$; expression$_{opt}$; expression$_{opt}$) statement

jump-statement
    goto *identifier* ;
    continue ;
    break ;
    return *expression*$_{opt}$;

External Definitions

file:
    external-definition
    file external-definition

external-definition:
    function-definition
    declaration

asm-statement
    asm *tokens newline*
    asm *tokens*;

function-definition:
    declaration-specifiers$_{opt}$ *declarator declaration-list*$_{opt}$ *compound-statement*

Preprocessing Directives

preprocessing-file:
    group

group:
    group-part
    group group-part

group-part:
    pp-tokens$_{opt}$ *newline*
    if-section
    control-line

if-section:
    if-group elif-groups$_{opt}$ *else-group*$_{opt}$ *endif-line*

if-group:
    #if *constant-expression newline group*$_{opt}$
    #ifdef *identifier newline group*$_{opt}$
    #ifndef *identifier newline group*$_{opt}$

elif-groups:
    elif-group
    elif-groups elif-group

elif-group:
    #elif *constant-expression newline group*$_{opt}$

else-group:
    #else *newline group*$_{opt}$

endif-line:
    #endif *newline*

control-line:
    #include *pp-tokens newline*
    #define *identifier replacement-list newline*
    #define *identifier lparen identifier-list*$_{opt}$ *) replacement-list newline*
    #undef *identifier newline*
    #line *pp-tokens newline*
    #error *pp-tokens*$_{opt}$ *newline*
    #pragma *pp-tokens*$_{opt}$ *newline*
    #pragma **warn** *action abbreviation newline*
    #pragma **inline** *newline*
    #   *newline*

action:
    +
    –
    .

abbreviation:

amb	dyn	pia	str
amp	dup	pro	stu
apt	eff	rch	stv
ans	fun	ret	sus
cln	ign	rpt	use
cpt	mod	rvl	voi
def	par	sig	zst

lparen:
    the left-parenthesis character without preceding white space

replacement-list:
  *pp-tokens*_{opt}

pp-tokens:
  preprocessing-token
  pp-tokens preprocessing-token

preprocessing-token:
  header-name (only within an `#include` directive)
  identifier   (no *keyword* distinction)
  constant
  string-literal
  operator
  punctuator
  each non-whitespace character that cannot be one of the preceding

header-name:
  <*h-char-sequence*>

h-char-sequence:
  h-char
  h-char-sequence h-char

h-char:
  any character in the source character set except
  the newline greater than (>) character

newline:
  the newline character

F

Customizing Turbo C

Turbo C comes ready to run, as soon as you make working copies of the disk files. There is no installation, *per se*. But you do have the option of changing many of Turbo C's default modes of operation by running this customization program. This program, TCINST.COM, lets you do six things:

- set up a path to your configuration and Help files
- customize your Editor commands
- modify your default edit modes
- set up your default screen mode
- change your screen colors
- change the size of Turbo C's windows

If you want to store your help (TCHELP.TCH) or configuration files (TCCONFIG.TC) in a directory other than the one where you do your work, you'll need to use the Turbo C directory option to set a path to those files.

If you're either unfamiliar with Turbo C's editor or inexorably tied to another editor, you can use the Editor commands option to reconfigure (customize) the editor keystrokes to your liking.

You can also use the Default editor mode option to set several defaults for the editor. You can choose to

- load and save a pick list
- work in insert or overwrite mode
- turn tabs *on* or *off*

- work with auto-indent *on* or *off*

You can set up the display mode that Turbo C will use when it is in operation and specify whether you have a "snowy" video adapter.

You can customize the colors of almost every part of the Turbo C screen output.

And finally, you can change the default sizes of the Edit and Message windows.

Running TCINST

To get started, type TCINST at the DOS prompt. The first (main installation) menu lets you select the **T**urbo C directory, **E**ditor commands, **D**efault edit modes, **S**creen mode, **C**olors, **R**esize windows, or **Q**uit/save/abort. You can either press the highlighted capital letter of the preferred option or use the *Up* and *Down* arrow keys to move to your selection and then press *Enter*; for instance, press *D* to modify the **D**efault edit modes. In general, pressing *Esc* (more than once if necessary) will return you from a submenu to the main installation menu.

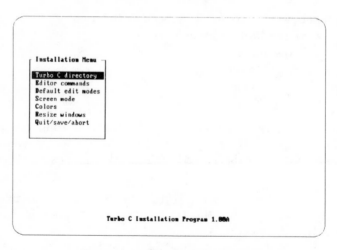

```
Installation Menu
┌─────────────────────┐
│ Turbo C directory   │
│ Editor commands     │
│ Default edit modes  │
│ Screen mode         │
│ Colors              │
│ Resize windows      │
│ Quit/save/abort     │
└─────────────────────┘


      Turbo C Installation Program 1.00A
```

Figure F.1: TCINST Installation Menu

The Turbo C Directory Option

You'll use the Turbo C directory option to specify a path to your standard configuration and Help files, so that they are accessible from wherever you call up Turbo C.

When you select the Turbo C directory option, you're prompted to enter the full path to your Turbo directory. (This is where your standard configuration and Help files are kept; see the Environment option in the Options pull-down menu in Chapter 2 of the *Turbo C User's Guide*. For example, if you want Turbo C to look for the standard configuration file in a directory called TURBOC (if it's not found in your current directory), then you might type for your path name

```
C:\TURBOC
```

After typing a path, press *Enter* to accept it, and the TCINST main installation menu will redisplay. When you exit the program, you're prompted whether you want to save the changes. Once you save the Turbo C path, the location is written to disk. (Note that the Quick-Ref line tells you which keystrokes to use when you're in this screen.)

The Editor Commands Option

This option allows you to change the default editing keys that you use while you're in the Turbo C editor. To modify the Editor commands, press *E* or move the selection bar to the option and press *Enter*. The help line at the top of the screen shows you which keys to use to move around and make changes. Most of these commands are simply movement commands; the **R** option, however, is useful when you want to restore the keystrokes to the factory defaults. You'll notice that you can modify only the secondary, or highlighted, keystrokes.

```
┌─────────────────────────────────────────────────────────────────┐
│ ═══════════════ Turbo C Installation Program ═══════════Command══ │
│      ←-backspace  C-clear  R-restore  ◄┘-accept edit  <Scroll Lock> literal │
│ ════════════════════════════════════════════════════════════════ │
│ New Line                  <Enter>              <Enter>            │
│ Cursor Left               <CtrlS>              <Lft>              │
│ Cursor Right              <CtrlD>              <Rgt>              │
│ Word Left                 <CtrlA>              <CtrlLft>          │
│ Word Right                <CtrlF>              <CtrlRgt>          │
│ Cursor Up                 <CtrlE>              <Up>               │
│ Cursor Down               <CtrlX>              <Dn>               │
│ Scroll Up                 <CtrlW>                                │
│ Scroll Down               <CtrlZ>                                │
│ Page Up                   <CtrlR>              <PgUp>             │
│ Page Down                 <CtrlC>              <PgDn>             │
│ Left of Line              <CtrlQ><CtrlS>       ▓<Home>▓▓▓▓       │
│ Right of Line             <CtrlQ><CtrlD>       <End>             │
│ Top of Screen             <CtrlQ><CtrlE>       <CtrlHome>        │
│ Bottom of Screen          <CtrlQ><CtrlX>       <CtrlEnd>         │
│ Top of File               <CtrlQ><CtrlR>       <CtrlPgUp>        │
│ Bottom of File            <CtrlQ><CtrlC>       <CtrlPgDn>        │
│ Move to Block Begin       <CtrlQ><CtrlB>                         │
│ Move to Block End         <CtrlQ><CtrlK>                         │
│ Move to Previous Position <CtrlQ><CtrlP>                         │
│ Move to Marker 0          <CtrlQ>0                               │
│ Move to Marker 1          <CtrlQ>1                               │
└─────────────────────────────────────────────────────────────────┘
```

Figure F.2: Changing Default Editor Commands

Once you press *Enter* to modify the keystroke(s), you'll see a selection bar next to the command you want to redefine. If you take another look at the top of the screen, you'll see that the help line now lists the available commands:

<- backspace **C** clear **R** restore ⏎ accept edit <**Scroll Lock**> literal

backspace　　Use the *Backspace* key to backspace or delete something in the keystroke box.

clear　　The **C** option clears, or erases, the whole box.

restore　　Use **R** to restore the original keystrokes before exiting from the screen.

accept edit　　The ⏎ stands for the *Enter* key; pressing *Enter* accepts the keystroke modification you've made.

<**Scroll Lock**>　　This is a toggle that lets you alternate between command and literal modes.

To understand the <**Scroll Lock**> option, take a look at the *Enter* key, which is used to modify and accept the editing of a key command. If you wanted, for example, to use *Enter* as part of Find String's keystrokes (*Ctrl-Q F*), you would have to follow these steps:

1. Make sure <**Scroll Lock**> is toggled to command (check the upper right-hand corner of your screen).

2. Press *Enter* at the Find String command line.

3. Press *Backspace* to delete the *Ctrl-F* part of the string.

4. Now toggle <**Scroll Lock**> to `literal` and press *Enter*— voilà.

5. Again, toggle <**Scroll Lock**> to `command` and press *Enter* to accept.

After you've defined the new keystroke(s) for a command, press *Enter* to accept them. If you've finished making changes, press *Esc* to exit. If you still have more changes to make, use the arrow keys to scroll up and down the list and select your next command.

At this point, if you've accidentally assigned a keystroke sequence that's been used as a control character sequence in the primary command column, the message

```
Command conflicts need to be corrected. Press <ESC>
```

will flash at the bottom of the screen. Any duplicated sequences will be highlighted, which enables you to easily search for any disallowed items and to reselect a sequence. If you change your mind, you can use the **R** option to restore all of the factory defaults.

Also, if you assign a hot key to one of the commands, the message

```
<function key> is a built-in hot key. Press <ESC>
```

flashes at the bottom of the screen. Pressing *Esc* takes you back to the command you were changing so that you can reselect a key assignment.

The Default Edit Modes Option

Press *D* to bring up the **D**efault edit modes menu. There are four editor modes you can install: Load/save pick list, Insert mode, Auto-indent mode, and **T**abs. These are all toggles.

Load/save pick list   With this option *on*, Turbo C will automatically save the current pick list when you exit Turbo C, and then reload that file upon reentering the program. If you have this option *off* when you exit Turbo C, your pick list will not be saved.

Insert   With Insert mode *on*, anything you enter at the keyboard is inserted at the cursor position, pushing any text to the right of the cursor further right. Toggling Insert mode *off* allows you to overwrite text at the cursor.

Auto-indent   With Auto-indent mode *on*, the cursor returns to the starting column of the previous line when you press *Enter*. When toggled *off*, the cursor always returns to column one.

Tab   With Tab mode *on*, a tab is placed in the text using a fixed tab stop of 8. Toggle it *off*, and it spaces to the beginning of the first letter of each word in the previous line.

When you load Turbo C, the default value for Load/save pick list is off; the default values for the other three modes are *on*. You can change the defaults to suit your preferences and save them back to Turbo C. Of course, you'll still be able to toggle these modes from inside Turbo C's editor.

Look at the Quick-Ref line for directions on how to select these options: Either use the arrow keys to move the selection bar to the option and then press *Enter*, or press the key that corresponds to the highlighted capital letter of the option.

The Screen Mode Option

Normally, Turbo C will correctly detect your system's video mode so you should only change the Screen mode option if

- you want to select a mode other than your current video mode
- you have a Color/Graphics Adapter that doesn't "snow"
- you think Turbo C is incorrectly detecting your hardware

Press *S* to select Screen mode from the installation menu. A pop-up menu will appear; from this menu you can select the screen mode Turbo C will use during operation. Your options include Default, Color, Black and white, or Monochrome. These are fairly intuitive.

Default   By default, Turbo C will always operate in the mode that is active when you load it.

Color   Turbo C will use color mode with 80 x 25 characters, no matter what mode is active, and switches back to the previously active mode when you exit.

Black and White   Turbo C will use black and white mode with 80 x 25 characters, no matter what mode is active, and switches back to the previously active mode when you exit.

Monochrome   Turbo C will use monochrome mode, no matter what mode is active, and switches back to the previously active mode when you exit.

When you select one of the first three options, the program conducts a video test on your screen; the Quick-Ref line tells you what to do. When you press any key, a window comes up with the query `Was there Snow on the screen?`. You can choose

- **Yes**, the screen was "snowy;"
- **No**, always turn off snow checking;
- **Maybe**, always check the hardware; look to the Quick-Ref line for more about **Maybe**.

Press *Esc* to return to the main installation menu.

The Color Customization Option

Pressing *C* from the main installation menu allows you to make extensive changes to the Colors of your version of Turbo C. After pressing *C*, you will see a menu with these options:

- **Customize colors**
- **1st color set**
- **2nd color set**
- **3rd color set**

Because there are nearly 50 different screen items that can be given their own customized colors, you will probably find it easier to choose a *preset* set of colors to your liking. Three preset color sets are on disk. Press *1, 2,* or *3* and scroll through the colors for the Turbo C screen items using the *PgUp* and *PgDn* keys. If none of the preset color sets is to your liking, however, you can still design your own.

To make custom colors, press *C* to Customize colors. Now you have a choice of 12 types of items that can be color-customized in Turbo C; some of these are text items, some are screen lines and boxes. Choose one of these items by pressing a letter **A** through **L**.

Once you choose a screen item to color-customize, you will see a pop-up menu and a *view port:* The first is an example of the screen item you chose; the second displays the components of that selection, and also reflects the change in colors as you scroll through the color palette. For example, if you chose **H** to customize the colors of Turbo C's error boxes, you would see a new menu with the four different parts of an error box: its **Title, Border, Normal** text, and **Inverse** text.

You must now select one of the components from the pop-up menu. Type the appropriate highlighted letter, and you're treated to a color palette for the item you chose. Using the arrow keys, select a color to your liking. Press *Enter* to record your selection.

Repeat this procedure for every screen item you want to change the color of. When you are finished, press *Esc* until you are back at the main installation menu.

Note: Turbo C maintains three internal color tables: one each for color, black and white, and monochrome. TCINST only allows you to change one set of colors at a time, based upon your current video mode. So, for example, if you wanted to change to the black and white color table, you would set your video mode to BW80 at the DOS prompt and then load TCINST.

The Resize Windows Option

This option allows you to change the respective sizes of the Edit and Message windows in Turbo C. Press *R* to choose **R**esize windows from the main installation menu.

Using the *Up* and *Down* arrow keys, you can move the bar dividing the Edit window from the Message window. Neither window can be smaller than three lines. When you have resized the windows to your liking, press *Enter*. You can discard your changes and return to the Installation menu by pressing *Esc*.

Quitting the Program

Once you have finished making all desired changes, select **Quit/save/edit** at the main installation menu. The message

```
Save changes to TC.EXE? (Y/N)
```

will appear at the bottom of the screen.

- If you press *Y* (for **Y**es), all the changes you have made will be permanently installed into Turbo C. (Of course, you can always run this program again if you want to change them.)
- If you press *N* (for **N**o), your changes will be ignored and you will be returned to the operating system prompt.

If you decide you want to restore the original Turbo C factory defaults, simply copy TC.EXE from your master disk onto your work disk. You can also restore the Editor commands by selecting the **E** option at the main menu, then press *R* (for Restore) and *Esc*.

G

MicroCalc

MicroCalc—written in Turbo C—is a spreadsheet program. Its source code files and an object file are provided with your TURBO C system as an example program. The spreadsheet program is an electronic piece of paper on which you can enter text, numbers and formulas, and have MicroCalc do calculations on them automatically.

About MicroCalc

Since MicroCalc is only a demonstration program, it has its limitations (which you may have fun eliminating):

- You cannot copy formulas from one cell to others
- You cannot copy text or values from one cell to others
- Cells that are summed must be in the same column or row

In spite of its limitations, MicroCalc does provide some interesting features. Among these are the following:

- Writing directly to video memory for maximum display speed
- Full set of mathematical functions
- Built-in line editor for text and formula editing
- Ability to enter text across cells

In addition to these, MicroCalc offers many of the usual features of a spreadsheet program; you can do all of the following:

- Load a spreadsheet from the disk
- Save a spreadsheet on the disk
- Automatically recalculate after each entry (may be disabled)
- Print the spreadsheet on the printer
- Clear the current spreadsheet.
- Delete columns and rows
- Set a column's width
- Insert blank columns and rows between existing ones

How to Compile and Run MicroCalc

Compiling MicroCalc is easy. All you need to do is copy all the MC*.* files from your distribution disk to your TURBOC directory (where TC.EXE and/or TCC.EXE reside). You can compile and run MicroCalc with either version of Turbo C. In both cases, compiling under a large data model (COMPACT, LARGE, or HUGE) will give you much more memory for your spreadsheets.

With TC.EXE

After you have set the INCLUDE and LIB directories in the O/Environment menu, do the following:

1. Run TC.EXE
2. In the Project menu, specify the project name "MCALC.PRJ"
3. From the main menu select the Run option

With TCC.EXE

Compile from DOS with the following command line:

```
TCC mcalc mcparser mcdisply mcinput mcommand mcutil mcmvsmem.obj
```

Note: You must also specify the INCLUDE and LIB directories with the -I and -L command-line options, respectively.

How to use MicroCalc

Once you have compiled MicroCalc, you can run it in one of two ways.

If you compiled with the **R**un command from TC, MicroCalc will come up on your screen; when you exit, you will return to Turbo C.

If you want to run MCALC.EXE from the DOS command line, just type MCALC. (If you already have a spreadsheet file, you can automatically load it by typing

```
MCALC <your_file>
```

at the DOS prompt.)

This is an example of what you will see once MicroCalc is loaded:

```
            A        B        C        D        E        F        G
1        22.00
2         1.00
3         2.00
4         3.00
5        28.00

...

20
A5 Formula
A1+A2+A3+A4
```

The MicroCalc screen is divided into cells. A cell is a space on the spreadsheet designated by a column-row pair. By default, each column is 10 characters wide; you can change this to a maximum of 77 characters (each).

The columns are named A-Z and AA-CV; the rows are numbered 1-100. This gives a total of 10000 cells. You can change these limits by modifying the constants MAXROWS and MAXCOLS in MCALC.H.

A cell may contain a value, a formula or some text; these are known as cell types. The type of the cell and its coordinates are shown in the bottom left corner of the screen:

`A5 Formula` Means that the current cell, A5, contains a formula.

`A1 Text` Cell A1 contains text.

`A2 Value` Cell A2 contains a value and no cell references.

In this example the line `A5 Formula` shows that the active cell is cell A5 and that it contains a formula. The last line, `A1+A2+A3+A4`, says the active cell contains the sum of A1 through A4. These two lines mean that the numbers in cells A1, A2, A3 and A4 should be added and the result placed in cell A5.

The formula can be abbreviated to `A1:A4`, meaning "add all cells from A1 to A4".

The following are examples of valid cell formulas:

`A1+(B2-C7)` subtract cell C7 from B2 and add the result to cell A1

`A1:A23` the sum of cells: A1,A2,A3..A23

The formulas may be as complicated as you want; for example:

`SIN(A1)*COS(A2)/((1.2*A8)+LOG(ABS(A8)+8.9E-3))+(C1:C5)`

To enter data in any cell, move the cursor to that cell and enter the data. MicroCalc automatically determines if the cell's type is value, formula, or text.

Standard MicroCalc Functions and Operators

+, -, *, /	addition, subtraction, multiplication, division
^ -	raises a number to a power (example: 2^3 = 8)
:	returns the sum of a group of cells (ex: A1:A4 = A1+A2+A3+A4)
ABS	absolute value
ACOS	arc cosine
ASIN	arc sine
ATAN	arc tangent
COS	cosine
COSH	hyperbolic cosine
EXP	exponential function
LOG	logarithm
LOG10	base 10 logarithm
POW10	raise argument to the 10th power
ROUND	round to the nearest whole number
SIN	sine
SINH	hyperbolic sine
SQR	square
SQRT	square root
TAN	tangent
TANH	hyperbolic tangent
TRUNC	return the whole part of a number

/	brings up the main menu

/SL	loads a spreadsheet
/SS	saves the current spreadsheet
/SP	prints the current spreadsheet
/SC	clears the current spreadsheet

/F	formats a group of cells
/D	deletes the current cell
/G	moves the cursor to a selected cell

/CI	inserts a column
/CD	deletes the current column
/CW	changes the width of the current column

/RI	inserts a row
/RD	deletes the current row

/E	edits the current cell

/UR	recalculates the formulas in the spreadsheet
/UF	toggles the display of the text of formulas in cells instead of the value of the formulas

/A	toggles AutoCalc on/off
/Q	quits from MicroCalc
DEL	deletes the current cell
HOME	moves to cell A1
END	moves to the rightmost column and bottom row of the spreadsheet

PGUP and PGDN	move up or down a full screen
F2	allows you to edit the data in the current cell.

While you're editing, the following commands work:

ESC	disregards changes made to the data.
←,→ ↑,↓,↵	The left and right arrow keys move to the left and right. The up and down arrow keys, and the Enter key, enter the input then return to the current cell.
HOME	moves to the start of the input.
END	moves to the end of the input.
DEL	deletes the character under the cursor.
INS	changes between insert/overwrite mode.
Backspace	deletes the character to the left of the cursor.

The MicroCalc Parser

This information is provided in case you want to modify the MicroCalc parser (for instance, you might want to add a function that takes two parameters). The state and goto information for the parser was created using the UNIX YACC utility. The input to YACC was as follows:

```
%token CONST CELL FUNC
%%
e : e '+' t
  | e '-' t
  | t

t : t '*' f
  | t '/' f
  | f

f : x '^' f
  | x

x : '-' u
  | u

u : CELL ':' CELL
  | o

o : CELL
  | '(' e ')'
  | CONST
  | FUNC '(' e ')'

%%
```

Index

C

cabs, 58
calloc, 157
Carriage-return/line-feed
  translation, *See* Mode
Carry flag, 140-41, 143
Case-sensitive link, 350
ceil, 58
cgets, 129
Character
  classification, 12, 147
  conversion 12, 248
  conversion type, in printf, 180-182
  conversion type, in scanf, 205-207
  delete, 268
  devices, 149
  insert, 268
  translation, 248
Characters conversion routines, 12
chdir, 59
_chmod, 60
chmod, 60
Classification routines, 12
_clear87, 62
clearerr, 62, 94
_close, 63
close, 63
Co-routines, 154
Color screen, customizing, 379
COMMAND.COM, 246
Command interpreter, *See*
  COMMAND.COM
Command lists in makefiles, 325
Command-line options, 298
  CPP, 311
  LINK, 343
  MAKE, 339
  TCC, 297
Command-line syntax
  MAKE, 336-337
Commands, DOS, 246
Commands, editor, 265
Comparison function
  user-written, 56, 194
Complex numbers, 31

CONIO.H, 10, 13
Console, ungetting characters,
  116-117
Constants, 358
Control-break interrupt, 135
Conventions, notational, *See*
  Typographic Conventions
Conversion
  character, 12, 248
  input, *See* scanf
  number to string, 79
  routines, 12
  specifications, 180
  string, 12, 40
  time, 16, 71, 77
  to integers & fractions, 101
  to numbers, 40
  to strings, 79, 149
  type characters, in printf, 180-183
coreleft, 157
cos, 65, 250
cosh, 65, 137
Cosine, 250
country, 66
CPP, 311-313
cprintf, 67, 177
cputs, 68, 193
_creat, 68
creat, 68
CR-LF translation, *See* Mode
cscanf, 71, 201
ctime, 71
ctrlbrk, 74
CTYPE.H, 10, 12
Cursor movement, 267-268
Customizing colors, 379-380
Customizing TC, 373-381

D

Data conversion, *See also* Conversion
  atof, 40
  atoi, 41
  atol, 41
  ecvt, 79
  fcvt, 93

F

G

K

kbhit, 150
keep, 150
Keystroke, testing for, 150
keywords, 358

L

labs, 30-31, 151
ldexp, 85, 151
Lexical grammar, 357
lfind, 55, 151
Libraries, 308, 347
LIMITS.H, 10
Linear searches, 55
Link map option, 308
Linker stand-alone, 343
Load/Save pick list, 377
localtime, 71
lock, 152
log, 85, 153
log10, 85, 153
Logarithmic functions
  log, 85
  log10, 85
longjmp, 74, 153
lsearch, 55, 155
lseek, 155
ltoa, 149, 157

M

Macros
  character classification, 147-148
  expansion, 311
  fileno, 97
  getc, 116
  getchar, 116
  inportb, 139, 140
  is..., 147
  outportb, 139, 172
  peek, 173
  peekb, 173
  poke, 175

pokeb, 175
putc, 191
putchar, 191, 192
_tolower, 248, 249
_toupper, 248, 249
va_end, 254, 256
va_start, 254, 258
Major version number, 26
MAKE directives, 332
MAKE, 314-342
MAKE macros
  $* Base file name, 330
  $d Defined test, 330
  $. File name and extension, 332
  $& File name only, 332
  $: File name path, 332
  $< Full file name, 331
  definitions, 327
  expansion, 328
  in makefiles, 328
  invocation, 329
MAKEFILE, *See* makefile
makefile, 314-343
makefile rules, 320-325
Make file name, 166
malloc, 157
map, link, 308, 348
Math errors, *See* matherr
Math routines
  absolute value, 30
  ceil, 58, 100
  error handling, 31, 85, 100, 138
  exponential functions, 85-87
  floor, 100
  fmod, 101
  hyperbolic functions, 137
  hypotenuse, 138
  in math.h, 15
  matherr, 159, 161
  modulo, 101
  polynomial, 176
  remainder, 101
  rounding, 100
  trig functions, 250
MATH.H, 10, 15
_matherr, 159
matherr, 161

U

ultoa, 149, 252
UNDERFLOW, 162
ungetc, 116, 252
ungetch, 116, 252
unixtodos, 77, 253
unlink, 253
unlock, 152, 254
Utilities, 311-354

V

va_..., 254
va_arg, 257
va_end, 257
VALUES.H, 11
Variable
  argument list, 257
  daylight, 21
  _doserrno, 21
  environ, 25
  errno, 21
  _fmode, 24
  global, 15-20
  _osmajor, 26
  _osminor, 26
  _psp, 25
  sys_errlist, 21
  sys_nerr, 21

timezone, 21
  _version, 26
va_start, 254, 258
Verify flag, 133
vfprintf, 177
vfscanf, 201, 258
vprintf, 177
vscanf, 201, 259
vsprintf, 179, 259
vsscanf, 201, 260

W

Warnings
  Linker, 352
  Compiler, 292, 305
Width specification
  printf, 186
  scanf, 210
Windows
  Edit, 263
  resizing, 380
WordStar vs. Turbo C editor, 263,
  274-76
Write
  randbwr, 197
  random block, 197
  to a file, 260
  _write, 260
write, 260

Borland
Software

BORLAND
INTERNATIONAL

4585 Scotts Valley Drive, Scotts Valley, CA 95066

Available at better dealers nationwide.
To order by credit card, call (800) 255-8008; CA (800) 742-1133;
CANADA (800) 237-1136.

SIDEKICK:® THE DESKTOP ORGANIZER

Whether you're running WordStar,® Lotus,® dBASE,® or any other program, SideKick puts all these desktop accessories at your fingertips—Instantly!

A full-screen WordStar-like Editor to jot down notes and edit files up to 25 pages long.

A Phone Directory for names, addresses, and telephone numbers. Finding a name or a number is a snap.

An Autodialer for all your phone calls. It will look up and dial telephone numbers for you. (A modem is required to use this function.)

A Monthly Calendar from 1901 through 2099.

Appointment Calendar to remind you of important meetings and appointments.

A full-featured Calculator ideal for business use. It also performs decimal to hexadecimal to binary conversions.

An ASCII Table for easy reference.

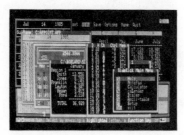

All the SideKick windows stacked up over Lotus 1-2-3.® From bottom to top: SideKick's "Menu Window," ASCII Table, Notepad, Calculator, Appointment Calendar, Monthly Calendar, and Phone Dialer.

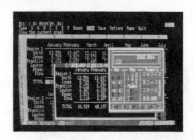

Here's SideKick running over Lotus 1-2-3. In the SideKick Notepad you'll notice data that's been imported directly from the Lotus screen. In the upper right you can see the Calculator.

The Critics' Choice

"In a simple, beautiful implementation of WordStar's block copy commands, SideKick can transport all or any part of the display screen (even an area overlaid by the notepad display) to the notepad."
—Charles Petzold, PC MAGAZINE

"SideKick deserves a place in every PC."
—Gary Ray, PC WEEK

"SideKick is by far the best we've seen. It is also the least expensive."
—Ron Mansfield, ENTREPRENEUR

"If you use a PC, get SideKick. You'll soon become dependent on it."
—Jerry Pournelle, BYTE

Suggested Retail Price: $84.95 (not copy protected)

Minimum system configuration: IBM PC, XT, AT, PCjr and true compatibles. PC-DOS (MS-DOS) 2.0 or greater. 128K RAM. One disk drive. A Hayes-compatible modem, IBM PCjr internal modem, or AT&T Modem 4000 is required for the autodialer function.

BORLAND
INTERNATIONAL

SideKick is a registered trademark of Borland International, Inc. dBASE is a registered trademark of Ashton-Tate. IBM, XT, AT, and PCjr are registered trademarks of International Business Machines Corp. AT&T is a registered trademark of American Telephone & Telegraph Company. Lotus and 1-2-3 are registered trademarks of Lotus Development Corp. WordStar is a registered trademark of MicroPro International Corp. Hayes is a trademark of Hayes Microcomputer Products, Inc. Copyright 1987 Borland International

BOR0060C

Traveling SIDEKICK®

The Organizer For The Computer Age!

Traveling SideKick is *BinderWare*,® both a binder you take with you when you travel and a software program—which includes a Report Generator—that *generates* and *prints out* all the information you'll need to take with you.

Information like your phone list, your client list, your address book, your calendar, and your appointments. The appointment or calendar files you're already using in your SideKick® can automatically be used by your Traveling SideKick. You don't waste time and effort reentering information that's already there.

One keystroke prints out a form like your address book. No need to change printer paper;

you simply punch three holes, fold and clip the form into your Traveling SideKick binder, and you're on your way. Because Traveling SideKick is CAD (Computer-Age Designed), you don't fool around with low-tech tools like scissors, tape, or staples. And because Traveling SideKick is electronic, it works this year, next year, and all the "next years" after that. Old-fashioned daytime organizers are history in 365 days.

What's inside Traveling SideKick

TABLET OF EXTRA FORMS
IN POCKET ON BACK FLAP, FOR USE IN ANY OF THE ORGANIZER SECTIONS.

ADDRESS BOOK SECTION
PREPRINTED ADDRESS FORMS WITH TABBED DIVIDERS FOR EASY REFERENCE.

MISCELLANEOUS SECTION
TO STORE ALL EXTRA PREPRINTED FORMS AND COMMONLY-USED RECORDS.

ROLLER BALLPOINT PEN
BLACK PEN THAT FITS IN FLAP FOR EASY ACCESS.

REFERENCE SECTION
CONTAINS MAPS THAT SHOW AREA CODES AND TIME ZONES, TOLL-FREE NUMBERS FOR TRAVEL ACCOMODATIONS, METRIC CONVERSION CHARTS.

FINANCE SECTION
MULTI-USE LEDGER FORMS, RECEIPT LOG AND STORAGE ENVELOPE, CREDIT CARD INFORMATION.

CALENDAR SECTION
YEARLY, MONTHLY, WEEKLY, AND DAILY ENGAGEMENT CALENDARS SUPPLEMENT THOSE YOU PRINT OUT WITH TRAVELING SIDEKICK

PENDING SECTION
A "TO BE CONTINUED" SECTION FOR CURRENT PROJECTS, MEETING NOTES, ETC.

CALCULATOR
IN ONE OF TWO BUSINESS-CARD-SIZE STORAGE POCKETS.

TRAVELING SIDEKICK SOFTWARE
GENERATES, UPDATES, AND PRINTS YOUR ADDRESS AND CALENDAR FILES.

What the software program and its Report Generator do for you before you go—and when you get back

Before you go:
- Prints out your calendar, appointments, addresses, phone directory, and whatever other information you need from your data files

When you return:
- Lets you quickly and easily enter all the new names you obtained while you were away into your SideKick data files

It can also:
- Sort your address book by contact, zip code or company name
- Print mailing labels
- Print information selectively
- Search files for existing addresses or calendar engagements

Suggested Retail Price: $69.95 (not copy protected)

Minimum system configuration: IBM PC, XT, AT, Portable, PCjr, 3270 and true compatibles. PC-DOS (MS-DOS) 2.0 or later. 256K RAM mimimum.

BORLAND
INTERNATIONAL

SideKick, BinderWare and Traveling SideKick are registered trademarks of Borland International, Inc. IBM, AT, XT, and PCjr are registered trademarks of International Business Machines Corp. MS-DOS is a registered trademark of Microsoft Corp. Copyright 1987 Borland International

BOR 0083A

SUPERKEY.® THE PRODUCTIVITY BOOSTER

RAM-resident
Increased productivity for IBM®PCs or compatibles

SuperKey's simple macros are electronic shortcuts to success. By letting you reduce a lengthy paragraph into a single keystroke of your choice, SuperKey eliminates repetition.

SuperKey turns 1,000 keystrokes into 1!
SuperKey can record lengthy keystroke sequences and play them back at the touch of a single key. Instantly. Like magic.

In fact, with SuperKey's simple macros, you can turn "Dear Customer: Thank you for your inquiry. We are pleased to let you know that shipment will be made within 24 hours. Sincerely," into the one keystroke of your choice!

SuperKey keeps your confidential files—confidential!
Without encryption, your files are open secrets. Anyone can walk up to your PC and read your confidential files (tax returns, business plans, customer lists, personal letters, etc.).

With SuperKey you can encrypt any file, *even* while running another program. As long as you keep the password secret, only *you* can decode your file correctly. SuperKey also implements the U.S. government Data Encryption Standard (DES).

- ☑ RAM resident—accepts new macro files even while running other programs
- ☑ Pull-down menus
- ☑ Superfast file encryption
- ☑ Choice of two encryption schemes
- ☑ On-line context-sensitive help
- ☑ One-finger mode reduces key commands to single keystroke
- ☑ Screen OFF/ON blanks out and restores screen to protect against "burn in"
- ☑ Partial or complete reorganization of keyboard

- ☑ Keyboard buffer increases 16 character keyboard "type-ahead" buffer to 128 characters
- ☑ Real-time delay causes macro playback to pause for specified interval
- ☑ Transparent display macros allow creation of menus on top of application programs
- ☑ Data entry and format control using "fixed" or "variable" fields
- ☑ Command stack recalls last 256 characters entered

Suggested Retail Price: $99.95 (not copy protected)

Minimum system configuration: IBM PC, XT, AT, PCjr, and true compatibles. PC-DOS (MS-DOS) 2.0 or greater. 128K RAM. One disk drive.

BORLAND
INTERNATIONAL

SuperKey is a registered trademark of Borland International, Inc. IBM, XT, AT, and PCjr are registered trademarks of International Business Machines Corp. MS-DOS is a registered trademark of Microsoft Corp.
BOR 0062C

If you use an IBM® PC, you need

TURBO
Lightning®

Turbo Lightning teams up with the Random House Concise Word List to check your spelling as you type!

Turbo Lightning, using the 80,000-word Random House Dictionary, checks your spelling *as you type*. If you misspell a word, it alerts you with a "beep." At the touch of a key, Turbo Lightning opens a window on top of your application program and suggests the correct spelling. Just press one key and the misspelled word is instantly replaced with the correct word.

Turbo Lightning works hand-in-hand with the Random House Thesaurus to give you instant access to synonyms

Turbo Lightning lets you choose just the right word from a list of alternates, so you don't say the same thing the same way every time. Once Turbo Lightning opens the Thesaurus window, you see a list of alternate words; select the word you want, press ENTER and your new word will instantly replace the original word. Pure magic!

If you ever write a word, think a word, or say a word, you need Turbo Lightning

The Turbo Lightning Proofreader

The Turbo Lightning Thesaurus

You can teach Turbo Lightning new words

You can *teach* your new Turbo Lightning your name, business associates' names, street names, addresses, correct capitalizations, and any specialized words you use frequently. Teach Turbo Lightning once, and it knows forever.

Turbo Lightning is the engine that powers Borland's Turbo Lightning Library®

Turbo Lightning brings electronic power to the Random House Concise Word List and Random House Thesaurus. They're at your fingertips—even while you're running other programs. Turbo Lightning will also "drive" soon-to-be-released encyclopedias, extended thesauruses, specialized dictionaries, and many other popular reference works. You get a head start with this first volume in the Turbo Lightning Library.

Suggested Retail Price: $99.95 (not copy protected)

Minimum system configuration: IBM PC, XT, AT, PCjr, and true compatibles with 2 floppy disk drives. PC-DOS (MS-DOS) 2.0 or greater. 256K RAM. Hard disk recommended.

BORLAND
INTERNATIONAL

Turbo Lightning and Turbo Lightning Library are registered trademarks of Borland International, Inc. IBM, XT, AT, and PCjr are registered trademarks of International Business Machines Corp. Random House is a registered trademark of Random House, Inc.   Copyright 1987 Borland International
BOR 0070B

Your Development Toolbox and Technical Reference Manual for Turbo Lightning®

LIGHTNING
WORDWIZARD™

Lightning Word Wizard includes complete, commented Turbo Pascal® source code and all the technical information you'll need to understand and work with Turbo Lightning's "engine." More than 20 fully documented Turbo Pascal procedures reveal powerful Turbo Lightning engine calls. Harness the full power of the complete and authoritative Random House® Concise Word List and Random House Thesaurus.

Turbo Lightning's "Reference Manual"

Developers can use the versatile on-line examples to harness Turbo Lightning's power to do rapid word searches. Lightning Word Wizard is the forerunner of the database access systems that will incorporate and engineer the Turbo Lightning Library® of electronic reference works.

The ultimate collection of word games and crossword solvers!

The excitement, challenge, competition, and education of four games and three solver utilities—puzzles, scrambles, spell-searches, synonym-seekings, hidden words, crossword solutions, and more. You and your friends (up to four people total) can set the difficulty level and contest the high-speed smarts of Lightning Word Wizard!

Turbo Lightning—Critics' Choice

"Lightning's good enough to make programmers and users cheer, executives of other software companies weep."
Jim Seymour, *PC Week*

"The real future of Lightning clearly lies not with the spelling checker and thesaurus currently included, but with other uses of its powerful look-up engine." **Ted Silveira, *Profiles***

"This newest product from Borland has it all." **Don Roy, *Computing Now!***

Minimum system configuration: IBM PC, XT, AT, PCjr, Portable, and true compatibles. 256K RAM minimum. PC-DOS (MS-DOS) 2.0 or greater. Turbo Lightning software required. Optional—Turbo Pascal 3.0 or greater to edit and compile Turbo Pascal source code.

 **BORLAND**
INTERNATIONAL

Suggested Retail Price: $69.95
(not copy protected)

Turbo Pascal, Turbo Lightning and Turbo Lightning Library are registered trademarks and Lightning Word Wizard is a trademark of Borland International, Inc. Random House is a registered trademark of Random House, Inc. IBM, XT, AT, and PCjr are registered trademarks of International Business Machines Corp. MS-DOS is a registered trademark of Microsoft Corp. Copyright 1987 Borland International
BOR0087B

REFLEX® THE DATABASE MANAGER

The high-performance database manager that's so advanced it's easy to use!

Lets you organize, analyze and report information faster than ever before! If you manage mailing lists, customer files, or even your company's budgets—Reflex is the database manager for you!

Reflex is the acclaimed, high-performance database manager you've been waiting for. Reflex extends database management with business graphics. Because a picture is often worth a 1000 words, Reflex lets you extract critical information buried in mountains of data. With Reflex, when you look, you see.

The **REPORT VIEW** allows you to generate everything from mailing labels to sophisticated reports. You can use database files created with Reflex or transferred from Lotus 1-2-3,® dBASE,® PFS: File,® and other applications.

Reflex: The Critics' Choice

". . . if you use a PC, you should know about Reflex . . . may be the best bargain in software today."
Jerry Pournelle, BYTE

"Everyone agrees that Reflex is the best-looking database they've ever seen."
Adam B. Green, InfoWorld

"The next generation of software has officially arrived."
Peter Norton, PC Week

Reflex: don't use your PC without it!
Join hundreds of thousands of enthusiastic Reflex users and experience the power and ease of use of Borland's award-winning Reflex.

Suggested Retail Price: $149.95 (not copy protected)

Minimum system configuration: IBM PC, XT, AT, and true compatibles. 384K RAM minimum. IBM Color Graphics Adapter, Hercules Monochrome Graphics CArd, or equivalent. PC-DOS (MS-DOS) 2.0 or greater. Hard disk and mouse optional. Lotus 1-2-3, dBASE, or PFS: File optional.

BORLAND
INTERNATIONAL

Reflex is a trademark of Borland/Analytica Inc. Lotus 1-2-3 is a registered trademark of Lotus Development Corporation. dBASE is a registered trademark of Ashton-Tate. PFS: File is a registered trademark of Software Publishing Corporation. IBM, XT, AT, and IBM Color Graphics Adapter are registered trademarks of International Business Machines Corporation. Hercules Graphics Card is a trademark of Hercules Computer Technology. MS-DOS is a registered trademark of Microsoft Corp.   Copyright 1987 Borland International   BOR 0066C

REFLEX: THE WORKSHOP™

Includes 22 "instant templates" covering a broad range of business applications (listed below). Also shows you how to customize databases, graphs, crosstabs, and reports. It's an invaluable analytical tool and an important addition to another one of our best sellers, Reflex: The Database Manager.

Fast-start tutorial examples:

Learn Reflex® as you work with practical business applications. The Reflex Workshop Disk supplies databases and reports large enough to illustrate the power and variety of Reflex features. Instructions in each Reflex Workshop chapter take you through a step-by-step analysis of sample data. You then follow simple steps to adapt the files to your own needs.

22 practical business applications:

Workshop's 22 "instant templates" give you a wide range of analytical tools:

Administration
- Scheduling Appointments
- Planning Conference Facilities
- Managing a Project
- Creating a Mailing System
- Managing Employment Applications

Sales and Marketing
- Researching Store Check Inventory
- Tracking Sales Leads
- Summarizing Sales Trends
- Analyzing Trends

Production and Operations
- Summarizing Repair Turnaround

- Tracking Manufacturing Quality Assurance
- Analyzing Product Costs

Accounting and Financial Planning
- Tracking Petty Cash
- Entering Purchase Orders
- Organizing Outgoing Purchase Orders
- Analyzing Accounts Receivable
- Maintaining Letters of Credit
- Reporting Business Expenses
- Managing Debits and Credits
- Examining Leased Inventory Trends
- Tracking Fixed Assets
- Planning Commercial Real Estate Investment

Whether you're a newcomer learning Reflex basics or an experienced "power user" looking for tips, Reflex: The Workshop will help you quickly become an expert database analyst.

Minimum system configuration: IBM PC, AT, and XT, and true compatibles. PC-DOS (MS-DOS) 2.0 or greater. 384K RAM minimum. Requires Reflex: The Database Manager, and IBM Color Graphics Adapter, Hercules Monochrome Graphics Card or equivalent.

BORLAND
INTERNATIONAL

**Suggested Retail Price: $69.95
(not copy protected)**

Reflex is a registered trademark and Reflex: The Workshop is a trademark of Borland/Analytica, Inc. IBM, AT, and XT are registered trademarks of International Business Machines Corp. Hercules is a trademark of Hercules Computer Technology. MS-DOS is a registered trademark of Microsoft Corp. Copyright 1987 Borland International

BOR 0088B

TURBOPASCAL®

Version 3.0 with 8087 support and BCD reals

Free MicroCalc Spreadsheet With Commented Source Code!

FEATURES:

One-Step Compile: No hunting & fishing expeditions! Turbo finds the errors, takes you to them, lets you correct them, and instantly recompiles. You're off and running in record time.

Built-in Interactive Editor: WordStar®-like easy editing lets you debug quickly.

Automatic Overlays: Fits big programs into small amounts of memory.

MicroCalc: A sample spreadsheet on your disk with ready-to-compile source code.

IBM® PC Version: Supports Turtle Graphics, color, sound, full tree directories, window routines, input/output redirection, and much more.

THE CRITICS' CHOICE:

"Language deal of the century . . . Turbo Pascal: it introduces a new programming environment and runs like magic."
—Jeff Duntemann, PC Magazine

"Most Pascal compilers barely fit on a disk, but Turbo Pascal packs an editor, compiler, linker, and run-time library into just 39K bytes of random access memory."
—Dave Garland, Popular Computing

"What I think the computer industry is headed for: well-documented, standard, plenty of good features, and a reasonable price."
—Jerry Pournelle, BYTE

LOOK AT TURBO NOW!

☑ More than 500,000 users worldwide.

☑ Turbo Pascal is the de facto industry standard.

☑ Turbo Pascal wins PC MAGAZINE'S award for technical excellence.

☑ Turbo Pascal named "Most Significant Product of the Year" by PC WEEK.

☑ Turbo Pascal 3.0—the fastest Pascal development environment on the planet, period.

Suggested Retail Price: $99.95; CP/M®-80 version without 8087 and BCD: $69.95

Features for 16-bit Systems: 8087 math co-processor support for intensive calculations. Binary Coded Decimals (BCD): eliminates round-off error! A *must* for any serious business application.

Minimum system configuration: 128K RAM minimum. Includes 8087 & BCD features for 16-bit MS-DOS 2.0 or later and CP/M-86 1.1 or later. CP/M-80 version 2.2 or later 48K RAM minimum (8087 and BCD features not available). 8087 version requires 8087 or 80287 co-processor.

BORLAND
I N T E R N A T I O N A L

Turbo Pascal is a registered trademark of Borland International, Inc. CP/M is a registered trademark of Digital Research Inc. IBM is a registered trademark of International Business Machines Corp. MS-DOS is a registered trademark of Microsoft Corp. WordStar is a registered trademark of MicroPro International. Copyright 1987 Borland International BOR 0061B

TURBO PASCAL
TURBO TUTOR®

VERSION 2.0

Learn Pascal From The Folks Who Created
The Turbo Pascal® Family

Borland International proudly presents Turbo Tutor, the perfect complement to your Turbo Pascal compiler. Turbo Tutor is really for everyone—even if you've never programmed before.

And if you're already proficient, Turbo Tutor can sharpen up the fine points. The manual and program disk focus on the whole spectrum of Turbo Pascal programming techniques.

- **For the Novice:** It gives you a concise history of Pascal, tells you how to write a simple program, and defines the basic programming terms you need to know.

- **Programmer's Guide:** The heart of Turbo Pascal. The manual covers the fine points of every aspect of Turbo Pascal programming: program structure, data types, control structures, procedures and functions, scalar types, arrays, strings, pointers, sets, files, and records.

- **Advanced Concepts:** If you're an expert, you'll love the sections detailing such topics as linked lists, trees, and graphs. You'll also find sample program examples for PC-DOS and MS-DOS.®

10,000 lines of commented source code, demonstrations of 20 Turbo Pascal features, multiple-choice quizzes, an interactive on-line tutor, and more!

Turbo Tutor may be the only reference work about Pascal and programming you'll ever need!

Suggested Retail Price: $39.95 (not copy protected)

Minimum system configuration: Turbo Pascal 3.0. PC-DOS (MS-DOS) 2.0 or later. 192K RAM minimum (CP/M-80 version 2.2 or later: 64K RAM minimum).

BORLAND
I N T E R N A T I O N A L

Turbo Pascal and Turbo Tutor are registered trademarks of Borland International Inc. CP/M is a registered trademark of Digital Research Inc. MS-DOS is a registered trademark of Microsoft Corp.
Copyright 1987 Borland International

BOR 0064C

TURBO PASCAL

DATABASE TOOLBOX ®

Is The Perfect Complement To Turbo Pascal®

It contains a complete library of Pascal procedures that allows you to sort and search your data and build powerful database applications. It's another set of tools from Borland that will give even the beginning programmer the expert's edge.

THE TOOLS YOU NEED!

TURBO ACCESS Using B+ trees: The best way to organize and search your data. Makes it possible to access records in a file using key words instead of numbers. Now available with complete source code on disk, ready to be included in your programs.

TURBO SORT: The fastest way to sort data using the QUICKSORT algorithm—the method preferred by knowledgeable professionals. Includes source code.

GINST (General Installation Program): Gets your programs up and running on other terminals. This feature alone will save hours of work and research. Adds tremendous value to all your programs.

GET STARTED RIGHT AWAY—FREE DATABASE!

Included on every Toolbox diskette is the source code to a working database which demonstrates the power and simplicity of our Turbo Access search system. Modify it to suit your individual needs or just compile it and run.

THE CRITICS' CHOICE!

"The tools include a B+ tree search and a sorting system. I've seen stuff like this, but not as well thought out, sell for hundreds of dollars." —*Jerry Pournell, BYTE MAGAZINE*

"The Turbo Database Toolbox is solid enough and useful enough to come recommended." —*Jeff Duntemann, PC TECH JOURNAL*

Suggested Retail Price: $69.95 (not copy protected)

Minimum system configuration: 128K RAM and one disk drive (CP/M-80: 48K). 16-bit systems: Turbo Pascal 2.0 or greater for MS-DOS or PC-DOS 2.0 or greater. Turbo Pascal 2.1 or greater for CP/M-86 1.0 or greater. 8-bit systems: Turbo Pascal 2.0 or greater for CP/M-80 2.2 or greater.

BORLAND
INTERNATIONAL

Turbo Pascal and Turbo Database Toolbox are registered trademarks of Borland International Inc. CP/M is a registered trademark of Digital Research, Inc. MS-DOS is a registered trademark of Microsoft Corp.   Copyright 1987 Borland International   BOR 0063C

TURBO PASCAL
GRAPHIX TOOLBOX®

A Library of Graphics Routines for Use with Turbo Pascal®

High-resolution graphics for your IBM˙ PC, AT,˙ XT,˙ PCjr˙, true PC compatibles, and the Heath Zenith Z-100.˙ Comes complete with graphics window management.

Even if you're new to Turbo Pascal programming, the Turbo Pascal Graphix Toolbox will get you started right away. It's a collection of tools that will get you right into the fascinating world of high-resolution business graphics, including graphics window management. You get immediate, satisfying results. And we keep Royalty out of American business because you don't pay any—even if you distribute your own compiled programs that include all or part of the Turbo Pascal Graphix Toolbox procedures.

 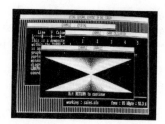

What you get includes:

- Complete commented source code on disk.
- Tools for drawing simple graphics.
- Tools for drawing complex graphics, including curves with optional smoothing.
- Routines that let you store and restore graphic images to and from disk.
- Tools allowing you to send screen images to Epson®-compatible printers.

- Full graphics window management.
- Two different font styles for graphic labeling.
- Choice of line-drawing styles.
- Routines that will let you quickly plot functions and model experimental data.
- And much, much more . . .

"While most people only talk about low-cost personal computer software, Borland has been doing something about it. And Borland provides good technical support as part of the price."
John Markov & Paul Freiberger, syndicated columnists.

If you ever plan to create Turbo Pascal programs that make use of business graphics or scientific graphics, you need the Turbo Pascal Graphix Toolbox.

Suggested Retail Price: $69.95 (not copy protected)

Minimum system configuration: IBM PC, XT, AT, PCjr, true compatibles and the Heath Zenith Z-100. Turbo Pascal 3.0 or later. 192K RAM minimum. Two disk drives and an IBM Color Graphics Adapter (CGA), IBM Enhanced Graphics Adapter (EGA), Hercules Graphics Card or compatible.

 **BORLAND**
INTERNATIONAL

Turbo Pascal and Turbo Graphix Toolbox are registered trademarks of Borland International, Inc. IBM, XT, AT, and PCjr are registered trademarks of International Business Machines Corporation. Hercules Graphics Card is a trademark of Hercules Computer Technology. Heath Zenith Z-100 is a trademark of Zenith Data Systems. Epson is a registered trademark of Epson Corp. Copyright 1987 Borland International

TURBO PASCAL
EDITOR TOOLBOX®

It's All You Need To Build Your Own Text Editor Or Word Processor

Build your own lightning-fast editor and incorporate it into your Turbo Pascal® programs. Turbo Editor Toolbox gives you easy-to-install modules. Now you can integrate a fast and powerful editor into your own programs. You get the source code, the manual, and the know-how.

Create your own word processor. We provide all the editing routines. You plug in the features you want. You could build a WordStar®-like editor with pull-down menus like Microsoft's® Word, and make it work as fast as WordPerfect.®

To demonstrate the tremendous power of Turbo Editor Toolbox, we give you the source code for two sample editors:

Simple Editor   A complete editor ready to include in your programs. With windows, block commands, and memory-mapped screen routines.

MicroStar   A full-blown text editor with a complete pull-down menu user interface, plus a lot more. Modify MicroStar's pull-down menu system and include it in your Turbo Pascal programs.

The Turbo Editor Toolbox gives you all the standard features you would expect to find in any word processor:

- Wordwrap
- UN-delete last line
- Auto-indent
- Find and Find/Replace with options
- Set left and right margin
- Block mark, move, and copy
- Tab, insert and overstrike modes, centering, etc.

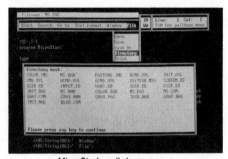

MicroStar's pull-down menus.

And Turbo Editor Toolbox has features that word processors selling for several hundred dollars can't begin to match. Just to name a few:

☑ **RAM-based editor**. You can edit very large files and yet editing is lightning fast.

☑ **Memory-mapped screen routines.** Instant paging, scrolling, and text display.

☑ **Keyboard installation.** Change control keys from WordStar-like commands to any that you prefer.

☑ **Multiple windows.** See and edit up to eight documents—or up to eight parts of the same document—all at the same time.

☑ **Multitasking.** Automatically save your text. Plug in a digital clock, an appointment alarm—see how it's done with MicroStar's "background" printing.

Best of all, **source code is included for everything in the Editor Toolbox.**

Suggested Retail Price: $69.95 (not copy protected)

Minimum system configuration: IBM PC, XT, AT, 3270, PCjr, and true compatibles. PC-DOS (MS-DOS) 2.0 or greater. 192K RAM. You must be using Turbo Pascal 3.0 for IBM and compatibles.

BORLAND
I N T E R N A T I O N A L

Turbo Pascal and Turbo Editor Toolbox are registered trademarks of Borland International, Inc. WordStar is a registered trademark of MicroPro International Corp. Word and MS-DOS are registered trademarks of Microsoft Corp. WordPerfect is a trademark of Satellite Software International. IBM, XT, AT, and PCjr are registered trademarks of International Business Machines Corp.

BOR 0067B

TURBO PASCAL GAMEWORKS®

Secrets And Strategies Of The Masters Are Revealed For The First Time

Explore the world of state-of-the-art computer games with Turbo GameWorks. Using easy-to-understand examples, Turbo GameWorks teaches you techniques to quickly create your own computer games using Turbo Pascal.® Or, for instant excitement, play the three great computer games we've included on disk—compiled and ready to run.

TURBO CHESS

Test your chess-playing skills against your computer challenger. With Turbo GameWorks, you're on your way to becoming a master chess player. Explore the complete Turbo Pascal source code and discover the secrets of Turbo Chess.

"What impressed me the most was the fact that with this program you can become a computer chess analyst. You can add new variations to the program at any time and make the program play stronger and stronger chess. There's no limit to the fun and enjoyment of playing Turbo GameWorks Chess, and most important of all, with this chess program there's no limit to how it can help you improve your game."

—*George Koltanowski, Dean of American Chess, former President of the United Chess Federation, and syndicated chess columnist.*

TURBO BRIDGE

Now play the world's most popular card game—bridge. Play one-on-one with your computer or against up to three other opponents. With Turbo Pascal source code, you can even program your own bidding or scoring conventions.

"There has never been a bridge program written which plays at the expert level, and the ambitious user will enjoy tackling that challenge, with the format already structured in the program. And for the inexperienced player, the bridge program provides an easy-to-follow format that allows the user to start right out playing. The user can 'play bridge' against real competition without having to gather three other people."

—*Kit Woolsey, writer of several articles and books on bridge, and twice champion of the Blue Ribbon Pairs.*

TURBO GO-MOKU

Prepare for battle when you challenge your computer to a game of Go-Moku—the exciting strategy game also known as Pente.® In this battle of wits, you and the computer take turns placing X's and O's on a grid of 19×19 squares until five pieces are lined up in a row. Vary the game if you like, using the source code available on your disk.

Suggested Retail Price: $69.95 (not copy protected)

Minimum system configuration: IBM PC, XT, AT, Portable, 3270, PCjr, and true compatibles. PC-DOS (MS-DOS) 2.0 or later. 192K RAM minimum. To edit and compile the Turbo Pascal source code, you must be using Turbo Pascal 3.0 for IBM PCs and compatibles.

Turbo Pascal and Turbo GameWorks are registered trademarks of Borland International, Inc. Pente is a registered trademark of Parker Brothers. IBM, XT, AT, and PCjr are registered trademarks of International Business Machines Corporation. MS-DOS is a registered trademark of Microsoft Corporation. Copyright 1987 Borland International

BOR0065C

TURBO PASCAL

NUMERICAL METHODS TOOLBOX™

New from Borland's Scientific & Engineering Division!

A complete collection of Turbo Pascal® routines and programs

New from Borland's Scientific & Engineering Division, Turbo Pascal Numerical Methods Toolbox implements the latest high-level mathematical methods to solve common scientific and engineering problems. Fast.

So every time you need to calculate an integral, work with Fourier Transforms or incorporate any of the classical numerical analysis tools into your programs, you don't have to reinvent the wheel. Because the Numerical Methods Toolbox is a complete collection of Turbo Pascal routines and programs that gives you applied state-of-the-art math tools. It also includes two graphics demo programs, Least Squares Fit and Fast Fourier Transforms, to give you the picture along with the numbers.

The Numerical Methods Toolbox is a must for you if you're involved with any type of scientific or engineering computing. Because it comes with complete source code, you have total control of your application.

What Numerical Methods Toolbox will do for you now:

- Find solutions to equations
- Interpolations
- Calculus: numerical derivatives and integrals
- Fourier transforms

- Matrix operations: inversions, determinants and eigenvalues
- Differential equations
- Least squares approximations

---

5 free ways to look at "Least Squares Fit"!

As well as a free demo "Fast Fourier Transforms," you also get "Least Squares Fit" in 5 different forms—which gives you 5 different methods of fitting curves to a collection of data points. You instantly get the picture! The 5 different forms are:

1. Power
2. Exponential
3. Logarithm
4. 5-term Fourier
5. 5-term Polynomial

They're all ready to compile and run "as is." To modify or add graphics to your own programs, you simply add Turbo Graphix Toolbox® to your software library. Our Numerical Methods Toolbox is designed to work hand-in-hand with our Turbo Graphix Toolbox to make professional graphics in your own programs an instant part of the picture!

Suggested Retail Price: $99.95 (not copy protected)

Minimum system configuration: IBM PC, XT, AT and true compatibles. PC-DOS (MS-DOS) 2.0 or later. 256K. Turbo Pascal 2.0 or later. The graphics modules require a graphics monitor with an IBM CGA, IBM EGA, or Hercules compatible adapter card, and require the Turbo Graphix Toolbox. MS-DOS generic version will not support Turbo Graphix Toolbox routines. An 8087 or 80287 numeric co-processor is not required, but recommended for optimal performance.

 **BORLAND** *INTERNATIONAL*

Turbo Pascal Numerical Methods Toolbox is a trademark and Turbo Pascal and Turbo Graphix Toolbox are registered trademarks of Borland International, Inc. IBM, XT, and AT are registered trademarks of International Business Machines Corp. MS-DOS is a registered trademark of Microsoft Corp. Hercules is a trademark of Hercules Computer Technology. Apple is a registered trademark of Apple Computer, Inc. Macintosh is a trademark of McIntosh Laboratory, Inc. licensed to Apple Computer. Copyright 1987 Borland International BOR 0219A

TURBO PROLOG™

the natural language of Artificial Intelligence

STEP-BY-STEP TUTORIAL AND DEMO PROGRAMS WITH SOURCE CODE INCLUDED!

Turbo Prolog brings fifth-generation supercomputer power to your IBM® PC!

Turbo Prolog takes programming into a new, natural, and logical environment

With Turbo Prolog, because of its natural, logical approach, both people new to programming *and* professional programmers can build powerful applications such as expert systems, customized knowledge bases, natural language interfaces, and smart information management systems.

Turbo Prolog is a *declarative* language which uses deductive reasoning to solve programming problems.

Turbo Prolog provides a fully integrated programming environment like Borland's Turbo Pascal,® the *de facto* worldwide standard.

You get the complete Turbo Prolog programming system

You get the 200-page manual you're holding, software that includes the lightning-fast Turbo Prolog six-pass compiler and interactive editor, and the free GeoBase natural query language database, which includes commented source code on disk, ready to compile. (GeoBase is a complete database designed and developed around U.S. geography. You can modify it or use it "as is.")

Turbo Prolog's development system includes:

- ☐ A complete Prolog compiler that is a variation of the Clocksin and Mellish Edinburgh standard Prolog.
- ☐ A full-screen interactive editor.
- ☐ Support for both graphic and text windows.
- ☐ All the tools that let you build your own expert systems and **AI** applications with unprecedented ease.

Minimum system configuration: IBM PC, XT, AT, Portable, 3270, PCjr and true compatibles. PC-DOS (MS-DOS) 2.0 or later. 384K RAM minimum.

Suggested Retail Price: $99.95 (not copy protected)

BORLAND
INTERNATIONAL

Turbo Prolog is a trademark and Turbo Pascal is a registered trademark of Borland International, Inc. IBM, AT, XT, and PCjr are registered trademarks of International Business Machines Corp. MS-DOS is a registered trademark of Microsoft Corp. Copyright 1987 Borland International   BOR 0016D

TURBO PROLOG™
TOOLBOX

Enhances Turbo Prolog with more than 80 tools and over 8,000 lines of source code

Turbo Prolog, the natural language of Artificial Intelligence, is the most popular AI package in the world with more than 100,000 users. Our new Turbo Prolog Toolbox extends its possibilities.

The Turbo Prolog Toolbox enhances Turbo Prolog—our 5th-generation computer programming language that brings supercomputer power to your IBM PC and compatibles—with its more than 80 tools and over 8,000 lines of source code that can be incorporated into your programs, quite easily.

Turbo Prolog Toolbox features include:

- ☑ Business graphics generation: boxes, circles, ellipses, bar charts, pie charts, scaled graphics
- ☑ Complete communications package: supports XModem protocol
- ☑ File transfers from Reflex,® dBASE III,® Lotus 1-2-3,® Symphony®
- ☑ A unique parser generator: construct your own compiler or query language
- ☑ Sophisticated user-interface design tools
- ☑ 40 example programs
- ☑ Easy-to-use screen editor: design your screen layout and I/O
- ☑ Calculated fields definition
- ☑ Over 8,000 lines of source code you can incorporate into your own programs

---

Suggested Retail Price: $99.95 (not copy protected)

Minimum system configuration: IBM PC, XT, AT or true compatibles. PC-DOS (MS-DOS) 2.0 or later. Requires Turbo Prolog 1.10 or higher. Dual-floppy disk drive or hard disk. 512K.

Turbo Prolog Toolbox and Turbo Prolog are trademarks of Borland International, Inc. Reflex is a registered trademark of Borland/Analytica, Inc. dBASE III is a registered trademark of Ashton-Tate. Lotus 1-2-3 and Symphony are registered trademarks of Lotus Development Corp. IBM, XT, and AT are registered trademarks of International Business Machines Corp. MS-DOS is a registered trademark of Microsoft Corp.   BOR 0240

TURBO BASIC®

The high-speed BASIC you've been waiting for!

You probably know us for our Turbo Pascal® and Turbo Prolog.® Well, we've done it again! We've created Turbo Basic, because BASIC doesn't have to be slow.

If BASIC taught you how to walk, Turbo Basic will teach you how to run!

With Turbo Basic, your only speed is "Full Speed Ahead"! Turbo Basic is a complete development environment with an *amazingly fast compiler,* an *interactive editor* and a *trace debugging system.* And because Turbo Basic is also compatible with BASICA, chances are that you already know how to use Turbo Basic.

Turbo Basic ends the basic confusion

There's now one standard: Turbo Basic. And because Turbo Basic is a Borland product, the price is right, the quality is there, and the power is at your fingertips. Turbo Basic is part of the fast-growing Borland family of programming languages we call the "Turbo Family." And hundreds of thousands of users are already using Borland's languages. So, welcome to a whole new generation of smart PC users!

Free spreadsheet included with source code!

Yes, we've included MicroCalc,™ our sample spreadsheet, complete with source code. So you can get started right away with a "real program." You can compile and run it "as is," or modify it.

A technical look at Turbo Basic

- ☑ Full recursion supported
- ☑ Standard IEEE floating-point format
- ☑ Floating-point support, with full 8087 coprocessor integration. Software emulation if no 8087 present
- ☑ Program size limited only by available memory (no 64K limitation)
- ☑ EGA, CGA, MCGA and VGA support
- ☑ Full integration of the compiler, editor, and executable program, with separate windows for editing, messages, tracing, and execution
- ☑ Compile and run-time errors place you in source code where error occurred
- ☑ Access to local, static and global variables
- ☑ New long integer (32-bit) data type
- ☑ Full 80-bit precision
- ☑ Pull-down menus
- ☑ Full window management

Suggested Retail Price: $99.95 (not copy protected)

Minimum system configuration: IBM PC, AT, XT, PS/2 or true compatibles. 320K. One floppy drive. PC-DOS (MS-DOS) 2.0 or later.

BORLAND
INTERNATIONAL

Turbo Basic, Turbo Prolog and Turbo Pascal are registered trademarks and MicroCalc is a trademark of Borland International, Inc. Other brand and product names are trademarks or registered trademarks of their respective holders.
Copyright 1987 Borland International

BOR 0265B

EUREKA: THE SOLVER™

The solution to your most complex equations—in seconds!

If you're a scientist, engineer, financial analyst, student, teacher, or any other professional working with equations, Eureka: The Solver can do your Algebra, Trigonometry and Calculus problems in a snap.

Eureka also handles maximization and minimization problems, plots functions, generates reports, and saves an incredible amount of time. Even if you're not a computer specialist, Eureka can help you solve your real-world mathematical problems fast, without having to learn numerical approximation techniques. Using Borland's famous pull-down menu design and context-sensitive help screens, Eureka is easy to learn and easy to use—as simple as a hand-held calculator.

$X + exp(X) = 10$ solved instantly instead of eventually!

Imagine you have to "solve for X," where $X + exp(X) = 10$, and you don't have Eureka: The Solver. What you do have is a problem, because it's going to take a lot of time guessing at "X." With Eureka, there's no guessing, no dancing in the dark—you get the right answer, right now. (PS: $X = 2.0705799$, and Eureka solved that one in .4 of a second!)

How to use Eureka: The Solver

It's easy.
1. Enter your equation into the full-screen editor
2. Select the "Solve" command
3. Look at the answer
4. You're done

You can then tell Eureka to
- Evaluate your solution
- Plot a graph
- Generate a report, then send the output to your printer, disk file or screen
- Or all of the above

Some of Eureka's key features

You can key in:
- ☑ A formula or formulas
- ☑ A series of equations—and solve for all variables
- ☑ Constraints (like X has to be $<$ or $= 2$)
- ☑ A function to plot
- ☑ Unit conversions
- ☑ Maximization and minimization problems
- ☑ Interest Rate/Present Value calculations
- ☑ Variables we call "What happens?," like "What happens if I change this variable to 21 and that variable to 27?"

Eureka: The Solver includes

- ☑ A full-screen editor
- ☑ Pull-down menus
- ☑ Context-sensitive Help
- ☑ On-screen calculator
- ☑ Automatic 8087 math co-processor chip support
- ☑ Powerful financial functions
- ☑ Built-in and user-defined math and financial functions
- ☑ Ability to generate reports complete with plots and lists
- ☑ Polynomial finder
- ☑ Inequality solutions

Minimum system configuration: IBM PC, AT, XT, PS/2, Portable, 3270 and true compatibles. PC-DOS (MS-DOS) 2.0 and later. 384K.

Suggested Retail Price: $167.00
(not copy protected)

Eureka: The Solver is a trademark of Borland International, Inc. IBM, AT, and XT are registered trademarks of International Business Machines Corp. MS-DOS is a registered trademark of Microsoft Corp. Copyright 1987 Borland International   BOR 0221B

SIDEKICK: THE DESKTOP ORGANIZER Release 2.0

Macintosh™

The most complete and comprehensive collection of desk accessories available for your Macintosh!

Thousands of users already know that SideKick is the best collection of desk accessories available for the Macintosh. With our new Release 2.0, the best just got better.

We've just added two powerful high-performance tools to SideKick—Outlook™: The Outliner and MacPlan™: The Spreadsheet. They work in perfect harmony with each other and *while* you run other programs!

Outlook: The Outliner

- It's the desk accessory with more power than a stand-alone outliner
- A great desktop publishing tool, Outlook lets you incorporate both text and graphics into your outlines
- Works hand-in-hand with MacPlan
- Allows you to work on several outlines at the same time

MacPlan: The Spreadsheet

- Integrates spreadsheets and graphs
- Does both formulas and straight numbers
- Graph types include bar charts, stacked bar charts, pie charts and line graphs
- Includes 12 example templates free!
- Pastes graphics and data right into Outlook creating professional memos and reports, complete with headers and footers.

SideKick: The Desktop Organizer, Release 2.0 now includes

- ☑ Outlook: The Outliner
- ☑ MacPlan: The Spreadsheet
- ☑ Mini word processor
- ☑ Calendar
- ☑ PhoneLog
- ☑ Analog clock
- ☑ Alarm system
- ☑ Calculator
- ☑ Report generator
- ☑ Telecommunications (new version now supports XModem file transfer protocol)

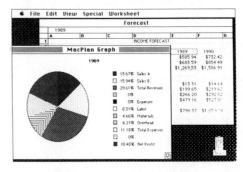

MacPlan does both spreadsheets and business graphs. Paste them into your Outlook files and generate professional reports.

Suggested Retail Price: $99.95 (not copy protected)

Minimum system configurations: Macintosh 512K or Macintosh Plus with one disk drive. One 800K or two 400K drives are recommended. With one 400K drive, a limited number of desk accessories will be installable per disk.

BORLAND
INTERNATIONAL

SideKick is a registered trademark and Outlook and MacPlan are trademarks of Borland International, Inc. Macintosh is a trademark of McIntosh Laboratory, Inc. licensed to Apple Computer, Inc. Copyright 1987 Borland International   BOR 0069D

REFLEX® THE DATABASE MANAGER

The easy-to-use relational database that thinks like a spreadsheet. Reflex for the Mac lets you crunch numbers by entering formulas and link databases by drawing on-screen lines.

5 free ready-to-use templates are included on the examples disk:

- A sample 1040 tax application with Schedule A, Schedule B, and Schedule D, each contained in a separate report document.
- A portfolio analysis application with linked databases of stock purchases, sales, and dividend payments.
- A checkbook application.

- A client billing application set up for a law office, but easily customized by any professional who bills time.
- A parts explosion application that breaks down an object into its component parts for cost analysis.

Reflex for the Mac accomplishes all of these tasks without programming—using spreadsheet-like formulas. Some other Reflex for the Mac features are:

- Visual database design.
- "What you see is what you get" report and form layout with pictures.
- Automatic restructuring of database files when data types are changed, or fields are added and deleted.
- Display formats which include General, Decimal, Scientific, Dollars, Percent.

- Data types which include variable length text, number, integer, automatically incremented sequence number, date, time, and logical.
- Up to 255 fields per record.
- Up to 16 files simultaneously open.
- Up to 16 Mac fonts and styles are selectable for individual fields and labels.

After opening the "Overview" window, you draw link lines between databases directly onto your Macintosh screen.

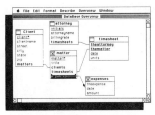

The link lines you draw establish both visual and electronic relationships between your databases.

You can have multiple windows open simultaneously to view all members of a linked set—which are interactive and truly relational.

Critic's Choice

". . . a powerful relational database . . . uses a visual approach to information management." **InfoWorld**

". . . gives you a lot of freedom in report design; you can even import graphics." **A+ Magazine**

". . . bridges the gap between the pretty programs and the power programs." **Stewart Alsop, PC Letter**

BORLAND
INTERNATIONAL

Suggested Retail Price: $99.95
(not copy protected)

Minimum system configuration: *Macintosh 512K or Macintosh Plus with one disk drive. Second external drive recommended.*

Reflex is a registered trademark of Borland/Analytica, Inc. Macintosh is a trademark of McIntosh Laboratory, Inc. and is used with express permission of its owner.
Copyright 1987 Borland International

BOR0149A

TURBO
PASCAL® MACINTOSH™

The ultimate Pascal development environment

Borland's new Turbo Pascal for the Mac is so incredibly fast that it can compile 1,420 lines of source code in the 7.1 seconds it took you to read this!

And reading the rest of this takes about *5 minutes*, which is plenty of time for Turbo Pascal for the Mac to compile at least *60,000 more lines* of source code!

Turbo Pascal for the Mac does both Windows and "Units"

The *separate* compilation of routines offered by Turbo Pascal for the Mac creates modules called "Units," which can be linked to any Turbo Pascal program. This "modular pathway" gives you "pieces" which can then be integrated into larger programs. You get a more efficient use of memory and a reduction in the time it takes to develop large programs.

Turbo Pascal for the Mac is so compatible with Lisa® that they should be living together

Routines from Macintosh Programmer's Workshop Pascal and Inside Macintosh can be compiled and run with only the subtlest changes. Turbo Pascal for the Mac is also compatible with the Hierarchical File System of the Macintosh.

The 27-second Guide to Turbo Pascal for the Mac

- Compilation speed of more than 12,000 lines per minute
- "Unit" structure lets you create programs in modular form
- Multiple editing windows—up to 8 at once
- Compilation options include compiling to disk or memory, or compile and run
- No need to switch between programs to compile or run a program
- Streamlined development and debugging
- Compatibility with Macintosh Programmer's

- Workshop Pascal (with minimal changes)
- Compatibility with Hierarchical File System of your Mac
- Ability to define default volume and folder names used in compiler directives
- Search and change features in the editor speed up and simplify alteration of routines
- Ability to use all available Macintosh memory without limit
- "Units" included to call all the routines provided by Macintosh Toolbox

---

Suggested Retail Price: $99.95   (not copy protected)

3 MacWinners from Borland!
First there was SideKick for the Mac, then Reflex for the Mac, and now Turbo Pascal for the Mac™!

Minimum system configuration: Macintosh 512K or Macintosh Plus with one disk drive.

BORLAND
INTERNATIONAL

Turbo Pascal and SideKick are registered trademarks of Borland International, Inc. and Reflex is a registered trademark of Borland/Analytica, Inc. Macintosh is a trademark of McIntosh Laboratories, Inc. licensed to Apple Computer with its express permission. Lisa is a registered trademark of Apple Computer, Inc. Inside Macintosh is a copyright of Apple Computer, Inc.
Copyright 1987 Borland International BOR 0167A

Borland
Software
ORDER TODAY

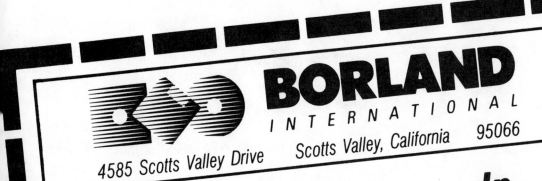

BORLAND

I N T E R N A T I O N A L

4585 Scotts Valley Drive   Scotts Valley, California   95066

To Order
By Credit
Card,
Call
(800)
255-8008

In
California
call
(800)
742-1133

In Canada call
(800) 237-1136

BOR 0234